vahili Modernities

Swahili Modernities

Culture, Politics, and Identity on the East Coast of Africa

Edited by

Pat Caplan and Farouk Topan

Africa World Press, Inc.

P.O. Box 1892

Trenton, NJ 08607

P.O Box 48

Asmara, ERITREA

Africa World Press, Inc.

P.O. Box 1892
Trenton, NJ 08607

P.O. Box 48
Asmara, ERITREA

Copyright © 2004 Pat Caplan and Farouk Topan
First Printing 2004

Book Design: Getahun Seyoum Alemayehu
Cover Design: Roger Dormann

Cataloging-in-Publication Data is available from Library of Congress

ISBN 1-59221-045-7 (hard cover)
ISBN 1-59221-046-5 (paperback)

CONTENTS

Contents

Contents

PREFACE

This volume arises out of the fifth conference in an on-going series of interdisciplinary Anglo-French Workshops, held alternately in Paris and London. The first of these took place in 1987 and its theme was 'Social Stratification in Swahili Society' (Parkin and Constantin 1989). Two years later, a conference was held on 'Networks and Exchanges in the Coastal Societies of East Africa' (Le Guennec-Coppens and Caplan 1991). The third conference was held in October 1992, and its theme was 'Continuity and Autonomy in Swahili Communities: inland influences and strategies of self-determination' (Parkin 1994). In 1995, the conference took place in Paris, with the theme of 'Authority and Power in the Coastal Societies of East Africa (Le Guennec-Coppens and Parkin 1998). Most of the scholars who presented papers at these gatherings were either British or French, although a small number were of East African origin.

The fifth conference was not held until 2001 in London, and it was decided that this time scholars would be invited from a wider spectrum of countries: France, Britain, Norway, America, Kenya, Tanzania, although several people currently working in Europe were from further afield: Mexico, Canada, Zanzibar, Kenya. The theme which the organisers chose was that of 'Modernity and the Swahili' and the call for papers read as follows:

> The theme of 'The Swahili and Modernity' will encourage us to consider the concepts of modernity and modernization in relation to the Swahili-speakers of the Coast and Islands of East Africa. How have the dramatic changes of recent years, including the influx of up-country migrants and the tourist boom, affected Swahili culture and society? What have been the effects of such factors as structural adjustment programmes, multi-party democracy, and political contestations?

Preface

We wanted to think about modernity, in all its many senses, in relation to the Swahili coast of East Africa. Our choice of this term in no way posited the existence of the usual counterpart to modernity – 'tradition', since noone working on this area could possibly imagine that the Swahili have, for at least the last millenium, lived in a timeless 'traditional' society, much less one isolated from the wider world. We did not want to participate in the kinds of narratives which locate people on one side or the other of a dualistic divide of modern/traditional and which tends to place Africa in the latter category. Rather, we wanted explorations of the impact of recent historical changes on the East Coast: globalization and its concomitant, localization; development and under-development; political changes, conflict and contests; and local understandings of and strivings towards the elusive goal of modernity.

During the two-day conference, thirteen papers were presented to an enthusiastic audience, several of whom had travelled long distances to attend. Sadly, one participant, Christine Walley, could not be present as she was due to fly out on September 11th 2001 from the USA, but her paper was discussed at the conference and is included in this volume.

Our contributors came from a range of disciplines: language and literature (Topan, Musau, Amidu, Mlacha, Saavedra), anthropology (Larsen, Caplan, Walley, Beckerleg, Le Guennec-Coppens, Saleh), and political science (Cameron). Furthermore, they had carried out research along the length and breadth of the East African littoral from Lamu in the north to the Comoros Islands in the far south: Amidu in Lamu, Beckerleg in Malindi, Cameron, Larsen and Saleh in Zanzibar, Mlacha in Bagamoyo, Caplan and Walley in Mafia, and Le Guennec- Coppens in the Comoros. All of us were aware that the East Coast is simultaneously many places and it is precisely the mixture of sameness and difference which made this conference, like the ones preceding it, so fascinating.

We are grateful to the British Academy and to the School of Oriental and African Studies for supporting this conference financially, to the contributors for their cooperation and contributions, and to Lionel Caplan for editorial assistance.

Pat Caplan and Farouk Topan,
London, May 2002

Bibliography

Le Guennec-Coppens, and Pat Caplan (eds.), 1991 *Les Swahili entre Afrique et Arabie*. Karthala, Paris, CREDU Nairobi.

Le Guennec-Coppens, F. and David Parkin (eds.), 1998. *Autorite et pouvoir chez les Swahili*. Karthala, Paris IFRA Nairobi.

Parkin, David (ed.), 1994. *Continuity and Autonomy in Swahili Communities: inland influences and strategies of self-determination*. Beitrage zu Afrikanstik Band 48, Wien, London SOAS.

Parkin, David and Francois Constantin (eds.), 1989 *Social Stratification in Swahili Society*. special edition of *Africa: Journal of the International African Institute*, 59. 2.

CONTRIBUTORS TO THIS VOLUME

Assibi Amidu taught Swahili language, literature and culture at the University of Ghana before becoming Associate Professor in Swahili at the Linguistics Department of the Norwegian University of Science and Technology, Trondheim, Norway. Publications: *Kimwondo: a Kiswahili Electoral Contest Vienna: Afro-Pub, 1990; Classes in Swahili: a Study of their Forms and Implications. Cologne: Rudiger Koppe Verlag, 1997.*

Susan Beckerleg is a social anthropologist and international development consultant on health projects in Africa and Asia, based at the London School of Hygiene and Tropical Medicine. She has been carrying out research on the Kenya coast since the mid-1980s on a wide range of topics including Swahili medicine, ethnicity, boat-building and the effects of international mass tourism and has published a number of journal articles and chapters. She is a co-founder of The Omari Project, a group that assists heroin users and their families living in coastal Kenya and runs a residential rehabilitation centre, the first of its kind in East Africa. In addition she has carried out medical anthropological research in Yemen, The Gambia, Palestine and Israel.

Greg Cameron lived in Tanzania for ten years, during most of which time he worked with the Tanzanian co-operative movement as an organizer and trainer stationed in Zanzibar. He has recently completed his Ph.D. in political science at the School of Oriental and African Studies, University of London, on modes of popular politics in the Zanzibar Co-operative Movement, post-1964. He returned to the Isles for follow up research on the recent elections in October 2000. He is presently teaching at the University of Asmara, Eritrea.

Pat Caplan is Professor of Anthropology at Goldsmiths College, where she has been teaching since 1977. She has been carrying out research on Mafia Island Tanzania since 1965, with subsequent visits in 1976, 1985, 1994, and 2002. She has researched kinship and descent, land tenure, spirit possession and healing, gender relations, food/health/fertility, personal narratives and other topics. Her books on Mafia include *Choice and Constraint in a Swahili Community* (OUP/IAI 1975) and *African Voices, African Lives: Personal Narratives from a Swahili Village* (Routledge 1997) as well as numerous articles and chapters. Her other fields of research are South India and West Wales.

Kjersti Larsen formerly taught anthropology at the Agricultural University of Norway and is currently Associate Professor at the Ethnographic Museum, University of Oslo. She has conducted extensive research in Zanzibar from 1984 until the present and has published a number of chapters and journal articles. She has had several assignments as a consultant on various development projects in a number of African countries and has also been a member of an official Committee on Citizenship Requirements reporting to the Norwegian Government.

Francoise le Guennec-Coppens is an anthropologist and Senior Research Fellow (*Chargee de Recherche)* at the LACITO laboratory of the CNRS in Paris. She has been carrying out research in East Africa for thirty years, and her topics have included women and their society in Lamu, Kenya, the Hadhrami diaspora, the *'grand mariage'* and notability in the Comoro Islands. She is co-editor (with Pat Caplan) of *'The Swahili between Africa and Arabia' (Les Swahilis entre Afrique et Arabie* – Paris, Karthala 1991) and co-editor (with David Parkin) of *Autorite et Pouvoir chez les Swahili (Authority and Power among the Swahili)* (Paris, Karthala 1998)

Shaaban Mlacha is Research Professor in Kiswahili Literature and Culture at the Institute of Kiswahili Research, University of Dar es Salaam, Tanzania of which he was formerly Director from 1994-2000. He has published three books on Kiswahili literature and an English-Kiswahili Legal Dictionary. He has also co-authored a book on Kiswahili literature, and co-edited an English-

Kiswahili dictionary. He has many articles in both local and international journals and chapters in several books. He is on the Advisory Boards of the Mali African Academy of Languages and the Journal of African Lexicography.

Paul M. Musau is a Senior Lecturer and a former Chair of the Department of Kiswahili and African Languages, Kenyatta University, Nairobi, Kenya. He teaches and publishes on Swahili literature, sociolinguistics and second language learning. He is the author of several books that are used in secondary and tertiary institutions in Kenya. He is a member of the Kiswahili Association of Kenya, the Writers Association of Kenya and the Association of Third World Studies, Inc.

José Arturo Saavedra has taught Swahili language, general historiography and the history of Africa in several Mexican universities and is currently a member of the academic staff of the Asian and African Studies Center at El Colegio de México. In 1998 he began work on his PhD at SOAS on the historiography of Swahili war poetry about the German conquest of East Africa (1888-1910). He has published several articles about African history, historiography, and Swahili poetry as an historical source. He is a member of the editorial board of the Journal *Estudios de Asia y Africa.*

Mohamed Ahmed Saleh was born in Zanzibar. He joined the *Ecole des Hautes Etudes en Sciences Sociales (EHESS)*, Paris, in 1988 to study social anthropology and is presently a doctoral candidate working on the theme of identity and nationalism in the Zanzibari diaspora. His fieldwork has taken place in traditional fishing communities in Zanzibar as well as in Swahili communities in East Africa, the Comoros and Europe on the topics of identity, marriage, and community development. He has published a number of articles and chapters on his research. He has recently been working for the French Public Television Channel 3 (France 3) on a documentary film on Zanzibar.

Farouk Topan is Senior Lecturer in Swahili at the School of Oriental and African Studies, University of London. He has taught at the Universities of Dar es Salaam and Nairobi where he introduced the teaching of Swahili literature in 1968 and 1972 respectively. He has edited two volumes of essays on Swahili literary criticism (*Uchambuzi wa Maadanishi* 1971 and 1978 OUP). Dr. Topan has also published three plays in Swahili, *Mfalme Juha* (Nairobi, OUP 1971), *Aliyeonja Pepo* (Tanzania Publishing House 1973, also translated into English, Italian and Esperanto) and *Siri* (Jomo Kenyatta Foundation 2000) and he is also the author of a number of academic publications. His research interests are in spirit possession and songs, Swahili oral and written literature, and religion in East Africa.

Christine J. Walley is an Assistant Professor of Anthropology at the Massachusetts Institute of Technology. She conducted research in Tanzania for 19 months between 1994 and 1997, and received her Ph.D. in 1999 from New York University (NYU). Her dissertation, *Making Waves: Struggles over the Environment, Development and Participation within the Mafia Island Marine Park, Tanzania* was jointly awarded the Dean's Outstanding Dissertation Award in the Humanities from NYU in 2000 and is currently being prepared for publication.

CHAPTER 1

INTRODUCTION

Pat Caplan

Modernity: contemporaneity, currency, fashionableness, freshness, innovation, innovativeness, newness, novelty, originality, recentness (Chambers Thesaurus)

Modernity: broad synonym for capitalism, or industrialization, or whatever institutional and ideological features are held to mark off the modern West from other traditional societies (Encyclopaedia of Social and Cultural Anthropology 1996: 378)

Concepts of modernity and development

The terms 'modern', 'modernization' and 'modernity' occur frequently in both academic and lay parlance, with the assumption that everyone understands what is meant. Yet their meanings are far from clear. In history, the 'modern' period starts with the end of the Middle Ages and continues to the present. In art, architecture, literature and music, the term is applied mainly to experimental work dating from the end of the nineteenth and through the twentieth century. In the social sciences, modernization has been defined as all those developments which have followed in the wake of industrialization and mechanization. It thus serves broadly as a synonym for capitalism, globalization, and those aspects of society which are held to differentiate the modern West from other 'traditional' or 'developing' societies (see Spencer 1996). Classic theories of modernity include those by Marx on the dynamics of class society, Weber on bureaucratic, psychological and cultural rationalization, and Durkheim on the growing complexity of the division of labour (Fischer 1997: 369).

Giddens, like Leach (1968) before him, has suggested that 'The modern world is a "runaway world": not only is the pace of social change much faster than in any prior system, so also is its *scope*, and the *profoundness* with which it affects pre-existing social practices and modes of behaviour' (1999: 16, see also 1991)

In a recent volume, Arce and Long have suggested that, while modernity is a tendency that populates all spheres of the globe, it is not received passively. Rather, local actors appropriate various aspects associated with modernity in order to construct their own social worlds:

> People, then, do not experience the 'arrival' of modernity as the disintegration of their 'old' worlds, marked by the establishment of an unproblematic new and 'pure' code of communication and rationality. Rather, they visualise reality as made up of 'living' ensembles of imagined and felt experiences that juxtapose and interrelate different materialities and types of agency embracing notions associated with aspects of both modernity and tradition (Arce and Long 1999: 14).

Such approaches as these inevitably question Rostow's highly influential earlier thesis (1971) which suggested the need to eradicate those 'traditional' cultural and institutional obstacles which were assumed to block progress towards modernity and development. They also suggest that some of the results of this previous modernization thesis, such as the production of a series of dichotomies which include modernity and tradition, civilization and barbarism/primitivism, developed and underdeveloped, and First World/Third World, are in fact untenable. Yet in common parlance, in the mass media, indeed even in much scholarly work, such dichotomies continue to be used, and inevitably, Africa tends to fall into the second part of each. Such stereotypical categorizations do little to help us understand much beyond Western ways of viewing the world, and if we are forced to make use of terms such as modernity, we need to do so in more nuanced ways. For example, following the work of the Comaroffs (1993), it is perhaps preferable to speak of 'multiple modernities' rather than modernity *tout court*.

Furthermore, there is no simple linear move from tradition to modernity. Recent commentators have shown how individuals and groups draw upon tradition in a way that enables them to accommodate to the modern world; in this way, as Chabal and Daloz note, one can be both 'traditional' and 'modern' at the same time (Chabal and Daloz 1999). Arce and Long also argue that 'the term "modern" connotes a sense of belonging to the present and an awareness of a past to which people can link and at the same time distantiate themselves' (1999: 4).

One way of looking at the relationship between 'tradition' and 'modernity' is in terms of the tension between cultural homogenization and cultural heterogenization. As many anthropologists have noted, '[A]s soon as forces from various metropolises are brought into new societies they tend to become indigenized in one way or another' (Appadurai 1990: 295). Appadurai suggests that one way of conceptualizing a globalizing world, with its concomitant localizing tendencies, is to think in terms of a series of 'scapes' which are not objectively given relations but 'deeply perspectival constructs, inflected very much by the historical, linguistic and political situatedness of different sorts of actors' (1990: 297). One such construct he terms 'ethnoscapes': 'the landscape of persons who constitute the shifting world in which we live: tourists, immigrants, refugees, exiles, guest-workers and other moving groups and persons [who] constitute an essential feature of the world' (ibid: 297). The East Coast of Africa is just such an ethnoscape, and its multiple modernities are the subject of this book.

Continuities and discontinuities on the East African coast

The coast of East Africa, as many scholars have noted, has long been an area of perpetual change. Recent work by archaeologists and historians suggests that some form of what we may broadly call Swahili culture has been discernible since the ninth century A.D. (Horton and Middleton 2000, Allen 1993). The East Coast has for over a millenium interacted with both the Indian Ocean littoral, especially the Persian Gulf, and the interior of Africa. Indeed, scholars have argued that it is precisely the role of coastal dwellers as intermediaries, traders, merchants and cultural brokers which has given this area its distinctive quality. In the course of the last millenium, the Swahili-speakers of the coast have adapted to numerous changes: incursions and migrations by the Portuguese, the Omanis, the Germans, the British, as well as African people coming from 'up-country'. Indeed, this last tendency has intensified in recent years to the extent that, in many coastal settlements, the Swahili now form a minority.

At the same time, although the East Coast shares a long common history and culture, it also forms part of at least two modern nation-states, and is subject to their laws, policies and political processes. Like other Kenyans and Tanzanians, coastal dwellers have felt the effects of major recent changes in their lives: structural adjustment programmes, the introduction of multi-party political systems, the growth of tourism and the increasing menace of AIDS and HIV infection. Furthermore, Kenya and Tanzania adopted very different policies and trajectories in the post independence period, thus a comparison of their respective coastal regions today reveals significant differences, as well as on-going similarities.

While it is important to be aware of the importance of history and historical processes, and the way in which these impinge upon the present, in this book we are also mindful of the fact that the present to some extent shapes the past. On the East Coast, as elsewhere, there are many versions of history, indeed many histories, and their writing is often not only contested, but also politicized.

Modernity on the Swahili coast

How then may we define 'the modern' on the Swahili coast? Indeed, should we be seeking it at all, or does this term risk ethnocentricity? During the discussions at the conference which gave rise to this volume, two of our contributors, Saavedra and Le Guennec-Coppens, both expressed discomfort with the concept, arguing that a clear demarcation between a 'modern' and a non-modern period is difficult to establish.

Yet it is clear that there do exist local concepts of modernity. As Talle has recently pointed out for an inland area of East Africa, in Swahili people draw contrasts between *ya kisasa* (of now) and *ya kizamani* or *ya asili* (of before, of olden times) (Talle 1998: 38). Some of our contributors, notably Walley, suggest that the term in Swahili closest to 'modernity' is *maendeleo*, which also means development. Yet for many on the coast modernity has not brought development in the sense of progress or improvements in their standard of living or quality of life. On the contrary, for many people, recent times are worse times, a theme taken up by both Caplan and Walley in their chapters on Mafia Island. It is also discussed by Beckerleg in her examination of the effects of the decline in tourism in Malindi – a decline which leads people there to say that nowadays 'It is always the off-season *(kusi)*'. Indeed, in our discussions at the conference, Beckerleg perceptively suggested that it is only the getting of tangible forms of development which enables people to claim to be 'modern'. This view resonates with Caplan's exploration of the symbolic and material importance of the construction of a 'proper road' in northern Mafia and Walley's discussion of the significance which Chole islanders in southern Mafia attributed to the construction of demarcated pathways and modern buildings. For the latter, such developments indicated the making of a 'proper town' and recalled the period when Chole Island was the capital of Mafia District during the German colonial period.

Several of the papers in this volume show clearly that the relationship between modernity and tradition is far from being an either/or matter. People may use 'modern' phenomena to pursue tradition, as Le Guennec-Coppen's examination of the institution of the Great Marriage in the Comoros reveals. The relatively recent phenomenon of migration to the metropolitan country, France, has resulted in the monetization of matrimonial prestations and led to high levels of inflation in these payments. Le Guennec-Coppens argues that, as long as capital is tied up in an endless round of ever-escalating expenses for 'Great Marriages' rather than being used productively, development, in a conventional economic sense, is likely to be impaired.

The effects of lack of development may be felt not only in terms of greater impoverishment, as Caplan suggests, but also, according to Cameron's analysis of recent events in Zanzibar, in the growth of political conflict, even violence. He argues that the process of encouraging a mono-crop clove economy, begun by the British and encouraged to an even greater extent by the post-

Revolutionary government, led to the increasing pauperization of rural dwellers in Zanzibar, especially on Pemba Island, and thus to increasing discontent. For him, an explanation of political conflict in Zanzibar needs to be sought as much in agrarian questions, as it does in other historical processes and questions of identity.

There was considerable discussion at the conference on the changing values associated with modernity: several participants noted that those who wish to be considered modern have to 'go with the times' (*kwenda na wakati*). This is a practice much criticized by some local people who wish to uphold what they see as traditional Swahili values. A number of other commentators on the coast have made similar observations: Peake, for instance, in his study of tourism in Malindi, notes the conflict between the values of beach-boys and hustlers, on the one hand, and their elders (1989), a topic on which Beckerleg has also written (1994, 1995). Porter's (1998) study of education in Mombasa also points to an apparent conflict in values between male elders, who see themselves as the guardians of tradition and gate-keepers to outsiders, and young women who seek to be both modern and respectable in traditional Swahili terms (e.g. by adopting a particular mode of dress) (see also Swartz 1991). In this volume, Saleh examines changing moral values in Tanzania, especially in Zanzibar, and a perceived increase in corruption. Saleh argues that long-established values such as *heshima* (respect), *uaminifu* (honesty, truthworthiness), *uadilifu* (ethics) and *ari* (honour) have for some people been superseded in the scramble for resources, and that corruption has even become an everyday aspect of behaviour. This discussion has resonances with another in this volume: Musau's analysis of the criticisms of some recent forms of *taarabu* songs. Some have even been banned from public radio for being overtly sexual or obscene, rather than relying for their meanings on nuance, innuendo and *double entendre*, the use of which places the songs on the proper side of *heshima*.

Several contributors to this volume approach notions of modernity by considering Swahili literature. Saavedra shows that even before the imposition of European colonial rule in the nineteenth century, Swahili verse had begun to borrow words from both English and German to express new ideas and new technologies. Musau examines *taarabu* songs and shows how modern changes are expressed through this medium. Amidu discusses a new form of poetry, *kimondo* (literally 'shooting star'), which was formulated during the 1975 elections in the Lamu East constituency of Kenya but which belongs to a widely known genre of Swahili poetry competitions (*mashairi ya kujibizana*) (See Biersteker 1995). Amidu argues that such competitive verses penned on behalf of candidates enabled communities to survive the potentially divisive process of campaigning. Topan examines changing gender relations by constrasting earlier Swahili texts centring upon women with their more recent depictions in modern Swahili plays. Literature read in these ways can thus provide us with a window on historical change.

It is clear from several of the papers which follow that aspects of modernity do not go uncriticized on the East Coast, and indeed, several contributors chronicle various forms of local resistance to practices deemed to be undesirable. While modernity and development, in the sense of getting ahead, are generally considered desirable goals, such a view is not shared by all those who spend time on the coast. Walley discusses the anti-modernist stance of Euro-American tourists who come to Mafia Island seeking somewhere 'unspoiled'. Here there is a paradox: tourism is supposed to bring development and yet the form of tourism being developed ('eco-tourism') seeks to maintain the pristine quality of the area.

In short, then, as Walley suggests, following the work of Pigg (1996), the term 'modernity' may perhaps best be viewed as an 'empty signifier' which only takes on meaning in particular contexts. Furthermore, it is a contested term with many different meanings, and its definition will depend to some extent upon the location of the definer. This brings us to a consideration of identities and their articulation with different forms of modernity.

Identity and self-identity: pluralism, multiculturalism and ethnicity

A number of commentators have noted that modernity, far from inevitably flattening difference, has often resulted in assertions of identity, especially ethnic identity. Identity refers to perceived qualities of sameness, as a result of which people associate themselves, or are associated by others, with particular groups or categories on the basis of some common features. But notions of the self and identity also presuppose the existence of the Other and thus are based upon notions of difference as well. In one sense, then, identity is about classification and categorization of the world and of social relations. But it is also about cognition and affect, and encompasses emotions from which individuals derive their perceptions of the self, self-esteem and belonging (see Cohen 1982). It is thus both social and personal.

The question of identities on the East Coast is a complex one which has generated a large literature. It is clear that identities have shifted over time, as an examination of the census data reveals. For instance, the numbers claiming 'Arab' status has shifted dramatically: during the British colonial period, it was advantageous to be classed as a 'non-native' (e.g. 'Arab') because legal jurisdictions were different and might be more favourable; in war-time, rations were also better. But in the immediate aftermath of the Zanzibar Revolution, it was not desirable to assert an 'Arab' identity, and so the numbers claiming that status decreased dramatically.

Horton and Middleton argue that the old question 'Who are the Waswahili?' is an 'undiscerning one based on a misunderstanding of what this mercantile system has been and remains' (2000: 4). Although they concede that the answer to this question is largely dependent upon the situation of the observer, they nonetheless contend that the Swahili are indeed a single people for a variety of reasons:

- they speak one language and have a written literature going back several centuries
- they lived in stone-built towns with particular kinds of architecture, some of which are still extant, others of which are now ruined
- they possessed a complex internal structure and system of stratification which was dependent upon being merchants or commercial middlemen, cultural brokers and mediators
- they had a particular religion (Islam) and system of morality; as well as specific notions of beauty and purity.

In all of these respects, the Swahili are like each other, but 'quite different from their neighbours' (ibid: 2). For these reasons, Horton and Middleton argue strongly that the Swahili have thus constituted a *single* African civilization.

Horton and Middleton see the major differences in status as lying between the *waungwana*, whom they term 'patricians', those who were formerly merchants and lived in the stone towns, and the *wenyeji* or 'commoners' who lived in the 'country towns'. But within these broad categories are other terms of identity, such as Shirazi, Bajuni, Comorians, various kinds of Arabs, and groups from the Indian sub-continent such as Ismaili and Bohoras. Thus as they note: 'No one element... can be envisaged and understood without reference to all the others... As with most social identities, their boundaries are there and have meanings, but they are permeable and changeable in many situations' (ibid: 23). In short, the Swahili have many identities from which they can select in different contexts.

For several hundred years, this Swahili mercantile civilization, based to a large extent upon slavery, flourished throughout the East Coast, but in the end it lost wealth and influence to predatory colonial states. Horton and Middleton argue that the Swahili have been used and exploited, then discarded, by both colonial powers and independent governments 'so that the term 'Swahili' has come to refer to a marginalized and internally divided category of people without any obvious sense of single political identity, an 'Other' conceived as a means of self-definition of those who so define them' (ibid: 14).

In their 1994 discussion of Swahili identity, Mazrui and Shariff criticize modern scholars for adding to the 'colonially created confusion' about Swahili identity which in turn, so they argue, came to serve as a 'lucrative research area'. This tendency is exemplified by an article by Eastman published in 1971 and entitled 'Who are the Waswahili?'. Mazrui and Shariff insist that such work 'raised further doubt about the substance and indeed the very reality of Swahili identity' (1994: 43) and go on to argue as follows:

> Even the seemingly innocent scholarly publications were now contributing to the legitimating ideologies of the different interest groups that have a stake in the identity of the Swahili people. Swahili identity thus became increasingly interwoven into the complex disarray of East African politics, and it has become impossible to talk of Swahili identity in terms that are neutral and nonpartisan' (ibid: 4-5).

They note that, recently, Swahili nationalists have emphasized the cultural unity of the Swahili and challenged the 'one-sided, Arab-

9

oriented claims' about Swahili identity, citing Chiraghdin's argument that the Swahili are indeed a 'tribe' because they have a specific ancestry through their own clans and lineages and that they constitute a 'united nation' because they have traditions that distinguish them from others (Mazrui and Shariff 1994: 46-7, Chiragdin 1974: 6).

It is perhaps scarcely surprising that a group which feels itself under pressure should seek to re-emphasize aspects of its cultural traditions, indeed to 'reinvent' itself. This 'invention' or 'reinvention' of tradition' (Anderson 1983) is, as Parkin points out, part of a widespread phenomenon of indigenous claims to authenticity (2001: 134).

The importance of identity, or rather the question of identities, constantly emerged from the papers and discussions at the conference, and is reflected in this volume. It is also an issue on which a number of scholars have recently commented.

Both western and East African scholars have argued for the recognition of a Swahili culture and identity (Arens 1975, Nurse and Spear 1985, Allen 1993, Middleton 1992, Horton and Middleton 2000, Mazrui and Sheriff 1994). Yet within the group termed Swahili, there are numerous differences: for example, between 'patricians' and 'commoners' or between townspeople and rural dwellers. The Swahili themselves distinguish difference in terms of origin and lineage: Wa-Arabu (a category also subdivided), Wa-Shirazi, Wa-Bajuni, Wa-Mbwera, Wa-Mrima and so on. The term 'Wa-Swahili' has also at various times signalled someone who cannot lay claim to any of these statuses, and who is therefore perhaps even of slave origin. More recently, however, there have been calls for the term to be applied to all those coastal dwellers who have lived there for a long time, practice Islam, and speak Swahili as their first language. Such a definition recognizes a common identity (Mazrui and Sheriff 1994) which subsumes some of the above differences, but distinguishes between coastal Swahili, with a particular history and culture, and Africans from inland areas.

In our discussions at the conference, we agreed that identity is rarely singular, much less homogenous, and that it is, rather, multiple, shifting both in terms of historical time and social context, and constantly negotiated. Identities are about the relationship between the self and the other, and they concern both self-identity and that attributed by others. An essentialist and primordialist view of identity was rejected as at best, unhelpful, and at worst, positively dangerous in certain situations. We preferred to regard identities as socially, culturally and historically constructed, and therefore fluctuating.

Both Larsen and Cameron, writing on Zanzibar, show how the attribution of particular ethnic identities, based upon ethnic essentialism, has been channeled into political conflict, leading to violence both during the 1964 Revolution, and in the aftermath of the elections in 2000. Yet Larsen also demonstrates, through her examination of spirit possession, that subjects can be the bearers of multiple identities. People may be possessed by several spirits of different 'origins', each reflecting different aspects of the island's history and culture. She rejects translation of the local term '*kabila*' as 'ethnicity' because she feels it risks the reification of patterns of difference and because the boundaries are complex.

Identity is also powerfully expressed through literature. Saavedra explains how coastal people sought to control, or 'tame' new concepts, technologies and threats emanating from European powers in the nineteenth century by devising ways of writing about them, including formulating new words. Musau shows that *taarabu* songs and performance can also reveal changing social circumstances, and consequent shifts in identities and self-perception, as well as audience boundaries. Topan, on the other hand, is concerned with gender identity. He compares a classic Swahili text on appropriate behaviour for women, the didactic poem of Mwana Kupona, with more recent texts, showing that playwrights writing in Swahili have allowed female characters very different roles and identities.

Assertion of identity is of course a political act, encompassing power relations. In exploring politics and power on the East Coast, we have been mindful of the many levels of power – from the global to the local and including the state, the region, the town, the village, the household – all of which are discussed in this volume. We have also been aware of the many ways in which political power is contested, at best through using competitive poetry to argue elections (Amidu), at worst in the use of violence during elections (Cameron, Larsen).

This discussion on identities has subsumed questions of culture, cultural concepts and values, and cultural difference, issues which we raised at the beginning of this chapter where we noted that contributors to this volume have worked in many different parts of the East Coast. Each of us recognizes something of the area we know in the work of others, yet we are also constantly struck by differences. We agreed at the conference that, rather than seeking to establish an all-encompassing model of Swahili culture, as has been attempted by some of the authors discussed above, we should rather think in terms of a cultural repertoire from which people select at different times, in different places, and in different social contexts.

We also recognized the co-existence of different aspects of culture, labelled in Swahili *dini* or *sharia* (religion or Islamic law) and *mila* or *desturi* (custom) (see Caplan 1982, 1995), a topic discussed in some detail by Ahmed Yassin in a paper given at the conference but which does not appear in this volume (Yassin 2001). In an examination of how marital disputes are resolved on the north Kenya coast, Yassin argued that customary practices, such as the involvement of elders, tends to disadvantage women, who tend rather to go to the Kadhis' courts in the hope of obtaining a divorce. Larsen too, in her discussion of spirit posssession in Zanzibar, notes that this phenomenon is thought of as being associated with *mila*.

Beckerleg draws attention to aspects of modern popular cultures in Malindi: viewing videos (see also Fuglesang 1994), shopping, and material forms such as dress, household equipment and decoration, and the use of modern technology. The consumption of such forms of popular culture does not preclude continued observance of older forms, indeed, as Walley notes in her chapter, those who achieve some development and thereby lay claims to modernity, may be in a stronger position to observe traditional norms and rituals. In some of her earlier work on Watamu, a relatively new settlement on the Kenya coast, Beckerleg has argued that the different Swahili groups who settled there are 'actively engaged in creating a new Swahili order out of the flux of unplanned development' (1994: 99). This is similar to the situation described by Mlacha writing in this volume about Bagamoyo. In her present contribution, Beckerleg argues that the Swahili have developed a peculiar ability to adapt to constant change and still retain a distinctive culture and identity. Her chapter on Malindi shows how 'modernity has been Swahili-ised', in other words, people in Malindi, as elsewhere on the coast, can be both modern *and* Swahili.

Scholarly identities and positionality

In recent work in both literature and the social sciences, the authority of the author has been interrogated and questions raised about his or her positionality. It has become almost *de rigeur* for authors in disciplines such as anthropology to explain themselves, their background, and how this has affected both their relations with informants and what they end up writing (Marcus and Fischer 1986, Clifford and Marcus 1986).

So who are we, the contributors to this volume? We are almost equal numbers of women (five) and men (seven). Our ages range from late twenties to sixties, so our personal experience of lived history is varied: for some of us, memory goes back to the colonial period, while for others, conscious memory lies entirely in the period since independence. All of us have a strong commitment to East Africa, whether we are locals or foreigners. All of us speak, read and write Swahili, although only a minority has known the language from childhood (Mlacha, Musau, Saleh, Topan); most of us have learned it as adults (Amidu, Beckerleg, Cameron, Caplan, Larsen, Le Guennec, Saavedra, Walley). All of us have spent years living there, although for some, residence has been equated mainly with research, while for others, it is a place of birth and/or current residence.

Does any of this make a difference to what we choose to investigate, and what we write? Certainly any attempt to make sense of current debates around Swahili identity needs to bear the positionality of speakers and writers in mind. It scarcely needs to be said that writing as a foreign scholar is in some imporant respects different from writing as a local scholar, and writing as a scholar with local origins who is resident abroad, and not 'at home' is different again. During the discussions at the conference, we became aware of the fact that while, for some of us, the debates around identity are largely of academic interest, for others they are highly personal. On occasion, our discussions would suddenly become rather politicized, a reflection not only of people's differing viewpoints and standpoints, but also of the extent to which identities themselves, including scholarly identities, have been politicized in recent years in this area.

A new term has come into use – the Swahili diaspora. Some Swahili scholars working abroad see themselves as transnational intellectuals 'who keep in touch via global cultural flows and who are not only at home in other cultures, but seek out and adopt a reflexive, metacultural or aesthetic stance to divergent cultural experiences' (Featherstone 1990: 9). But others consider themselves to be part of an on-going community, albeit a de-territorialized one, with significant links to the home area. Thus when we read, for example, Saleh's chapter in this volume, we have to understand it in a number of ways: as a statement about Swahili values and their changing nature, as a personal note of regret for the passing of the values of his childhood, and a statement of what Swahili who live in the diaspora should seek to hold on to. This is equally true of those scholars writing in the diaspora who are seeking, like Mazrui and Shariff, to argue for a clear ethnic and territorial identity for the Swahili, even as Swahili society becomes yet more de-territorialized, with significant numbers living in other parts of East Africa and further afield: the USA, Europe, the Gulf States for example.

The volume

The twelve chapters in this book consider the themes of modernity, identity, and politics on the East African coast and islands. Written by anthropologists, political scientists, and literature specialists, it covers a variety of locations in Kenya, Tanzania (including Zanzibar) and the Comoros. Today, this area is undergoing rapid change as 'globalization' (a short-hand term for a variety of processes) makes its impact. Tourism, increased monetization, emigration from and immigration to the area, and the varying policies of multinational agencies and local states are all significant. What then has been the effect on the identity of a people who have never seen themselves as a single entity, but who nonetheless have differentiated themselves as coastal dwellers and Swahili speakers from other Africans of inland origin? This volume reveals some of the ways in which the Swahili seek to maintain their boundaries, even as they adapt their cultural practices, including their language and literature, to new realities. It also explores the tensions which can arise when ethnic differences are essentialized and politicized as they have been on Zanzibar.

We have divided this volume into three sections. In the first, a series of micro-level studies, mainly by anthropologists, examines the effects of recent economic and social changes in towns such as Bagamoyo (Mlacha) and Malindi (Beckerleg), the north and south of Mafia Island (Caplan and Walley), and the Comoro Islands (Le Guennec-Coppens). Part Two focuses upon Zanzibar, long a multicultural society which underwent a Revolution in 1964, and has recently once again experienced violent political confrontations, this time between the ruling party and its opposition rivals, a dispute which has at times appeared to threaten the unity of Tanzania. The three chapters in this section by Cameron (a political scientist), Larsen and Saleh (both anthropologists), all examine identities in a highly politicised context. In the third part of the book, the emphasis shifts to the expression of Swahili identity in poetry and song, with Amidu discussing poetry contests as part of political contests, Musau considering changes in *taarabu*, a long-established genre of song on the coast, Saavedra looking at the early incorporation of European loan words into Swahili, while Topan examines the representation of women in Swahili literature.

Bibliography

Allen, James de Vere, 1993. *Swahili Origins: Swahili Culture and the Shungwaya Phenomenon.* London: James Currey, Nairobi: EAEP, Athens: Ohio UP.

Anderson, Benedict, 1983. *Imagined Communities: Reflections on the origin and spread of nationalism.* London: Verso.

Appadurai, Arjun 1990. 'Disjuncture and Difference in the Global Cultural Economy', *Theory, Culture and Society* 7, 295-310.

Appadurai, Arjun, 1991. 'Global ethnoscapes: notes and queries for a transnational anthropology' in R.G. Fox (ed.) *Recapturing Anthropology: Working in the Present.* Santa Fe, Mexico: School of American Research Monographs.

Arce, Alberto and Norman Long, 1999. *Anthropology, Development and Modernities.* London and New York: Routledge.

15

Arens, William, 1975. 'The Waswahili: the social history of an ethnic group' *Africa* 45, 426-37.

Beckerleg, Susan, 1994. 'Watamu: lost land but a new Swahili town' in D. Parkin (ed.) *Continuity and Autonomy in Swahili Communities*. Wien, Beitrage zu Afrikanstik Band 48, London: School of Oriental and African Studies: 99-110.

Beckerleg, Susan, 1995. "Brown Sugar or Friday Prayers? Youth Choices and Community Building in Coastal Tanzania" *African Affairs* 94: 23-38.

Biersteker, Ann, 1995. *Kujibizana: Questions of Land and Power in Nineteenth and Twentieth-century Poetry in Kiswahili*. East Lansing, Michigan: Michigan State University Press.

Caplan, Pat, 1982. 'Gender, ideology and modes of production on the East African coast' in J. de Vere Allen (ed.) *From Zinj to Zanzibar: History, Trade and Society on the Coast of East Africa*. Wien: Franz Steiner Verlag: 29-43.

—— 1995b 'Law and custom: marital disputes on Mafia Island, Tanzania' in P. Caplan (ed.) *Understanding Disputes: the Politics of Law*. Oxford: Berg Publishers: 203-22.

Chabal, Patrick and Jean-Pascal Daloz, 1999. *Africa Works: Disorder as Political Instrument* London: International African Institute; Oxford: James Currey; Bloomington Indiana: Indiana University Press.

Chiragdin, Shihabuddin, 1974. 'Kiswahili na wenyewe' *Kiswahili* 44, 1: 48.

Clifford, James and George Marcus (eds.), 1986. *Writing Culture: the Poetics and Politics of Ethnography*. Berkeley: University of California Press.

Cohen, Anthony (ed.), 1982. *Belonging: Identity and Social Organisation in British Rural Cultures*. Manchester: Manchester University Press.

Comoraroff, Jean and John Comaroff, 1992. *Ethnography and the Historical Imagination* Boulder CO: Westview Press.

——, (eds.) 2001. *Millenial Capitalism and the Culture of Neoliberalism*. Durham and London: Duke University Press.

Featherstone, Mike 1990. 'Global Culture: an Introduction', *Theory, Culture and Society* 7: 1-14.

Fischer, Michael, 1997. 'Postmodern, postmodernism' in Thomas Barfield (ed.) *The Dictionary of Anthropology*. Oxford: Blackwell.

Fuglesang, Minou, 1994. *Veils and Videos: Female Youth Culture on the Kenyan Coast*. Stockholm Studies in Social Anthropology.

Giddens, Anthony, 1991. *Modernity and Self-Identity: Self and Society in the Late Modern Age*. Cambridge: Polity Press

Giddens, Anthony, 1999. *A Runaway World?* The Reith Lectures. London: BBC Publications.

Horton, Mark and John Middleton, 2000. *The Swahili: The Social Landscape of a Mercantile Society*. Oxford: Blackwell.

Larsen, Kjersti, 2000 'The other side of "nature": expanding tourism, changing landscapes and problems of privacy in urban Zanzibar' in Vidgis Broch-Due and Richard Scroeder (eds.) *Producing Nature and Poverty in Africa*. Nordisk Afrikan Institut.

Larsen, Kjersti, 1998. 'Spirit possession as historical narrative: the production of identity and locality in Zanzibar Town' in Nadia Lovell (ed.) *Locality and Belonging*. London and New York: Routledge

Leach, Edmund. 1968. *A Runaway world? The Reith Lectures, 1967*. London: BBC Publications

Le Guennec-Coppens, Francoise and Pat Caplan (eds.), 1991. *Les Swahili entre Afrique et Arabie*. Paris, Karthala, Nairobi CREDU. (OC)

Le Guennec-Coppens, Francoise and David Parkin (eds.), 1998. *Autorite et pouvoir chez les Swahili*. Paris, Karthala; Nairobi, IFRA.

Lovell, Nadia (ed.), 1998. *Locality and Belonging*. London and New York: Routledge.

Marcus, George, and Michael J. Fischer, 1986. *Anthropology as Cultural Critique: an Experimental Moment in the Human Sciences*. Chicago: University of Chicago Press.

Mazrui, Alamin and Ibrahim Noor Shariff, 1994. *The Swahili: Idiom and Identity of an African People*. Trenton, NJ: Africa World Press.

Middleton, John, 1992. *The World of the Swahili: an African Mercantile Civilization*. New Haven and London: Yale UP.

Nurse, Derek, and Thomas Spear, 1985. *The Swahili: Reconstructing the History and Language of an African Society, 800-1500*. Philadelphia: University of Pennsylvania Press.

Parkin, David (ed.), 1994. *Continuity and Autonomy in Swahili Communities: Inland Influences and Strategies of Self-determination*. Wien: Beitrage zu Afrikanstik Band 48; London: SOAS.

Parkin, David, 1995. 'Blank banners and Islamic consciousness in Zanzibar'. In Anthony Cohen and Nigel Rapport (eds.) *Questions of Consciousness*. London and New York: Routledge.

Parkin, David, 2001. 'Escaping cultures; the paradox of cultural creativity' in J. Liep (ed.) *Locating Culture and Creativity*. London, Pluto Press.

Parkin, David and Francois Constantin (eds.) 1989. *Social Stratification in Swahili Society*. Special edition of *Africa: Journal of the International African Institute*, 59. 2.

Peake, Robert, 1989. 'Swahili stratification and tourism in Malindi old town, Kenya', *Africa* 59, 2: 209-230.

Pigg, S. 1996. 'The credible and the credulous: the question of villagers' beliefs in Nepal', *Cultural Anthropology* 11(2): 160-201.

Porter, Mary A, 1998. 'Resisting uniformity at Mwana Kupona Girls' School: cultural productions in an educational setting', *Signs: Journal of Women in Culture and Society* 23, 3, 619-43.

Prins, A.H.J., 1961. *The Swahili-Speaking Peoples of Zanzibar and the East African Coast (Arabs, Shirazi and Swahili)*. London: International African Institute.

Rostow, W.W., 1960. *The Stages of Growth: a Non-Communist Manifesto*. Cambridge: Cambridge University Press.

Spencer, Jonathan, 1996. 'Modernism, modernity and modernisation' in A. Barnard and J. Spencer (eds.) *Encyclopaedia of Social and Cultural Anthropology*. London and New York: Routledge.

Swartz, Marc, 1991. *The Way the World Is: Cultural Processes and Social Relations among the Mombasa Swahili*. Berkeley and Los Angeles: University of California Press.

Talle, Aud, 1998. 'Sex for leisure: modernity among female bar workers in Tanzania' in Simone Abram and Jacquie Waldren (eds.) *Anthropological Perspectives on Local Development*. London and New York: Routledge.

Yassin, Ahmed, 2001. 'The changing patterns and structures of settling disputes among the Swahili of Kenya'. Paper given at the Fifth Anglo-French Swahili Workshop, School of Oriental and African Studies, London, September 2001.

CHAPTER 2

MODERNITY HAS BEEN SWAHILI-ISED: THE CASE OF MALINDI

Susan Beckerleg

Introduction

The notions of 'modernity', 'globalization' and 'westernization' are problematic. According to Chabal and Daloz (1999), the understanding of African modernity has been hampered by the tendency of social scientists to view Africa as backward and over-attached to tradition. They argue that, because Western countries were the first to become technologically and managerially efficient, 'westernization' and 'development' are often confused with modernity (p. 50). 'Modernity' is also often merged with 'globalization', as for example by many of the contributors to the edited volume *Modernity on a Shoestring* (Fardon, 1999). Furthermore, the modern state has been largely defined as one that produces individuals who are discrete citizens operating within the democratic process. However, in Europe, as elsewhere, globalization has been accompanied by the re-emergence of ethnicity and nationalism as important components of individual and group identities. Within the African context, Chabal and Daloz suggest, modernity should not simply be opposed to tradition. Individual and group identities and their expression draw on traditions that are instrumental to survival and success in the modern world: 'It is thus not a question of Africans being more 'traditional' (meaning backward) than others. Rather it is the much more pertinent fact that being both traditional and modern is at once justifiable and instrumentally profitable' (Chabal and Daloz, 1999: 147).

Malindi, a town of about 83,000 people, provides an excellent case study of the Swahili talent for adaptation to change and provides a vibrant illustration of what it means to be modern *and* Swahili. The old town area, named Shela after the settlement on Lamu Island, remains a Swahili enclave amidst the great ethnic diversity that characterises the rest of Malindi. Apart from a few Meru *miraa* (khat) traders who provide a commodity that has become part of modern Swahili culture, almost everybody residing in Shela is Swahili. Many of the poorer families are Bajuni and originate from the Lamu archipelago. Other, usually more prosperous, Swahili claim Arab ancestry. Like other Swahili, the Swahili of Malindi have numerous kin ties along the East African coast, inland, in Arabia and beyond. But unlike many other Swahili, such as the old families of the former city-states of Mombasa and Lamu, those living in Malindi all appear to have roots elsewhere. If there are any patrician Swahili in Malindi I have not met them nor heard them mentioned. Perhaps this lack of patrician identification with the town has contributed to the modernity of Swahili in Malindi. Unlike Lamu, for example, there is no sense of old families living out a glorious past and no pressure to conserve a precious, vulnerable way of life (Middleton, 1992; Swartz, 1991).

Many Shela households have family members involved in the fishing industry, but greater numbers of men are either unemployed or work in the informal tourist industry as 'beachboys'. In recent years Shela has also gained a reputation, partly deserved, as the centre of illicit drug dealing and using in Malindi. Non-Swahili health workers and teachers routinely single out the area as one with more than its fair share of social problems and refer to its inhabitants as 'hard to reach', problematic Muslims who do not know how to bring up their children.

This paper considers the ways that the Swahili of Malindi have engaged with the modern world. The first part examines their responses to the tourist boom and bust, while the second discusses Swahili identity and popular cultural expression.

20

Part 1: Tourist Boom and Bust

When the Portuguese arrived five hundred years ago in Malindi, they found a thriving town of about 6,000 Swahili-speaking Muslim traders and fishermen (Robertson, 1998). Horton and Middleton (2000) include Malindi as one of the old Swahili towns that participated in the complex interactions between rival city-states and competing colonial powers. In the twentieth century, however, Malindi lost its status as a centre of Swahili culture and became a somewhat disreputable tourist centre. Since the 1960s, the Swahili of Malindi have been joined by numerous migrants from other parts of the country and by European residents of Kenya, particularly Italians. In 1997 the district of Malindi was created and the town expanded again to accommodate local government officers, their families and those who service their needs.

In the early 1980s Peake found Malindi to be a major tourist destination and the fishing industry to be in decline (1989). Since then, the town has endured an Italian-led tourist boom that started in the 1980s and involved the purchase of land and the development of hotels, restaurants, bars and casinos. Even the coral reef was plundered for sale to aquaria in Europe. Italian business people worked with local partners who often fronted the businesses.

In the early years of Italian investment many Swahili became rich through land deals and numerous business ventures, which ranged from the legitimate to the illegal. According to Malindi people now in their thirties and forties who have both worked and relaxed with Italians, they desire good food and drink, adventurous sex, and casinos and drugs, including heroin.

The turndown started gradually in the 1990s, and, although some Italians remain, many businesses are failing and the town is now facing sharp declines in tourist numbers and revenue. 'Off season' is the modern meaning of *kusi*, the Southern monsoon, and the complaint of the town's people is that 'It is always *kusi* these days'.

Local people and migrants from afar serviced the Italians, and consequently numerous social problems have accompanied both the boom and the bust. Unemployment, prostitution and drug abuse are features of most African towns but Malindi has been particularly affected in recent years. AIDS is also taking a heavy toll in Malindi, as throughout Kenya. According to the District Medical Officer, about 20% of the adult population of Malindi is estimated to be HIV positive (personal communication).

In June 2001 some families were experiencing hunger during the *kusi* month when the tourist and fishing off-seasons coincide. Year-round catches are reportedly reduced due to competition from commercial trawlers and because some fishing grounds are now part of the Marine National Park and therefore off limits. Such restrictions on the traditional craft of fishing have pushed men into the modern enterprise of taking tourists snorkelling in the Marine Park (Beckerleg, 1994). Nevertheless, both traditional sailing dhows (*mashua*) and modern dinghies are still being built and the fish caught from them sold in two wholesale markets. Opportunities also exist for fishermen to go on longer expeditions into fish-rich, but pirate-infested, Somali waters (Beckerleg, 2001).

The local response

One response to economic hard times has been for families to exploit links with Arabia, particularly Yemen and Oman. Young Swahili men travel to the oil wealthy countries of the Arabian Gulf for work and some young women become expatriate wives. Such expatriate Swahili are an important source of remittance money. These overseas Swahili supplement the funds that flow from Europe to many Swahili households from business partners, absent spouses or lovers. Foreign funds that keep many families afloat reach once prosperous Malindi courtesy of Western Union Money Transfer, transactions which are a key part of modern life in Malindi and an example of the forces of globalization. Money thus attained can, however, be used to underwrite tradition, for example to pay for lavish weddings, or to fund modernity by the purchase of consumer goods.

In recent years, development agencies and donors have embraced the notion of civil society, but the meaning of the term remains hotly debated (Harrington, 1999). Some consider a developed civil society important as a means of countering the effects of the hegemonic state, while others see it a bulwark against the excesses of the market economy. Chabal and Daloz (1999) find the term civil society to be nebulous and problematic in the modern African context where the state is poorly developed and where local associations have always acted in their own interests. However, given the tendency of Swahili society towards factionalism and competition, the recent formation of outside-funded, welfare associations should not be taken for granted as a normal part of Swahili society, but as a key aspect of adaptation to life in modern Kenya. In Malindi, the growth of small local welfare and development organizations run by Swahili, or with significant Swahili membership, points to an active engagement with the modern world.

Twenty years ago Peake conducted fieldwork in Shela. He writes of young educated Swahili men who talked of Islamic revival as a means of coming to grips with tourism and with the challenges of living in modern Kenya (1989: 216). Perhaps some of those young men translated talk into action, for a number of Muslim-led welfare organizations and societies have been formed in recent years. Mostly, these organizations are supported by funds from wealthy Arab countries that are used to provide education, training and medical expenses to needy families. Tawfiq Muslim Youth and Tawfiq Hospital access money from Arab countries and and from organizations such as the UK charity Muslim Aid to fund a range of health projects such as eye clinics and the rehabilitation of glue-sniffing children. They also collaborate with The Omari Project, a self-help group tackling heroin abuse.

Heroin abuse is perceived by Swahili elders to be overwhelmingly a Muslim problem affecting coastal Kenya (Beckerleg, 1995). Following the lead of Mombasa and Watamu where strong local action – some would say vigilantism – has taken the form of aggressively targeting known drug dealers, a local branch of the Council of Imams and Preachers was formed specifically to try and control the supply of heroin to Malindi (Nyahah, 2001). The members comprise not only imams and preachers, but also concerned Muslim men of the Swahili community. Members of the Council have, with the police, raided known heroin dealers, with limited success. In July 2001 the Malindi branch of the Council hosted a coast-wide meeting to discuss their strategy towards drug abuse.

But not all Swahili-led organizations are overtly Islamic in their approach, although they focus on the problems facing the Islamic (Swahili) community. The Malindi Education Development

Association (MEDA) aims to serve disadvantaged youth from all communities living in Malindi. Recently MEDA members have become concerned with tackling an issue first raised by UNICEF, that of the heavy educational load of Muslim children who often attend secular schools during the week and Muslim schools at weekends. They are seeking new ways to integrate religious and secular education.

Swahili women are also active. The Shela branch of the Maendelo ya Wanawake, a women's organization with close links to the ruling party KANU, is concerned with health issues and also micro-credit. Another organization, SOLWODI, has international funding to provide new economic opportunities for sex workers and has the enthusiastic support of many Swahili women activists from Shela. In addition, some Swahili women have joined the multi-ethnic Society of Women Against AIDS – Kenya (SWAK) formed in 2000. The Society is concerned primarily with provision for AIDS orphans and with raising awareness of the need for HIV prevention throughout the Malindi area.

With AIDS increasingly acknowledged to be the cause of many deaths in the community, associations such as Tawfiq Hospital and SWAK provide a bridge between the conservative Islamic establishment, the Ministry of Health and donor agencies. In collaboration with the Ministry of Health, and as part of national HIV prevention efforts, Tawfiq Hospital provides free treatment services for sexually transmitted diseases. A new project for voluntary counselling and testing for HIV was opened in July 2001 with the approval of Tawfiq Hospital. Other initiatives that attempt to slow the spread of HIV remain controversial. As Bujra found in Tanzania, Muslim leaders in Malindi are grappling with the issues of condom promotion and sex education (Bujra, 2000).

These initiatives are primarily responses to local problems. By attempting to address specific problems in Malindi, the Swahili who are engaged in health or welfare project work are, to some extent, uniting to override the factionalism and divisions that often characterise Swahili communities. Thus while heeding the reservations of Chabal and Daloz (1999) regarding the development of civil society in Africa, it appears necessary to concede that these organizations *are* an example of civil society. To a greater or lesser extent they serve the wider community of Malindi and not just kin groups, other Swahili or co-religionists.

Such activism is a modern response to local social and economic problems. This activism sometimes runs in parallel, and sometimes overlaps with, conventional Swahili charitable movements that are based on kinship, Islamic charity and patron-client relationships.

Part 2: Swahili Identity and Cultural Expression

In modern Africa, as elsewhere, ethnic identity is expressed in terms of tradition, culture and use of language in ways that are instrumentally useful for individuals and the groups to which they owe allegiance. In Kenya, ethnicity has long been and remains a vital part not only of an individual's identity, but also a marker of social status and occupation. The colonial administration imposed the 'tribe' as the only accepted form of social identity (van Nahl, 1999). The term 'Swahili' was more both embracing and even more problematic than 'tribe', but remains an important part of modern self-identification in the town of Malindi.

While Shela remains overwhelmingly Swahili, it is a small area and many Swahili live in other parts of Malindi where they trade and often socialise with other ethnic groups. The Swahili of Malindi participate fully in the commercial and political life of the town in a way that characterises many aspects of modern Kenya and cross-cuts ethnic divides. As van Nahl found amongst the Kalenjin, commercial interests and the market economy sometimes overrule ethnic loyalty (1999). However, the continuing, contrary trend of ethnic-based loyalty should not be underestimated, nor labelled as 'backward'.

The leading Swahili families run thriving businesses such as bus companies, workshops, fish markets or petrol stations. They may also own land either within the town or in the hinterland on the old slave plantations of earlier centuries. Many of these wealthy families have their roots in Yemen or Oman, whence their forefathers migrated in the nineteenth or twentieth centuries. Horton and Middleton note that many families who formerly claimed Arab descent now assert that there are no Swahili 'patricians' and that they are all equally members of the traditional Swahili elite (2000, 203). In Malindi this interpretation of contemporary Swahili society appears to be widely accepted.

Modern Swahili Culture

Chabal and Daloz note that Africans have never been slow to adopt technological innovations such as videos and mobile telephones and write of the 'Africanization of Western modernity' (1999: 146). Of modern Africans they comment that: 'They cast themselves as mobile phone-wielding businessmen while keeping in contact with village spirits. They reinterpret Rambo from the memory of their initiation ceremonies' (Chabal and Daloz, 1999: 51).

Similarly, over the centuries a wide range of goods and popular cultural movements from Arabia, India and the West has been incorporated into Swahili culture. For example, a hundred years ago the development of the Maulidi movement in Lamu by Habib Saleh produced new forms of religious and cultural expression that drew on Yemeni ritual and also undermined the Lamu 'patrician' elite (Middleton, 1992).

Other imported, populist cultural movements may have had less impact on Swahili politics, but nevertheless, provide new forms of self-expression. The cultural import may vary, but the process of Swahiliization remains constant. In the early twentieth century the *beni* band movement parodied the marching bands of British colonial power. Rival associations competed in terms of their costumes and music in large-scale marches and displays (Ranger, 1975). At the time *beni* was a modern manifestation of the traditional division of Swahili towns into competing 'moieties', as well as an enjoyable means of mocking the colonialists. Such competition survives today in the form of football clubs that are centred on town quarters in all Swahili settlements. In Malindi, 'Liverpool' is the main rival of 'Young Stars', with players and supporters drawn from different areas within Shela. Important match wins are celebrated by a procession through town led by a *beni*-style band. Supporters of local clubs named after world-class clubs such as Liverpool and Arsenal also support the 'parent' teams. Matches are keenly watched on satellite television, with a small charge made by some owners of large screens to view important matches. Thus, in Shela support for Liverpool, for example, involves both the modern expression of spatially-based Swahili competitive tendencies, but also inclusion in the world-wide following of foreign clubs through the global medium of television.

Amongst the Swahili, football is largely, but not exclusively a male youth passion. Young Swahili women attend important matches in Shela and in Lamu and, heavily veiled, they stand together as patches of black amongst the multi-coloured dress of the men and boys. However, female youth culture entails activities that take women less into the public sphere than a football ground. Fuglesang (1994) has written about the leisure of young women in Lamu as centred on the viewing of videos. Since then, satellite television has arrived in Lamu, as in Malindi, and videos no longer represent the acme of modern leisure pursuits.

Commentators who bemoan the imminent decline of the Swahili under the assault of modernity should note that there is nothing new about innovations within Swahili culture. However, mass global communications have speeded up this process so that the modern Swahili must adapt to change more quickly than earlier generations. They share this technological brave new world with the vast majority of cultural groups throughout Africa and the rest of the world. The Swahili may be better equipped for dealing with rapid change than other societies that have been less exposed over the centuries to outside influences. As Horton and Middleton point out:

> Few societies in the world have lasted as long as that of the Swahili, and few have retained the same basic forms and institutions. It has never been isolated from the remainder of Africa or from Asia; and, facing in both directions, it has taken ideas and items of cultural behaviour from both places and also given others to them. Yet it has formed and kept its own civilisation based on exchange between its constituent groups and between those of a wider system of trading networks of both Africa and Asia. (Horton and Middleton, 2000: 203)

Dress

Contemporary links with the Arabian Gulf and Europe have stimulated local forms of Swahili self-expression. Modern Swahili dress reflects styles from both areas, but owes little or nothing to the mainstream Kenyan fashion that draws on both West African or pan-African textiles and styles and global trends. With their distinctive dress, the Swahili of Malindi are able to express their own identity and to differentiate themselves from other ethnic groups inhabiting the town. There is considerable scope for individual self- expression for both men and women and therefore the efforts of Swahili elders to maintain an Islamic dress code are largely successful.

Fashionable men's dress exhibits a mix of western and Arabian influences. In particular the Omani *dishdasha*, a white, pastel or lilac coloured robe, has become the most popular style of *kanzu*, worn mostly on Fridays, but daily by some men. Although fashions worn on Fridays and at religious festivals, such as Maulidi recitations and processions, tend to display links with Arabia and Islam, many Swahili men wear western dress at other times. The young are interested in trainers and jeans, but may top the outfit with an embroidered *kofia* rather than a baseball cap, thereby indicating that they are Muslim. Shorts are avoided by Swahili men as shameful, and as the apparel of non-Muslims such as Giriama servants and tourists.

In Malindi, Islamic dress that covers the head and body continue to be mandatory for the vast majority of Swahili women and girls once they reach puberty. Posters regularly appear on the premises of Swahili-run businesses and organizations such as Tawfiq Hospital depicting the correct way for Muslim women to dress, and cautioning against the sloppy use of the veil. While twenty years ago, virtually all women wore the *buibui* in public spaces, a choice of modest clothing is now available. The term 'veil' is generic and includes everything from wearing a headscarf and loose coat to complete covering of the body and face including hands and feet. Swahili women in Malindi wear all kinds of veil and none but there are considerable pressures to conform to what is seen as a badge of Swahili identity. Even the handful of Swahili women who work in the sex industry and/or are heroin users come under heavy social pressure from elders and family members to keep their hair covered and to observe the other basic rules of modesty.

In Malindi the vast majority of Swahili women use the veil not as a means as pursuing a career in the sex industry but as a strategy for being modern and Swahili. The diversity of modern veiling styles provides greater scope for self-expression than the *buibui* that dominated twenty years ago. Nevertheless, the *buibui* remains the definitive Swahili veil, to the extent that young Swahili men refer to young Swahili women as '*buibui*', although many of the latter do not wear this attire. Current fashions associated with modesty include the *hijabu*, which allows greater freedom of movement. It enables women to use their hands in the operation of computers in offices and banks and makes it easier to ride on the back of a motorcycle than would the *buibui*. The *hijabu*, combined with a total face covering (*ninja*), also allows greater freedom, not of movement but of self-expression. Some women wear the *ninja* style to conceal their bodies from men and to express their piety. Such intentions are signalled by the inclusion of socks and gloves in the woman's assemblage. But most of the increasing numbers of *ninja* wearers in Malindi are followers of Swahili fashion rather than Islamicists. Like their Zanzibari sisters, they play with dress as a marker in an environment where tourism, characterised by immodest dress and behaviour, is seen by many as threatening the Swahili way of life (Parkin, 1995).

Under the *buibui* or *hijabu* most younger women wear western clothing, including trousers and short skirts that may or may not be visible, and modern wedge shoes that are easily discernible. Even older women have largely abandoned the use of traditional *khanga* cloths outside the home. The height of fashion for Swahili women, thus, combines influences from both the west and from the wider Islamic world. The continuing use of veiling fashions satisfies the still-influential Swahili elders and provides an expression of a clear Swahili identity in a multi-ethnic town. In Zanzibar too Parkin (1995) found that men contrasted the scanty dress of tourists with the modest attire of their sisters in a way that drew on the Swahili ethic of concealment: 'The threat to concealment is disclosure. Stripping turns a virtuous woman into a whore according to the ethic' (Parkin, 1995: 202).

However, some women working in the sex industry have exploited veiling to their commercial advantage. The clients of sex workers, be they Africans or Europeans, appear to be attracted by the apparent contradiction of veiled woman being sexually available (Lindisfarne-Tapper and Ingham, 1997). Hence, being demurely dressed and available for commercial sex becomes a unique selling point. According to informants, some Italian men have expressed a desire to have sexual relations, not with any Kenyan women in Malindi, but with heavily-veiled Swahili women. The *ninja* style, in which the face is covered, may thus be sometimes used as a lure to attract foreign men, but the wearer is not always either Swahili or

29

Muslim. Other women play on the ambiguity of veiled sex by wearing black, see-through *hijabu* and headscarves. Some women in Malindi have skilfully played on the juxtaposition of the male requirement for women to be protected and male consumer fantasies of stripping concealed flesh. As Lindisfarne-Tapper and Ingham point out, "veiling' may be held to indicate virtually anything informants *and* analysts want' (1997: 16). Swahili elders require certain standards of dress for Muslim women in their community. However, Swahili women use the veil to assert themselves and to convey messages about their identity, independence, sexual availability and degree of piety.

Popular culture and language

Satellite television, video and audio-cassettes all bring outside influences. Indeed, the greater the variety of foreign influences, the greater the viewing and listening choices. Some imports, such as *taarabu* cassettes from Zanzibar and mainland Tanzania by the very popular Tanzania One Theatre, promote quintessentially Swahili cultural forms (Topp, 1994). Other popular music cassettes, mostly from Lebanon and Egypt, enable the Swahili to enjoy music that also helps them to identify with the Arab world. Hindi films and the songs that feature prominently in them continue to be popular. Kenyan *taarabu* singers copy both popular Arabic songs (such as those of Yusuf Mohammed Tenge) and Hindi film music (such as that sung by Juma Bhalo). Although Bhalo is reputed to have started his long career in Malindi, the town has not produced any recent *taarabu* stars. Nevertheless, the Swahili of Malindi remain enthusiastic about this modern Swahili form of expression.

In Malindi, Swahili people watch Arabic language satellite TV stations and CNN, but rarely the domestic Kenyan stations. A popular soap opera, showing characters who appear to be Latin American and is probably dubbed from Spanish or Portuguese, is shown on an Arabic language station. It is daily viewing in many Swahili households, although the majority of the viewers will understand no more than a few words of the Arabic dialogue. Videos cassettes of both Bollywood and Hollywood films are viewed mostly by the youth in video parlours that charge a modest entry fee.

English and Swahili are taught in government schools, while those attending Muslim schools may learn an Arabic that is useful for purposes beyond the recitation of the Quran. These formal linguistic influences combine with those of the foreign media and with face-to-face interaction with foreign tourists to influence day to day speech. *Sheng*, the street talk of Nairobi, derived from mixing Swahili and English grammatical forms, is popular throughout Kenya but in Malindi, Swahili street talk and slang incorporates English and Italian words mixed with Arabic. The result is a form of speech that is partly unintelligible to non-native speakers of Swahili, is particular to Malindi, and is enjoyed predominantly by the Swahili youth of the town. For example, a *mushkila* (Ar: problem) requires a *solutio* (English: solution). English loan words are also fitted into Swahili phrases in novel ways. In relating the story of a death, somebody may be referred to as '*aka* dead', and of somebody who is sleeping heavily one might say, '*amelala flat*'. As I speak no Italian, loan words in that language are more difficult to discern. However, when I heard young men calling each other *telo* I asked what it meant, and was told that it was Italian for 'friend'. I have also heard hybrid phrases such as: '*tilia* (Swahili) *aqua* (Italian)', meaning 'pour (me) some water'.

Such a creative use of foreign loan words is nothing new. In this volume, Saavedra describes how English and German words were incorporated into poetry at the eve of colonisation. Some of the terms he mentions, such as *sitimu*, which probably derived from the word 'steam' and denotes drunkenness, remain in common use. Indeed, *sitimu* in contemporary Malindi is also used to denote the pleasurable effects of a heroin 'high'.

Houses and their contents

Donley (1987) excavated eighteen-century coral houses in Lamu and interpreted what she found by analysing ethnographic information. This exercise showed that the spatial organization of such Swahili houses and the rituals that took place in them were concerned with the maintenance of privacy and the continual need to secure the space against outsiders. Archaeological and ethnographic evidence showed that the house was the domain of women, who were active in supervising servants. The inner area of the house was an arena for private, female-centred activities.

During fieldwork, Donley observed that it was still rare for a strange man to enter a house (1987: 186) and that men spent most of their time out of the house.

In Malindi many Swahili who have made money recently have moved into newly-built villas or apartments. These modern dwellings are still the domain of women, who, finances permitting, manage non-Swahili, mostly Giriama servants. However, the new dwellings are laid out according to international design conventions that do not take into account Swahili requirements for gendered space. As in other parts of the world, modern residences typically have a large reception room opening off the entrance. In the larger villas there may also be a veranda, a garage and extensive grounds, while apartments are more cramped, and tend to have smaller rooms. Hence, these new dwellings are very different in layout to either the traditional stone houses that Donley (1987) describes, or to the more modest traditional, square, thatched homes with rooms opening off a central corridor that also serves as a reception area.

Although the layout is new, many key decorative features have been incorporated into modern residences and their interiors. Doors are an important decorative feature of Swahili houses and elaborately carved 'Lamu doors' stand at the entrance of many modern villas in Malindi. Inside, traditional carving techniques are on display in items of modern furniture such as coffee tables and cabinets for the television and video player. In one house I visited, reproduction carved niches of the style found in old Lamu houses adorned one wall of the sitting room, while photographs depicting male family members in Arabian settings were prominently displayed. We watched Arabic-language pop-videos on satellite television, while a Giriama servant served sodas which were placed on carved coffee tables. This modern style effortlessly combined the use of modern consumer goods with Arabian influences while evoking a strong Swahili material heritage.

In Zanzibar, too, Parkin (1995) found that those who refurbished their homes displayed art that expressed the contradictions between the traditional and modern. In these pictures:

> ..... new buildings act as a background for old ones, and vice versa; audiovisual equipment lies within reach of ancient house interiors, whose elderly occupants can be seen clad in Islamic dress; a Swahili wooden fishing vessel lies off-shore next to a

powered motor boat, with tourists and Swahili fishermen on the beach; and most evocative of all, a scantily clad, blond young tourist woman standing outside the door of an old Stone Town house faces a Muslim woman of the same age dressed in the *hijab* (Parkin, 1995: 214).

Compared to Malindi the tourist boom in Zanzibar is new. Parkin describes a setting where Swahili people are grappling with contradictions that appear insoluble. In Malindi the boom is over, but the Swahili do appear to have found ways of successfully combining old and new elements of material culture in a way that does not allow their culture and society to disintegrate.

Conclusion

Kenyan Swahili retain a strong sense of identity, despite or because of their perception of themselves as a marginalised group in national life (Cruise-O'Brien, 1995; Mazrui and Shariff, 1994). The Swahili of Malindi have endured the full onslaught of mass tourism combined with a form of re-colonisation by wealthy Italians. Social problems, common to African towns in general and to Malindi in particular, abound. The town has become multi-ethnic, and the Swahili are no longer in the majority. Yet, they retain a strong sense of identity as Muslims and as Swahili. Financial links with Arabia and Europe have been exploited to respond to contemporary economic and social challenges and to express their cultural identity. The Swahili of Malindi remain easily distinguishable from their non-Swahili neighbours in terms of language, dress, house-style and leisure pursuits. All these cultural forms have been influenced by global or western trends, yet remain recognisably Swahili. Modernity has thus been Swahiliised, in the same sense that Chabal and Daloz (1999) write of the Africanisation of 'Western modernity' (146). For the Swahili, who have absorbed and adapted influences from three continents for over a millennium, this is nothing new.

Acknowledgements

Fieldwork in Malindi was carried out between 2000 and 2001 in three periods of about three months each, as part of an ESRC-funded research project, 'Risking Independence? Swahili Women

Heroin Users'. Additional time was spent in Malindi in 2001 on Omari Project business.

Bibliography

Beckerleg, Susan, 1994. 'Watamu: lost land, but a new Swahili town' in David Parkin (ed.) *Continuity and Autonomy in Swahili Communities: Strategies of Self Determination.* Afro-Pub, Institüt für Afrikanstik, University of Vienna: 99-109.

Beckerleg, Susan, 1995. 'Brown Sugar or Friday Prayers: Youth Choices and Community Building in Coastal Kenya' *African Affairs* 94, 23-38.

Beckerleg Susan, 2001. 'Continuity and Adaptation by Contemporary Swahili Boatbuilders in Kenya,' in Parkin, David and R. Barnes (eds.) *Ships and the Development of Marine Technology in the Indian Ocean.* Richmond, Surrey: Curzon: 258-276.

Bujra, Janet, 2000. 'Risk and Trust: Unsafe Sex, Gender and AIDS in Tanzania,' In Caplan, Pat (ed.) *Risk Revisited.* London: Pluto Press: 59-83.

Chabal, Patrick and Jean-Paul Daloz (1999) *Africa Works: Disorder as Political Instrument.* Oxford: IAI; Oxford: James Currey; Bloomington: Indiana University Press.

Cruise O'Brien, Donal, 1995. 'Coping with Christians: The Muslim predicament in Kenya' in Hansen, Holger Bernt and Michael Twaddle (eds.) *Religion and Politics in East Africa.* London: James Currey: 200-219.

Donley, L. W. (1987). 'Life in the Swahili town house reveals the symbolic meaning of spaces and artefact assemblages,' *The African Archaeological Review* 5: 181 -192.

Fardon, Richard, 1999. *Modernity on a Shoestring.* London: Eidos.

Fuglesang, Minou, 1994. *Veils and Videos: Female Youth Culture on the Kenyan Coast.* Stockholm: Stockholm Studies in Social Anthropology.

Harrington, J. A., 1999. 'Between the state and civil society: medical discipline in Tanzania,' *The Journal of Modern African Studies:* 37, 2; 207-239.

Horton, Mark and John Middleton, 2000. *The Swahili: The Social Landscape of a Mercantile Society.* Oxford: Blackwell Publishers.

Lindisfarne-Tapper, Nancy and B. Ingham, 1997. 'Approaches to the Study of Dress in the Middle East' in Nancy Lindisfarne-Tapper, and B. Ingham (eds.) *Languages of Dress in the Middle East*. Richmond, Surrey: Curzon: 1-39.

Mazrui, Alamin and Ibrahim Noor Shariff, 1994. *The Swahili: Idiom and Identity of an African People*. Trenton, NJ: Africa World Press.

Middleton, John, 1992. *The World of the Swahili*. New Haven and London: Yale University Press.

Nahl, van Andreas, 1999. 'Market expansion, globalized discourses and changing identity politics in Kenya,' in Richard Fardon (ed.) *Modernity on a Shoestring*. London: Eidos: 303-313.

Nyagah, Robert, 2001. 'Malindi people winning the war against drug abuse'. *Daily Nation* 7th May.

Parkin, David, 1995. 'Blank Banners and Islamic Consciousness in Zanzibar', in Anthony P. Cohen and Nigel Rapport (eds.) *Questions of Consciousness*. ASA Monograph 33. London and New York: Routledge: 198-216.

Peake, Robert, 1989. 'Swahili stratification and tourism in Malindi old town, Kenya', *Africa* 59, 2: 209-220.

Ranger, Terence, 1975. *Dance and Society in Eastern Africa*. London: Heineman.

Robertson, S. A., 1998. *Malindi and Vasco da Gama*. Booklet printed by Malindi Museum Society.

Swartz, Marc, 1991. *The Way the World Is: Cultural Processes and Social Relations Among the Mombasa Swahili*. Berkeley: University of California Press.

Topp, Janet, 1994. 'A history of *taarab* music in Zanzibar: a process of Africanisation', in David Parkin (ed.) *Continuity and Autonomy in Swahili Communities: Strategies of Self Determination*. Afro-Pub, Institüt für Afrikanistik, University of Vienna/ SOAS: 153-165.

CHAPTER 3

CULTURAL PLURALISM IN A COASTAL TOWN OF EAST AFRICA: A STUDY OF BAGAMOYO

S.A.K. Mlacha

Cultural pluralism implies the existence of a community made up of people of different backgrounds who in some respects retain their separate identities but in others create a new form of culture with shared ideas and values. In such a context, relations between the different constituent groups may be either hostile or harmonious. This paper considers the socio-cultural development of Bagamoyo, an old town on the coast of Tanzania, and the ways in which its inhabitants have created a relatively harmonious yet culturally plural society.

Bagamoyo is one of the most important towns in the history of East Africa. Although today its population does not exceed 50,000 people, its history as a trading centre goes back many centuries. In fact, the Kaole ruins of Bagamoyo indicate that Arabs had settled in Bagamoyo as early as the fourteenth century A.D. and that by this time Islam was already the dominant religion. But even more closely connected to our theme is the fact that Bagamoyo has had links with peoples of other cultures for many centuries, a factor that contributed to its development as one of the early coastal settlements. According to Allen, in the later part of the nineteenth century Bagamoyo could be compared to Lamu in that 'Both were relatively large and prosperous Swahili communities depending heavily upon trade' (1993: 200). Commercial links thus built relations between the people of Bagamoyo and communities coming from very different parts of the world. By the 1870s Bagamoyo already had many newcomers 'some of whom were Hindus or Shiite Muslims from the Indian sub-continent' (ibid.: 200). Furthermore, by the same period Roman Catholic Christians had started the construction of the first Roman Catholic Church in East Africa.

Bagamoyo's communication with the interior already existed through the slave trade. Slaves from the interior were brought to the coast for shipment abroad and to this town in particular, since it had the largest slave market in East Africa and the largest number of slaves and slave traders. Bagamoyo was also the place to which the famous porters, Susi and Chuma, managed to bring the body of Dr. David Livingstone all the way from Ujiji in Western Tanganyika and it was from here that the body was sent back to Europe.

Like other coastal towns, Bagamoyo is essentially a Swahili town which Middleton (1992) defines as a plural society composed of many elements of disparate origins that have for centuries intermingled, intermarried and interbred. Bagamoyo fits this definition when we look at the customs and cultures, cuisine and clothing, architecture and activities, history and traditional beliefs. But above all it is Swahili in the sense that it is a settlement established by a mixture of people from different cultures and origins. These include Arabs and Asians on the one hand and the African Zaramo, Doe, Kwere and Zigua, their major trading partners, on the other. Intermarriage took place between them thereby forming a mixed race, while their cultures mingled to form a complex constellation of experiences and beliefs. African traditions and beliefs were relocated into the social-cultural contexts of other traditions, specifically here, as elsewhere on the East Coast, the Arab traditions and beliefs based on religious books.

Nonetheless, the African groups remained tied together for many reasons. In the first place they were in general terms treated as inferior by the Arabs and Asians and later by the Europeans in terms of social and political relations. As Middleton (1992: 11) suggests, their long subjection to colonial political systems brought them together and created a sense of solidarity. Secondly, they were either middlemen or victims of the slave trade while later, with the imposition of colonial rule, they were victims of the colonial masters and thus shared with each other similar attitudes towards the rulers. For all of these reasons, Africans maintained in effect a somewhat separate community of their own.

Yet cultural links in Bagamoyo town were also formed by religion. Islam had been well established in Bagamoyo at an early stage, as mentioned above, and for local Africans the Moslem faith became a uniting factor not only between them but also with the Arabs. Under the umbrella of Moslem brotherhood people of different cultural backgrounds were brought together. However, although Islam has been in Bagamoyo since as early as the fourteenth century, it should not be forgotten that the Africans have continued to be guided by their own beliefs and ethics, including beliefs in spirits and the supernatural powers of magic. This is what they had inherited from their traditions which, as Vansina states 'have passed from mouth to mouth, for a period beyond the life time of the informants' (1985: 13). In a culturally plural society such as Bagamoyo, both the Islamic and the traditional African culture have continued to coexist, thereby fostering the development of what we may today term Swahili culture. When Christianity was introduced in the 1860s, the church was at the forefront of the emancipation of the slaves. The emancipated slaves were saved and maintained by the church, which enabled people of different ethnic backgrounds to see themselves as one.

Another factor which has been significant in unifying the inhabitants is language. Bagamoyo developed with a single language, Swahili, which Mazrui and Mazrui (1995) suggest has served as a means of mediation and communication between people. Thus speaking the same language and having the same African background allowed people from different ethnic groups to consider themselves as people with shared traditions. They developed as one, as Swahili, with a shared culture different from that of the 'foreigners' and shared a sense of belonging to a particular locality, rather than to the place where they (or their ancestors) were born.

Tolerance is a distinguishing feature of Swahili communities. This is because the `self' in African societies has always been very closely tied to the `other', and in many cases, to the ancestors and to the tribal chief. This means that the individual's actions and activities tend to reflect his or her position and role in society and participation based on the expectations and reactions of the `other'. Thus the level of tolerance and the degree of accommodation of the `other' has been high, resulting in peace and harmony among people of different ethnic backgrounds living as a single community. In Bagamoyo, the personal and cultural experience and knowledge of each other's ethnic groups (Zaramo, Zigua, Doe, Kwere, Arabs) has been reflected in intermarriage and joint activities which have contributed to the maintenance of harmonious relationships. While there has been recognition of differences between individuals and ethnic groups, interpersonal bonds and a strong sense of togetherness has also been established through joking relations, shared folklore, celebrations and economic activities.

The development over many centuries of the art of living together and accommodating others has given Bagamoyo a way of life totally different from the antagonistic relations seen in other parts of Tanzania, such as Kilimanjaro, Morogoro and Mara, where cultural pluralism has been a source of deaths and fighting. It therefore becomes possible to state that Bagamoyo people formed a community in a Swahili town and although they had originally come from or were brought from other places at different times gradually learned to live together and see each other as members of a community. All of the factors mentioned above – religion, inter-marriage, political contests, and language – have allowed them to live together for centuries in harmonious cultural pluralism.

The latter part of the twentieth century exposed Bagamoyo to different influences. Dar es Salaam had taken over as a major trading centre many years before and Bagamoyo was no longer directly exposed to the outside world. Furthermore, during this period, the town became famous (or notorious) throughout East Africa as a centre of witchcraft (*uchawi*) based upon a combination of traditional mainland African beliefs and Islamic magical powers, especially in spirits (*majini*) based on Islamic and Arabic influence. Such beliefs have for many years affected `foreigners', namely people from other ethnic groups, by making them fear to come to Bagamoyo. Bagamoyo was labelled as one of the most difficult towns to live in because it was said that the inhabitants practised their own beliefs which could not accommodate outsiders. Threatening as this powerful hybrid culture was to people from other places, it provided yet another unifying factor for the inhabitants of Bagamoyo. Yet at the same time, the fear engendered among locals by such beliefs hindered social development. Therefore, when we talk about positive aspects of Bagamoyo culture we also have to include the belief in witchcraft and evil-spirits which slowed down modern changes in the town.

However, like many other old Swahili settlements which had survived for centuries with a very conservative tradition and whose development has been stunted for centuries, Bagamoyo is now reviving and reacting to modernity. The fear that kept most people away from Bagamoyo is no longer there. Witchcraft is now left to those in the rural areas while in Bagamoyo town what was once a regular practice is now only regarded as part of myth or legend.

Modernization has in fact been taking place in Bagamoyo for several decades now. Today it is a town open to communities other than those with which it has traditionally had links and there are avenues for members of other ethnic groups to settle in the town and share certain social contexts with longer-established residents. Bagamoyo citizens are now becoming more aware of individual and collective rights and the need to open up participation in development to all regardless of their cultural background. Labelling people by their ethnicity, such as Arabs, Zaramo, Doe, Zigua and Kwere, is no longer a viable basis for either identity or the forms of knowledge which in the past were used to create common beliefs between them. Instead, there is a rapid development and understanding of each other's cultures. Geographical mobility, intermarriage, global communication and economic transactions are all contributing to the creation of a modern Bagamoyo reflected in a myriad of ways from art and architecture to economic and social activities. What is happening now in Bagamoyo as a result of communication with the outside world is a cross-cultural interplay where, building on its previous experience of cultural pluralism, new forms are being produced by further hybridization. In today's world of multi-party systems, such a pluralistic society could be well placed in the development of democracy.

Bibliography

Allen, James de Vere, 1999. *Swahili Origins*. London: James Currey.

Mazrui, Ali and Mazrui, Alamin, 1995. *Swahili State and Society*. Nairobi: East African Educational Publishers.

Middleton, John, 1992. *The World of the Swahili*. New Haven and London: Yale University Press.

Vansina, Jan, 1985. *Oral Tradition as History*. Madison: University of Wisconsin Press.

Wagner, Roy, 1975. *The Invention of Culture*. Chicago: The University of Chicago Press.

CHAPTER 4

'STRUGGLING TO BE MODERN': RECENT LETTERS FROM MAFIA ISLAND

Pat Caplan

Introduction

In this paper, I consider the meanings of modernity for the people of Mafia Island, Tanzania, one of the least developed areas of one of the world's poorest countries. In a recent article, Janet Bujra comments on the applicability for Africa of the theories of globalization and modernity by writers such as Beck and Giddens and writes:

> [N]owhere in Africa could we legitimately speak of conditions of 'late modernity'... Even 'modernity' cannot be said to be securely established... with industrial development limited and halting in many areas, the penetration of capitalism incomplete, the nation state built on insecure foundations, and "regularised control of social relations across..time-space distance" (Gidddens 1991, p. 16) extremely shaky...These features appear to set Africa outside of the theoretical frame within which Beck and Giddens operate (2000: 63).

Yet Tanzania, like other parts of Africa, is subject to the same globalizing tendencies as the rest of the world. As Arce and Long have recently noted, modernity is 'a tendency that populates all spheres and interstices of the globe' (2000: 3) and the lives and life-chances of the residents of Mafia Island are influenced by its processes. Arce and Long define the term 'modern' as connoting 'a sense of belonging to the present and an awareness of a past to which people can link and at the same time distantiate themselves' (ibid: 4). It is a 'metaphor for new or emerging "here and now" materialities, meanings and cultural styles seen in relation to the past state of things' (ibid: 2).

That people on the coast and islands of East Africa should be affected by wider social processes is not, of course, a new phenomenon. The inhabitants of the area, who have long had relations of many kinds not only with other parts of the coast and islands but also with the Arabian Gulf and further afield in the Indian Ocean, have been colonized in turn by the Omanis, the Germans and the British. It would thus be fallacious to assume that there was ever any period in which Mafia, or indeed any other part of the coast, was isolated from the wider world. For this reason, any simplistic dichotomy of 'modern' with 'traditional' distorts the complexities of history, as well as risking perpetuating an evolutionary, Western-centric view of development.

At the same time, it is difficult to posit any unitary notion of 'Swahili culture'. The Swahili have never had a single state, nor have they sought one. Their culture has often been described as a 'syncretic' or 'hybrid' mixture of African and Arab, yet it might be preferable to talk of Swahili *cultures* or even of cultural *repertoires* to indicate the very large menu from which the Swahili select and construct local cultures. Furthermore, the East Coast, whether of Kenya or Tanzania, has increasing numbers of people living there who do not identify as Swahili, while the Coast itself is part of modern nation-states, to whose laws and policies its residents are as much subject as those who live 'up-country'.

In the by now 35 years during which I have been carrying out research on Mafia Island, beginning soon after Independence, there have been many changes on Mafia and in Tanzania more generally. The country has moved from an emphasis on African socialism (*ujamaa*) and self-reliance (*kujitegemea*) under a one-party state to economic liberalization, structural adjustment and multi-partyism. The price of the major cash crops which Tanzania exports has, for the most part, fallen in relation to the cost of imports. On Mafia, the returns on coconuts and cashew-nuts has fluctuated during this period, but generally, they have decreased, even as the price of bought food and other goods purchased for cash has increased.

Some of the gains of the Nyerere period, such as improvements in health and education, have been put at risk, with charges for schooling and medicines being imposed.

At the same time, a view which posits recent macro-developments as totally determining removes agency from the lives of people such as the inhabitants of Mafia. It denies the multiple ways in which they, like local actors elsewhere, 'have appropriated and internalised the symbols, trappings and practices associated with modernity in an attempt to construct their own social worlds' (Arce and Long ibid: x). This paper, then, examines how people from one village, Minazini, in the north of the island, define modernity and seek to obtain what they see as its benefits. It also shows the extent to which their choices are constrained, and the diverse ways in which they attempt to deal with such constraints, arguing that in the current economic and political circumstances, there is relatively little room for manoeuvre.

Mafia Island

Mafia, and especially the north of the island where I have been carrying out fieldwork since 1965, is one of the least developed parts of Tanzania. Contact with the mainland for most people is by *mashua* (small dhow), airlines are erratic, generally overbooked and too expensive for the majority. Even within the island itself, communication is not easy: the two main roads which run north-south from Kilindoni, the District Capital in the south, to Bweni, the northernmost village, and east-west from Kilindoni to Utende, have for many years been in a poor state of repair and are frequently impassable in the rainy season. Only Kilindoni has electricity, telephone or postal services.

Ever since the Arab and German colonial periods the chief cash crop has been coconuts, with some production of cashew nuts. In addition, rice, sweet potatoes, millet, maize, pumpkins and other crops are grown primarily for subsistence. There is some small-scale fishing, both for local consumption and, increasingly in some areas, for export to Dar, especially of lobster and prawns. Records suggest that Mafia was a food deficit area for most of the twentieth century and that rice and other staples had regularly to be imported from the mainland (see Van Spengen 1979, Caplan 1999).

Although during the post independence period a number of primary schools were constructed on the island, until around 1990 secondary education was unavailable other than by children attending boarding schools on the mainland, or else staying with relatives in Dar or Zanzibar. Very few children from Minazini village, which has been the focus of my research, have gone on to secondary school, much less to university.

There are few opportunities on the island for regular paid work other than government jobs such as civil servants, teachers, agricultural officers and medical staff, or as labourers on the half dozen commercial coconut plantations, although there is sometimes local casual work available in cultivation, road repairs etc.

Like other African states, Tanzania has in recent years implemented a structural adjustment programme and has liberalized its economy. For the vast majority of people on Mafia, neither has brought benefits: services which were formerly free, such as education and health, now have to be paid for, while they have seen the prices of their main cash crop, coconuts, tumble on the world market. Villagers who live and work in Dar es Salaam find that the steeply rising cost of living is not met by commensurate wage increases and that work is more difficult to find.

Correspondence and Correspondents: *Barua ni nusu ya kuonana* (letters are half-way towards seeing someone face to face)

Ever since I returned from my first fieldtrip to Mafia Island in 1967, I have been in regular correspondence with a number of the villagers, both those who have remained on Mafia and others who live away. My last visit was in 1994, and in this paper, I consider the hundred or so letters sent and received from that time to the present. I examine these texts for what they say about how people view their own lives and problems, and how they see the world in its present state.

The letters are written in Swahili in Roman script (*Kizungu*); some are on aerogrammes, others on pages torn from exercise books. Their writers fall into four categories, based upon residence:

a) Those who remain living in the village, although they may travel regularly to the District Capital Kilindoni, and as far afield as Dar es Salaam or Zanzibar. Here my main correspondents are three men:
- Musa, who is in his sixties.
- Silima who is around the same age.
- Mohammed, the subject of my monograph *African Voices, African Lives* (Caplan 1997), who is also in his sixties.

b) Those who are living away from the village:
- Mwinyi, now in his forties, who maintains a house in the village and visits regularly, but who also has a house in Dar where his wife and children live.
- Sheha who has a good skilled job in Dar and who visits very rarely.
Both of these last have recently acquired email accounts of their own and some of our correspondence is now through this medium.

c) Those who are living abroad temporarily:
- Ali, a villager who was sent to Egypt for his secondary and university education.
- Juma, another who went to Ghana to do an M.Sc.
- Hassan, who came to take a short course in London and visited me.
- A Tanzanian student, Ahmed Kipacha[1], carrying out research for his London University Ph.D. in linguistics, who lived in the village from early April to the end of July 1999, and kindly wrote me a report, as well as furnishing me with other information on his return.

It should be noted that almost all of my correspondents are male. During this period I have only ever received two letters from women: one from a close friend (who has since died) soon after I left in 1994 and the other from a girl who had managed to get to secondary school. Although more women in this area are literate than when I first began research here in 1965, few women have either time to write, or money for stamps.

Topics in the letters: *Maisha yamekuwa magumu sana* **(life has become very hard)**

Most letters begin in the customary way, with inquiries after my health and those of my family, and information about the writer's own family and its members' health. They end in a similarly formulaic way with greetings to me and my family from the writer and members of his family, often mentioned by name, and sometimes add additional greetings from other named people[2]. The central part of the letter contains news about the writer and happenings in the village or further afield. There are four major topics: the weather and its effects on crops and harvests, prices, illness and its treatments, and death.

a) Weather, crops and harvests

During this period Mafia suffered several years of drought (*'jua kali sana', ukame)*, followed by rains so heavy that there were floods. Silima writes:

> The drought (*ukame*) of 1997 was very bad. Many coconut trees died, as did cattle, and even bush animals. In 1998, we got so much rain that there were floods and those who had cultivated rice got nothing.

Mohammed writes in similar vein:

> This year (1998) the cultivation of rice was very difficult because we had so much rain, and the rice rotted in the water. I cultivated with my daughter but she did not get a thing.

A year later in 1999, the weather was better, and Mohammed notes:

> Here at our place the harvest of rice was very good for those people who had the strength to cultivate big fields, and it was also good in terms of sweet potatoes, bananas and papaya. Unfortunately, there was no market for these goods because of a lack of cash with which to buy them. So there was plenty of food. But for shops the big problem is that money is very scarce and difficult to get, not like before.

b) Prices

During my last visit in 1994, there were frequent complaints about steep rises in the prices of bought goods. Ahmed Kipacha's report indicates that in 2001 an equally severe problem is the drop in the price of goods produced locally:

> The prices for goods sold like coconuts has dropped tremendously. A big coconut now only costs T.Sh. 15, while a basket of fish [sold locally to traders from Dar es Salaam] will fetch only Sh. 2000, while the same [basket] will cost more than T.Sh. 12,000 at the ferry in Dar es Salaam [and presumably even more at the market].

Yet money has to be found not only for day to day expenses, but for ceremonies such as weddings. Mohammed wrote about the cost of his son's marriage:

> My son married the daughter of AM from the next village. The girl had been brought up in Minazini by the chief shaman. Her *mahari* was Sh. 15,000. I paid all of it and the expenses of the *kadhi* Sh. 2,000, and Sh.3,000 for the food. And I bought wedding clothes to a total of 26 *khanga*, and paid the 'birth money' (*pesa za uzaliwa*) to my ex-wife (mother of the groom) and her daughters, and the men's *upatu* (tip) was Sh. 3,000.

A constant topic of complaint is that of making ends meet, whether people are living in the country or the town: living costs have gone up, including the costs of education and medical treatment, both no longer free. People complain that 'there is no work', that the price for which they sell their coconuts has dropped. Mwinyi, a man in his forties, writes of life in Dar in 1998:

> I have not managed to get any work, and the state of the coconut crop is bad. Living expenses are going up, and the costs of educating children even more. I don't know if I will be able to educate my children properly. My younger daughter is in Form I and her fees are Sh.10,000 ($10) per month. My older daughter is in Form IV and needs Sh. 4,000 ($4) per month. To feed my family on Mafia and in Dar requires Sh.150,000 ($150) per month. My income at present is Sh.90,000 ($90) per month [mainly from the sale of coconuts from his Mafia trees]. My wife would like to start a small business selling sewing materials and cloth, things for tailoring and sewing, and also perfume. But unfortunately, she has no capital. She wants to set up a business so that we can educate our children.

A year later, he sends me an email to say that he owes Sh.148,000 in school fees and that his children have been sent away from school as a result. Later in 1999: 'The state of our life is not good, I

49

can't get work, coconuts have no worth. Living expenses are still going up and the cost of education and medical treatment even more so. I try every conceivable means to make money but I am defeated, I just can't get together any capital'.

c)   *Illness and its treatment*

Illness is another frequent topic, scarcely surprising given the high morbidity rates and the number of serious illnesses: TB, malaria, even, in 1997, a suspected cholera outbreak when many people died. Correspondents write about who has been sick, what their problems are, and how they were treated: whether they went to hospital in Kilindoni or even to Dar es Salaam, or whether they were treated by local medicine, including spirits.

For example, Mohammed writes of his illness:

> I still have that hip problem, and I am not yet better from my cough. And my legs swelled up and for nine days I did not leave the house. Each time there is a divination at a spirit dance (*ngoma*) our guardian spirit [says] he wants a *mwingo*[3] dance with a cow [sacrificed] and if this cow is obtainable, there will be a dance. My [classificatory] son Saidi is always getting ill. Every two days he is sick again. My daughter and her children are in the same state. But now it is difficult because a cow costs not less than Sh 40,000. And the children of my [classificatory] sister in Baleni are also all sick because of this same problem... When I go to bed at night and I am asleep, the old man (i.e. the spirit) comes to me and I do not get to sleep because I need to perform a *mwingo*. My state is very bad, and will not improve until I have performed a *mwingo*.

A year on, and the situation remains the same:

> I want to inform you that I have many problems. My grandson has been given a spirit and I have been treating him myself. And my 'old one' (spirit) wants a cow, and I have not yet decided to sacrifice one because of my penniless state.

Not all people in Mafia see spirits as either the cause of their illness or the route to a cure. Musa, for example, has only contempt for spirit possession, which he describes as *upuuzi* (foolishness), and when ill, seeks hospital treatment:

> Your sister in law (*wifi*) has been having trouble with her cough. I took her to Dar [to Muhimbili hospital] and now she is

somewhat better, but her cough is still troubling her. I have also had some trouble with my eyes which are getting dim.

Later letters from other correspondents note that Musa went again to Dar and had a cataract operation.

Silima similarly has always sought allopathic medicine for one of his sons who is epileptic, and is treated both by the hospital in Kilindoni and also at Muhimbili Hospital in Dar es Salaam. The problem for him is that the drugs which his son needs to stop his seizures cost a great deal of money – in 1997 he quoted a price of Sh. 2-300 per tablet - and are often unobtainable in Tanzania. He relies on friends from abroad – the anthropologist and some Germans who once visited the village and stayed in his house – to send them regularly.

d) Death

Almost every letter contains news of a death in the village. Some of these are of people whom I knew and who would have been quite elderly but there are also frequent mentions of deaths of children and younger people, including three of my closest female friends, women in their thirties and forties[4]. Silima writes in April 2001:

> It is true what you heard about the death of my daughter, who died on Feb 24th, after being in Kilindoni hospital for a while with stomach problems. She had been going there for treatment without getting any better. And before that my granddaughter Latifa, who was still at school, died in Dar es Salaam on Feb. 3rd, and then the daughter of my older brother died in Dar on the 8th leaving small children. Three bereavements in one month.

Inevitably, in this scenario, the anthropologist herself is viewed as a resource and the letters often contain requests for financial help, medicine, books, and for information about courses and scholarships to study abroad. The following extract from a man related to one of my more regular correspondents is not atypical:

> I your elder brother am not well. I am here in Zanzibar for treatment. For this reason I ask for your help, by your kindness, so that I can start a business. As you know the main business here is our small village shops. So I hope that I will get your help, sister, and I will thank you very much if you assist me in

51

my difficulties. I hope I will get something from you, God willing, by your efforts.

In his first letter written to me from Minazini in 1999, Ahmed Kipacha, summarized the situation as he saw it: 'Life in general [in Minazini] is pathetic. Abject poverty is clearly seen though people here still take pride in themselves'. In the next section, I discuss how people deal with this increasing poverty.

Mipango na miradi (plans and projects i.e. coping strategies)

In this arena of struggle what are the survival strategies for my correspondents? They are surprisingly varied. For Mohammed, survival is largely through the help of kin, especially that of the adult son and daughter who live with him, the first newly married, the second long divorced. But he also looks to the spirit world, and especially to his guardian spirit to whom he takes offerings (see Caplan 1997). For Musa and Silima, on the other hand, the answer lies in seeking to take advantage of local opportunities: they mention such projects as improving their water supply by digging a well, or planting orange trees to get a new cash crop.

For those living in the city, strategies are different. For Musa's older sons, long resident in Dar, and for Sheha, also a Dar resident, everything depends on their ability to keep their jobs. One of Musa's sons lost his post after an industrial accident, and, when I met him in 1994, was trying to set up a small business with the compensation received. He had requested my help in obtaining an item of equipment and wrote later:

> Please do whatever you can to help me by sending that machine which I need badly to improve my standard of living here in the city. If I don't get it, I will probably be forced to return to Mafia, because here things have become really difficult (*mambo magumu mno*), especially since I had that accident.

For those who do have jobs, the need to improve their qualifications and knowledge in order both to retain them and to gain promotion is vital, and for this reason Sheha has asked several times for particular books relating to his occupation to be sent to him from London.

For many people, education is seen as the way out of poverty, yet several villagers who have received education are not able to get work. In 1994, a young woman wrote me from her boarding school in Mtwara, full of hopes and plans for her future, including learning English. But several years after she had completed secondary school, her guardian Mwinyi wrote that she was sitting at home because he did not have sufficient funds to send her on a course and she had not been able to get any work.

Ahmed Kipacha commented in his report that secondary schooling on the island, long awaited, had proved problematic for a number of reasons. One is that the children from the north attending secondary school in the south had difficulties with accommodation, often having to rely on the hospitality of kin living in the area. Secondly, that the exam results of the school were not impressive and that the school lacked important facilities such as science laboratories. Finally, even if they completed their schooling up to Form Four:

> They have nothing to do back in the village. Worse, no one in the northern villages is interested in marrying a Form Four leaver. They are [considered] 'too delicate [ie unable to cope with heavy work-loads]'. I have witnessed Form Four leavers selling *mandazi* (fried cakes) and without anyone to marry them, even their close kin[5].

But it is perhaps in an examination of the letters of my most frequent correspondent, Mwinyi, that the widest variety of coping strategies is to be found. Mwinyi, as already mentioned, divides his time between the village and the city. He has dependents in both places: his wife and two daughters live in the city, together with some of the children of a deceased brother and sister for whom he is responsible; in the village, he has had the care of his elderly parents and father's sister.

Mwinyi had his schooling in both Zanzibar and Dar, and later undertook a vocational course. He then did national service, after which he joined government service, working in the city, but he left in order to concentrate upon setting up an NGO concerned with development projects on Mafia. The NGO had a notable success when the island's first Secondary School was opened largely thanks to its efforts. During my last visit in 1994, he and his supporters were seeking funding from foreign donors for a number of projects (see Caplan 1998). They did not succeed in obtaining funds, and he left his post as Secretary of the NGO.

He then tried to obtain work as a plantation manager, both on the island and the mainland, but again without success. For a short time, he was an agent for a company on a commission basis, but this did not last. He wrote about plans for setting up a business buying the mats which are made by women on Mafia for export to the mainland, but lacked the capital to do so, and then of obtaining bee-hives to try and produce enough honey to sell. Recently, he has been planting orange trees in Minazini, and has also obtained land in a nearby village on which to plant trees which would yield firewood and building materials.

Finally, recognizing that he did not wish to return to the first NGO, which appeared to have been distintegrating since his departure, Mwinyi set up another NGO with an emphasis on health (especially AIDS) education, tree planting and fishing, and was again seeking funds through contacts with foreign NGOs in Dar es Salaam.

During this period, Mwinyi has also been trying to set up another secondary school, a *madrasa* based upon Islamic education, which would also serve as a centre for short vocational courses. The inspiration for this school was the existing Koran school run for many years by his late father, and for which Mwinyi has taken responsibility since the latter's death. In June 1997 he wrote on headed notepaper:

> The main work with which I am concerned at the moment is the building of the *madrasa* next to my house in Minazini. Up to now I've got 3,600 building blocks, but I need 6,000 before I can start building. At the moment I'm preparing the plan and specifications. My intention is to build a secondary school which will give both religious and general education up to Form IV. And later on I also want to start short courses in sewing by machine, electricity, typing, carpentry and computing. I will send you the plan and specifications, together with some pictures of the things I have got together so far (building blocks, stones etc.) And I hope that even you will send me some help...this is the headed notepaper which we are using to send information out about the school which is being built. All the people of the village and of Mafia are united on this topic. I have already set up a Building Committee and a School Board.

Fund-raising has proved problematic, with sponsors sought for sufficient funds to construct a brick building in the expectation that the school would be self-supporting from fees once it was set up. A couple of years ago, I received a set of photos of the bricks so far collected, and of the new Koran school of mud and wattle and with a thatched roof, built as a temporary measure pending the completion of the *madrasa* proper, which seems to be still far away. In June 2000 he wrote that 'The building work has stopped because I did not get any benefactor. I am still looking for benefactors and I am carrying on building huts, but I need a lot more money before I can finish this work'.

Mwinyi's attempts to make available to the children of northern Mafia a form of education which would be 'modern' and wide-ranging and yet based on Islamic values reflects a mode of thinking which sees no incompatibility between the two.

Given all of these problems and the frequent mention in letters of *maisha magumu, maisha mabaya* (a hard life, a poor life) it is scarcely surprising that when an Italian company arrived in the village and offered to buy land in two areas in order to construct hotels, people were willing to sell their trees, their main source of capital, and thus their land. Mwinyi wrote as follows:

> A number of people agreed to sell their coconut trees so that an Italian hotel could be built. My NGO did its best to persuade them not to agree but POVERTY and hunger made them sell. I was not a bit happy about it (Capitals in original).

In another letter, there are hints that people were persuaded to sell their trees for less than they had wanted. Silima writes: 'People wanted Sh. 50,000 for each tree, but the then MP for Mafia Island said they should sell them for Sh. 20,000 each', commenting philosophically that he hoped the hotels would bring some work to the village, at least in their construction. Later, however, Ahmed Kipacha reported that the actual price received fluctuated between Sh. 7,000 and Sh. 20,000 per tree, but that people still hoped for benefits:

> Some consider any foreign involvement in their areas as a blessing, since there would be economic activities that would involve the circulation of money. They would be able to sell fish, they will be given employment and [the setting up of hotels] would probably solve the long-term trouble of reliable transport to Kilindoni.

But, like Mwinyi, he also sounds a warning note:

Others are a bit worried about foreign involvement. More land will be taken and [there will be] intrusion of foreign culture. Utende (the resort area in the south of the island which has three hotels) has changed completely, the next place would be Minazini[6].

It will be noted that a major resource on which people depend is their social relationships, and their personal contacts, including with potential benefactors or patrons.

Maendeleo gani? What does modernity mean in this context?

The word mainly used in Swahili to translate 'progress' or 'development' is *maendeleo,* literally 'going forward' (see Walley, this volume). My correspondents have a number of ideas about what *maendeleo* means for them. In the village, it means producing cash crops which fetch sufficient income to pay for their needs; it means having an all-weather road so that they can travel to the District Capital to deal with government officials and obtain medical treatment; it means availability of good local clinics as well as a District hospital; it means sufficient school places, including at secondary level, for their children; finally it also means having jobs available commensurate with one's level of education. For those in the city, it means above all having work, and work which pays sufficient to cover the high costs of living in a situation where even water has to be purchased, and where new consumer goods, such as television, have become available and are much desired. There is increasing recognition of the need to speak and write English, which is seen as the international language and the path to a wider world, and to gain knowledge of computing. Development, in other words, is the *sine qua non* of modernity; unless people 'have' development, they cannot think of themselves as modern.

Yet even when *maendeleo* arrives, as it did finally in the much-heralded construction of the road from the north to south of the island, improvements may be transitory. During this period, money had been obtained from the World Bank by the Tanzanian government to improve the roads on the island, and many correspondents write about the progress of this work. In fact, scarcely a letter does not mention the road-building, and locally it clearly became a powerful metaphor for development. In June 1996, Silima writes

And about the road: it is completed in dirt form right up to the lighthouse (the northernmost point of the island) but they have not yet put any hard surface on it – I don't know if they plan to do that.

Sheha, visiting the island from Dar in 1996, writes:

As far as Mafia is concerned, there is no progress (*maendeleo*) at all since the road has been built badly to the point where the man who was in charge was thrown out because he didn't know how to build a road.

Sure enough, the road did not withstand the rains and in February 1998 Silima writes:

Please forgive me for the delay in writing you a letter. This was because of the problems we had in travelling out of Minazini to go to Kilindoni. The road was in a very bad state and vehicles could not get through even up to Kirongwe (in the centre of the island). So we had no postal service as it was very difficult to get to Kilindoni.

Three months later the situation has not improved. Silima again:

As far as the road is concerned here on Mafia the situation is very bad. The bus can't even get through to Kirongwe, so we have to walk to Baleni (about four hours) if we want to get to Kilindoni. The road engineers are still here on Mafia but I can't see them doing any work.

At the beginning of 1999, he writes again:

The road is completed right from Ras Mkumbi (northernmost point) to Kildinoni and it looks very good. It will be fine in the sun, but I don't know if it will withstand the rain because they have put very little gravel on it. But for the moment it is good and we are pleased.

But a road is of little use without vehicles. Ahmed Kipacha, wrote in May 1999: 'We have only one private bus to Kirongwe, known as *Mtu Kwao* [lit. 'a person at home' or 'home is best']. The previous bus owned by Minazini village is out of order'. This was the bus (or rather lorry) for the purchase of which in the early 1990s the villagers had exerted so much effort (Caplan 1999).

Later that year Silima says that more work was done on the road, but in 2000 he writes again:

> The road isn't too bad but there is no transport. There is just one bus which keeps breaking down and so it only goes to Kirongwe, not up to Minazini and Bweni.

There are veiled hints that the building of the road might have involved 'corruption' of various kinds: one of the contractors was an MP, insufficient hardcore had been used, the engineers were 'around' but 'not doing anything', the way in which the two contractors (one for the northern and one for the southern stretches) had constructed the surface was very different, one of the engineers had been dismissed because he did not know how to do his job. It is perhaps for this reason that plans to build hotels in the north of the island have not yet been realized.

Conclusion

For the majority of people on Mafia Island, notions of modernity and development (*maendeleo*) remain dreams, caught as they are in an economic situation which is increasingly difficult. This does not mean that they are purely victims of a situation not of their own making, on the contrary, what is striking is their resilience in the face of such difficulties. People are constantly planning and scheming to find ways to get what they want and need for themselves and their children. They utilize whatever links they have with others in many localities: kinship, friendship, sponsorship and patronage in order to obtain the resources they want. At the same time, the search for 'modernity' certainly does not mean eschewing such important aspects of their culture as Islam or, for many, the spirit possession cults. Using such aspects of modernity as allopathic medicine, secondary and higher education, and new cash crops, is certainly not seen as antithetical to other, more localized practices, which indeed, may acquire new meanings.

In much of the recent literature on development and modernity, there is, rightly, an emphasis on indigenous knowledge and on local processes and individual agency. Rather than being seen as victims, people's resourcefulness is celebrated, as is their resistance to the forces which threaten to overwhelm them. In some respects this is a welcome tendency, but there is a real risk of exaggerating the success of coping strategies or romanticizing resistance. In the context of Mafia Island, and indeed, I suspect, of much of the rest of sub-Saharan Africa, the odds are just overwhelming. Frequently people write, as I have often heard them say, '*Nimeshindwa*' (lit. 'I am defeated'). The fact is that people die needlessly and people's lives are much harder than they should be. Modernity remains elusive.

Notes

[1] I am extremely grateful to Ahmed Kipacha for making time to seek answers to the list of questions with which I furnished him, for letters from the field, and for writing me a short report on his return. I should also like to thank Lionel Caplan for reading early drafts of this paper, and the participants in the Swahili Workshop 2001 for their useful comments.

[2] Interestingly, I note that the style has changed completely when writers use email, with fewer formulaic greetings and greater concentration upon matters in hand, getting straight to the point.

[3] In northern Mafia, there are two main types of *ngoma* healing rituals which involve spirit possession: one involves spirits of the sea (*majini ya bahari*), the other spirits of the land (*mashaitani*). Land spirits have two types of *ngoma: kitanga* and *mwingo*. In both types participants become possessed by spirits and an animal, usually a cow, is sacrificed. For further details see Caplan 1997.

[4] Both the fertility and maternal mortality rates remain high – see Caplan 1995, 1999.

[5] People in northern Mafia, like most coastal dwellers, practice preferential cousin marriage.

[6] For a discussion of the effects of tourism on the Utende and Chole areas of southern Mafia, see Walley 1999 and Palazzo 1999, and for northern Kenya, see Beckerleg, this volume.

Bibliography

Arce, Alberto and Long, Norman (eds.), 2000. *Anthropology, Development and Modernities: Exploring Discourses, Counter-tendencies and Violence*. London and New York: Routledge.

Beck, Ulrich, 1995. [1992] *Risk Society: towards a new modernity*. London: Sage.

Bryceson, Deborah Fahy, 1999. *Sub-Saharan Africa Betwixt and Between: Rural Livelihood Practices and Policies.* Leiden: Afrika Studie Centrum, Working Paper 43.

Bujra, Janet, 2000. 'Risk and trust: unsafe sex, gender and AIDS in Tanzania', in P. Caplan (ed.) *Risk Revisited.* London and Sterling, Virginia: Pluto Press.

Caplan, Pat, 1995. '"Children are our wealth and we want them": a difficult pregnancy on Mafia Island, Tanzania', in Deborah Bryceson (ed.) *Women Wielding the Hoe: Lessons from Rural Africa for Feminist Theory and Development Practice.* Oxford: Berg Press.

———, 1997. *African Voices, African Lives: Personal Narratives from a Swahili Village.* London and New York: Routledge.

———, 1998. 'La vie politique en mutation d'un village cotier de la Tanzanie', in Francoise le Guennec-Coppens and David Parkin (eds.) *Autorite et Pouvoir chez les Swahili.* Paris: Karthala; Nairobi: IPRA.

———, 1999. 'Where have all the young girls gone? Gender and sex ratios on Mafia Island, Tanzania', in Peter Forster and Sam Maghimbi (eds.) *Agrarian Economy, State and Society in Contemporary Tanzania.* Avebury Press.

Giddens, Anthony, 1991. *Modernity and Self-identity: self and society in the late modern age.* Cambridge: Polity Press.

Palazzo, Katia, 1999. 'Social Change e sviluppo tutistico nel parco marino di Mafia (Tanzania)'. Tesi di laurea: Universitá degli Studi di Roma "La Sapienza".

Van Spengen, Wim, 1979. 'Structural Characteristics of Underdevelopment in the Mafia Archipelago: an Historical Analysis', *Cahiers d'Etudes Africaines*, XX (3): 331-53.

Walley, Christine, 1999. 'Making Waves: Struggles over the Environment, Development and Participation in the Mafia Island Marine Park, Tanzania', unpublished Ph.D. thesis in Anthropology, New York University.

CHAPTER 5

MODERNITY AND THE MEANING OF DEVELOPMENT WITHIN THE MAFIA ISLAND MARINE PARK, TANZANIA

Christine J. Walley

As scholars have increasingly noted, the concept of modernity is associated with a particular 'narrative' according to which geographic regions, people and even time are located on one side or another of a dualistic divide that marks the supposedly antithetical state of the 'modern' from the 'traditional'. History, in this scenario, is depicted in evolutionary and progressive terms. It is assumed to be characterized by ever increasing rationality and prosperity, and to be powered by the expanding forces of science, bureaucratic rationalization and the modern production systems of capitalism or, until recently, socialism. It perhaps goes without saying that this narrative is a powerful one in nearly all parts of the world today.

Some might argue that the concept of the modern is powerful because it embodies universal values - itself a modernist trope. However, it might be more accurate to attribute this widespread influence to the fact that the concept of the modern is, as Stacey Pigg notes, a cosmopolitan one (1996). It has gained widespread currency travelling via historical routes such as colonialism and contemporary ones including development institutions, and it serves to signal the worldly and progressive orientation of those who claim to be 'modern'. Despite the ubiquity of the term, Pigg argues that the 'modern' is an empty signifier, one that only takes on meaning within particular cultural, historical and social contexts. Describing the 'modern' as a 'representational adapter kit suitable for international travel', she argues that '...it becomes cosmopolitan not because "Western" ideas spread through the world, homogenizing it, but because heterogeneous meanings and social concerns can be organized through it' (1996: 192).

In recent years, a number of anthropologists have sought to understand these heterogeneous meanings, exploring what the 'modern' means to people in various parts of the world and how such understandings relate to local, national and international dynamics (Donham 1999, Rofel 1999). While there is a wide range of scholarship on the history and symbolism of the modern within Europe and the United States, analysts of the modern in formerly colonized and poorer countries must look in a different direction. As Pigg (1996) notes, the 'modern' in countries such as Nepal where she conducted her research has been largely synonymous with ideas of development. For both individuals and polities, 'development' has come to express hopes for a better life achievable through a 'modernity' that promises economic and political equality on a world stage.

The reality, however, that 'development' is not a self-evident process or idea but is open to a range of negotiated meanings became strikingly clear in my own research on Mafia Island which lies off the coast of East Africa. In recent years, tourism has been expanding throughout the Swahili coast (see Beckerleg, this volume). There have also been newer understandings of development that merge conservation and economic planning into 'sustainable development'. The Mafia Island Marine Park, Tanzania's first national marine park, had been conceived by international and national planners in the early 1990s as a cutting-edge example of a joint conservation and development project centring around environmentally-sensitive 'eco-tourism'. Unlike earlier wildlife reserves on the Tanzanian mainland, which were premised on preservationist models mandating the segregation of nature from human beings, Mafia's park was depicted as a new kind of national park which would both allow residents to live within park boundaries and encourage their 'participation'. Despite this innovative image, the implementation of the park was nonetheless marked by widespread contention among island residents, national government officials and representatives of international organizations. My own research, conducted during the mid-1990s, focused on this political conflict to which I elsewhere refer as the 'social drama' of the Mafia Island Marine Park (1999).

In this paper, rather than examining such overt contestation, I consider a more subtle phenomenon. Although largely unremarked upon, the differing understandings of development offered by various park actors profoundly shaped day-to-day interactions within the marine park. Among Euro-Americans, tension existed between those who advocated 'development' (albeit in revisionist forms that centred upon participation and eco-tourism), and those, particularly tourists, who viewed Mafia through an anti-modernist lens that sought to maintain the island as 'pristine' and free from development. National government officials, in contrast to both groups of Euro-Americans, strongly supported state-centred interpretations of development and were often preoccupied with the role that 'development' played in marking status distinctions both nationally and internationally. Finally, Mafia residents expressed a strong desire for development, or *maendeleo* in Swahili, interpreting it in ways that simultaneously resonated with and contradicted the viewpoints of national officials and Euro-American tourists and NGO workers. Overall, residents did not view history as progressing through evolutionary stages, nor did they depict 'development' as society-wide in orientation. Instead, for them, development signified the ability of individuals to 'get ahead' economically, a situation upon which tourism and the marine park were having an ambiguous impact.

In this paper, I examine this range of usages and what is at stake in them. I argue that such explorations allow us to move beyond abstract understandings of the goals of development to more socially-grounded considerations of how particular individuals and groups of people *use* the concept. By interpreting and appropriating 'development' in ways shaped by their own socioeconomic and historical situations, they are also able to refashion self-identities as well as relationships with others. In a ground-breaking work, James Ferguson has argued that development discourses erase the political dimensions of development by portraying it in naturalized terms as a technical process that merely requires proper 'management' (1994). By focusing on how different actors within the Mafia Island Marine Park use the concept, 'development' emerges in this article not only as a political phenomenon but as one fundamentally bound up in the negotiation of class relationships on both national and international levels. In the broadest terms, these conflicting understandings challenge us to rethink hegemonic interpretations of the 'modern' and 'development' originating in Europe and the United States and instead to direct our attention to the power-laden social dynamics of daily life - a level of analysis too often obscured within discussions of development.

Maendeleo: the meanings of 'development' for Mafia residents

For those people whom I knew on Mafia, development or *maendeleo* was a continuing preoccupation. Their acute sense of the lack of 'development' on Mafia was exacerbated by a sense of isolation, not only from other parts of the world, but from other parts of Tanzania as well. This situation was particularly striking since it contrasted sharply with Mafia's long history as part of the extensive and cosmopolitan Indian Ocean trading world in which the East African coast had played a vital role (Abu Lughod 1989, Chaudhuri 1985, Sheriff 1987). By the eighteenth century, the Mafia archipelago had become a dominion of Zanzibar Island to the north. However, after the British formed a protectorate over the Zanzibari sultan's domains in 1890, Mafia was traded to the Germans who were then consolidating their hold on Tanganyika. Destined to become an anomalous part of Tanzania's 'mainland', Mafia has since been marginalized both politically and economically and is currently considered to be a 'remote' region both by Mafia residents and other Tanzanians. Economically, Mafia residents have long depended upon the sale of coconuts, a situation stemming from the establishment of Arab and later European-owned coconut plantations on southern Mafia in the nineteenth and early twentieth centuries (Baumann 1895, Sunseri 1993). However, the falling price of copra in recent decades, combined with the impact of currency devaluations, has made the current economic period a precarious one. Consequently, many Mafia residents, particularly those living in ocean-front villages and on the smaller islands, are increasingly turning to the sale of fish for their livelihoods.

Chole Island, where I conducted my fieldwork, formed one 'village' within the broader Mafia archipelago which is home to approximately 50,000 people. The smallest inhabited island in the region, Chole is only three-quarters of a square mile in size and has a population of approximately 800. Although the stone ruins that litter the island testify to Chole's historical role as the urban centre for all of Mafia, at present most people eke out a meagre living based on fishing, subsistence farming, and growing oranges and coconuts for sale. In the early to mid-1990s, people on Chole regularly complained that they had 'no development at all' (*hatuna maendeleo yo yote*). Indeed, Chole residents had little access to schooling, health care or dependable transportation to the main island, relying upon a single old *mashua* or wooden sailing boat that served as a ferry. Residents found this situation particularly galling given Chole's history as a prosperous nineteenth century town with a port and market, paved roads, and even, as residents remarked, candle-lit street-lamps installed by the Germans.

Not surprisingly, given its relational connotations, discussions of development invariably led Chole residents to compare themselves with others. Indeed, they were acutely aware of their low-ranking position on an imagined ladder of development conceptualized in both international and national terms; they also regularly contrasted their situation with that of more 'developed' regions, such as Europe and the United States, as well as other areas within Tanzania and even other villages on Mafia. As a result, residents at times expressed embarrassment that 'outsiders' (*wageni*) might perceive them as lacking development, worrying, for example, that tourist photographs of Mafia would be displayed in Europe to demonstrate the poverty of Africans. Such concerns also encouraged some Mafia residents to stress the ways in which they did have some degree of 'development,' even on what they felt to be an internationally meagre scale. For example, when visiting other villages on Mafia, friends from Chole would invariably take me to sites they felt signalled 'development' such as clinics, schools, government and party offices, and water collection tanks.

While donor organizations and residents might agree that Mafia lacked development in comparison to other places, the connotations of 'development' on Chole both paralleled and differed from those meanings common among international organizations. When asked in the abstract how they defined 'development' or what kind of 'development' they would like to see on Mafia, people on Chole mentioned many of the things which Euro-Americans also equated with development. They emphasized their desire for electricity, better transportation (particularly a motorized ferry for travel between Chole and Mafia's main island), improved roads, a secondary school, and 'modern' boats and fishing equipment. In other words, they hoped for the infrastructure and technology commonly associated with 'developed' countries which could make their lives easier and serve as potential sources of upward mobility.

However, in day-to-day usage, Chole residents often used the word *maendeleo* in a variety of ways that differed from international discourses. Rather than considering development in terms of the transformation of societies as a whole (a historical vestige of the concept's nineteenth century origins in European evolutionary thought), 'development' was consistently used on Chole to refer to individuals 'getting ahead' in highly concrete ways. While this differing orientation was widespread, it was not a subject of explicit exegesis but rather emerged in often subtle differences in the use of language. For instance, one afternoon when I was teaching English to adults on Chole, an elderly woman in the class joked with curious passers-by that she was busy 'getting a little development'. Spoken in a simultaneously proud and self-deprecating tone, this comment, along with others like it, was perceived as humorous for underscoring the role that formal education played in marking the relative 'development' of individuals within Tanzania as well as Mafia residents' marginalization from such arenas. Intriguingly, people on Chole also referred to the small-scale entrepreneurial activities they commonly engaged in, such as selling bread or sweets, raising chickens or collecting shells, as *miradi* or 'projects' - the same word used for development projects organized by international donors. In general, commonplace usages of development on Chole served to draw attention to the marginalization of Mafia residents while simultaneously implying that the surest route to 'development' was for residents to glean what scraps they could through individual initiative.

Chole residents also used the term *maendeleo* to refer to historical understandings of wealth that posed a sharp contrast to 'modern' understandings. In one instance, Mzee Maarufu[1], the village chairman of Chole, drew upon historical ideas of people as wealth when he described the '*maendeleo ya kuzaa*' or 'the "development" of giving birth' on Chole. He recalled how, after the demise of Chole as an urban area when he was a child, the island had become radically depopulated. Happily, he noted, the few remaining members of the younger generation had borne children and now their children had repopulated the island - a usage which offers a distinct departure from the discourse of international organizations which equates 'development' with having fewer rather than more children. Historical understandings of wealth also appeared in a sarcastic comment made by Fatuma Fadhili to fellow anthropologist, Rachel Eide. Fatuma remarked that the only *maendeleo* occurring on Mafia these days involved those men who were earning money in the budding tourism industry taking second wives. As in Mzee Maarufu's comment, Fatuma's witticism drew upon the historical value of people as wealth (spouses as well as children). She playfully contrasted this historical understanding of wealth with contemporary 'development' procured through wage labour. In doing so, she suggested that Chole residents continue to be marginalized from 'real' development while simultaneously offering a gendered critique which hints that the only 'development' occurring on Chole harkens back to older models and benefits men more than (and potentially at the expense of) women[2].

Still other usages of development were even more unusual to my American ears. For example, Mzee Bakari once told me that the *wazee*, or former generations of people on Chole, used to 'bury their *maendeleo* in the ground'. This usage was so dissonant with my own cultural preconceptions of the term 'development' that, at the time, I simply assumed I had misunderstood his Swahili. However, upon repeatedly replaying a tape of our conversation after I returned to the United States, I realized there had been no mistake. Here, *maendeleo* had been transformed into a hoped-for object of 'getting ahead' - money. In his comments, Mzee Bakari described how, since there were no banks on Mafia in the past, if a person died suddenly, his or her heirs might not know where to locate the deceased's buried *maendeleo* (leading him into a discussion of how people on Mafia have been castigated as 'backward' for not putting their money in banks and his defence of why they chose not to do so).

What is most interesting in Mzee Bakari's discussion is how *maendeleo* differs from commonplace narratives of modernity. In this account, there is no divide between the modern and the traditional, nor is there an assumption of inevitable 'progress' as time passes. From this perspective, residents' ancestors also had access to *maendeleo*, contradicting narratives of history that presuppose earlier periods to be characterized precisely by their lack of development. When I returned to Mafia last summer, I continued my conversation with Mzee Bakari, asking what term Chole residents had used before *maendeleo* gained ascendancy in the period around Tanzania's independence in 1961. Without hesitation, he answered *'uchumi,'* referring to the business activities in which he himself had engaged when younger and which had a long history along the East African coast. When I asked whether he saw any differences between the two, he quickly stated there was none and demonstrated his surprise that I would ask.

In sum, the usages of 'development' put forward by Chole residents, in some cases, paralleled, and in others, contrasted with commonplace narratives of modernity. By demonstrating how residents reworked the concept of development in accordance with their own social and historical concerns, such usages underscore the concept's historically contingent nature while also pointing to the possibility of non-modernist interpretations. Such interpretations do not suggest that Mafia residents are not 'modern' (indeed, they are thoroughly embedded in 'modern' dynamics [see Walley 1999]), but rather that the term 'modern' itself fails to live up to its own universalist assumptions and that alternative histories continue to be an integral part of the 'modern' era.

Development and national elites

National government officials, whether assigned to the marine park or Mafia's district government offices, had their own views of development. Shaped by the particular social contexts in which they operated, such views once again alternately resonated and conflicted with those of others, in this case of Mafia residents and Euro-American NGO workers and tourists. Government officials agreed with Mafia residents that such things as better roads, improved houses, electricity, a motorized ferry, and the other 'modern' accoutrements which Mafia residents desired, would all constitute development. Like residents, they also considered development in explicitly relational terms, operating from the uncomfortable position by which Tanzania was defined internationally in terms of what it was perceived to lack. The tensions of this position surfaced, for example, in debates between donors and government officials over the new Mafia Island Marine Park headquarters. When government officials commissioned elaborate architectural plans for a state-of-the-art office, donors were angered by what they saw as extravagant and wasteful planning which was both out of proportion to the project and which contravened its populist goals. Donor representatives privately suggested that such actions were indicative of government officials' refusal to acknowledge more progressive views of development which stressed basic needs and community participation. The wish for an opulent headquarters, however, might alternately be 'read' as a desire for international recognition and prestige by a national elite which felt itself to be marginalized on a world stage.

At the same time, government officials offered a far more state-centered view of development than either Mafia residents or donors. In contrast to Chole residents' focus on individuals 'getting ahead' or NGOs interest in reforming development through an emphasis on environmental sustainability and community participation, national officials continued to support the state-oriented views of development that had first gained international prominence in the immediate post-World War II era (Finnemore 1997). Drawing upon the language of the post-independence socialist period, in which it was assumed that cadres must 'teach' the citizenry about development, government officials commonly attributed Mafia's lack of development to residents' ignorance, to their stubborn and irrational devotion to 'tradition' or to a refusal to work hard (see also Caplan 1992, Snyder 2001). In a context in which money was largely lacking for development initiatives (or in which donor funds routinely disappeared from such projects as paving the road between Utende and Kilindoni or tarmac-ing the tiny sand-covered airstrip in Kilindoni), it was also easier to offer lectures about development rather than substantial action. Indeed, government officials regularly chastised Mafia residents for numerous activities which were viewed, much as they had been by their colonial predecessors, as impediments to 'development' or signs of the 'backwardness' of the region. For example, in 1997, a mainland government minister who was visiting the marine park offered a stern lecture to residents on the continuing practice of clearing land by burning, the failure properly to weed coconut trees, and for keeping children out of school to help with chores, injunctions that residents had clearly heard numerous times before.

In contrast to Mafia residents, government officials also shared the evolutionary assumptions of development common in international discourses which posited societies as in a process of progressive social transformation. Within Tanzania, this meant not only that different countries could be characterized as more or less developed, but that particular people and regions within the nation-state were perceived as more 'developed' than others. Although government officials clearly believed that development should be directed by the nation, officials were also quick to assert that the citizenry unjustly expected the government to do 'everything' and that the people needed to 'learn' that their own hard labor was required. In short, much like international discourses, the language of national elites was readily able to attribute internal differences in 'development' to hard work and the proper attitudes toward development rather than to social marginalization or varying class positions.

Such perceptions partially stem from the ways in which ideas of development have been mapped onto particular categories of people, and how such mapping intersects with - and supports - other social divisions, including class relations, within Tanzania. On Mafia, for example, a strong social divide separates island residents from appointed government officials. In the post-independence period, such officials were almost invariably educated Christians from the mainland, many of whom hailed from more prosperous regions of Tanzania such as Kilimanjaro, and who were only temporarily posted in the region. During the course of my fieldwork, it quickly became clear that the officials I met viewed themselves as more 'developed' than Mafia residents. Some made a point of stressing to me how 'undeveloped' Mafia was, asking how I could stand to live in such a place. Others hinted, some more subtly than others, at the apparent backwardness, laziness and lack of interest in education they found among coastal Muslims, explicitly contrasting this situation with regions like Kilimanjaro which they deemed much more 'developed'. In addition, those few who had studied abroad were quick to point out this fact to me, aligning their sensibilities as closer to my own as a citizen of a 'developed' country, while simultaneously distancing themselves from Mafia residents.

In large part, derogatory views of Mafia residents as 'traditional,' non-modern, or 'backward' centred on their relative lack of education[3]. Indeed, within the Tanzanian national landscape, education served as the crucial social fault-line. Not only did it serve as the entry criteria into Tanzania's post-independence elite, those whom Shivji (1976) has acerbically labeled the 'bureaucratic bourgeoisie', but it also served symbolically to mark those who are considered to be more 'developed' from those considered to be less so. Chole residents themselves identified the division between the educated and the uneducated as the primary social divide in their interactions with non-islanders. Tellingly, during my research, residents repeatedly referred to themselves as '*sisi tusiosoma*' ('we, the uneducated') and explicitly stated that it was their lack of education which made officials scorn them.

The reality that Mafia residents had less education - and thus were perceived as less 'modern' - stemmed from a relative lack of access to formal education which had its roots in the post-World War I British colonial period. Colonial policy had for the most part relegated education to Christian missionaries, thereby marginalizing coastal areas which were populated by Muslims resistant to proselytization (Iliffe 1979). Despite government efforts vastly to expand access to primary schools after independence, most adults on Mafia had only obtained a few years of elementary schooling. Indeed, Mafia is widely rumoured to be the last district in all of Tanzania to have a secondary school, the first being built outside the capital of Kilindoni in the mid-1990s during the course of my fieldwork. In contrast, regions which were early sites of Christian missionary activity, such as Kilimanjaro, have historically had far greater access to education and hence a preponderance of national elites hail from such regions (Iliffe 1979).

While government officials often attributed the lack of development on Mafia to the ignorance of residents themselves, those living on Chole instead ascribed this condition to marginalization and neglect by these very same officials. Residents argued that officials from more developed regions such as Kilimanjaro were 'jealous' *(wanaona wivu)* of other regions gaining

71

development and hence sought to block Mafia residents from obtaining *maendeleo*. They supported such contentions by pointing out that some district government officials attempted to halt the community-based eco-tourism project that European expatriate hotel developers had proposed for Chole. Later when the project developers agreed to help build an expanded primary school and a health clinic on Chole, officials in Kilindoni sought to block the clinic claiming that it would make the government hospital in Kilindoni obsolete. When community groups on Chole began collecting fees from tourists to help with these projects, district officials showed up on the island, demanding that a portion of the money be turned over to them. Chole residents argued that because government officials had 'already got their own education' *(wameshapata elimu zao)* (with the implication that they were using it for their own social advancement), they refused to help residents in potentially useful ways, such as identifying tree diseases or halting dynamite fishing. Instead, in the words of one Chole resident, they preferred 'to sit in their offices in Kilindoni, taking naps and collecting their salaries'. Indeed, residents argued that 'big people' such as government officials regularly used their positions to extract money for their own purposes *(watu wakubwa wanakula tu*; literally 'the big people just eat')[4]. In short, while for government officials, the language of development was a modernist one that focused on the necessity of further education to attain new levels of 'development', for Chole residents, development and education were languages of social access and exclusion.

From alternative development to discourses of ruin: Euro-Americans within the Marine Park

While 'development' was highly valued by both Chole residents and government officials, Euro-Americans within the park were markedly ambivalent. To understand this situation, it is necessary to consider how conflicting views of development among Euro-Americans stem from long-standing tensions within European thought. Beginning in the late colonial period, development gained ascendancy as the reformist idea of bringing planned 'progress' to the non-Western world by transforming such regions in Europe's own image via capitalism (and, later, socialism) and other 'modern' political and social institutions (Cooper and Packard 1997, Cowen and Shenton 1996). This perspective, based on discourses rooted in nineteenth century Europe and the United States which presumed the superiority of 'modern' life, symbolically underscored European dominance and naturalized international economic and political inequality. At the same time, however, 'development' could also be appropriated as a language of rights and entitlement by formerly colonized peoples (Cooper and Packard 1997, Peters 2000). Today, developmentalist perspectives remain powerful among Euro-Americans, both in popular discussions and in the policies and viewpoints of numerous international institutions including the IMF, World Bank, and many donor organizations. In reaction to the failures and unintended consequences of many development policies and projects, however, some activists, academics and others have put forward critiques of mainstream development which have since become incorporated into the language of development itself. Donors involved in the Mafia Island Marine Park, for example, have followed an increasingly popular path in seeking to wed development with conservation through such activities as 'eco-tourism' and by stressing the need for 'community participation'.

In addition, there has been a long counter-history of anti-modernist discourses within Euro-American symbolic traditions (indeed, reform efforts stem in part from such discourses). Arising in reaction to modernist conceptions of the world, anti-modernist discourses have been promulgated by critics from across the political spectrum and form a powerful strand in Euro-American thought. Such discourses focus on arenas perceived to be outside modernity, such as nature and the 'traditional' cultures of non-western peoples, and seek to preserve sites and ways of life viewed as 'pristine' or 'authentic' by virtue of their supposed distance from modernity. Such discourses are widely apparent within the tourism industry. Indeed, advertisements for places like the Mafia Island Marine Park are premised upon such ideas, promising visitors an escape from the development of the modern world, at the same time that the park ironically promises Mafia residents its exact opposite. Indeed, debates concerning development, and whether it should be viewed as a harbinger of progress or as a source of cultural and environmental ruin, were commonplace among Euro-Americans within the marine park, whether as tourists, tour operators or environmentalists working with NGOs.

On Mafia, Euro-American tourists and expatriates commonly characterized the region as 'unspoilt,' and many expressed worries that the expanding tourism industry would 'ruin' the island and its 'friendly' residents. Such worries were common even among tour operators who stood to benefit from such developments. Yet, the anti-modernist discourses embodied in ideas of 'ruin' were not shared by Chole residents. Most people I knew on Chole welcomed Euro-American visitors and the tourism trade, a reflection both of the cosmopolitan legacy of the coast and residents' desire for jobs promised by the tourism industry [5].

Differing conceptions of 'development' often resulted in a mutual sense of bewilderment between Chole residents and Euro-Americans. For example, when visiting Mafia, Euro-American tourists did not seek out the schools, office buildings and water collection tanks considered important sites to visit by Mafia residents, but rather explored the regions' abundant reefs and marine life, its beaches and coral atolls, and the stone ruins on Chole or at Kua - all sites which signaled valuable forms of 'nature' and 'culture' within Euro-American symbolic traditions. In addition, in places where Mafia residents perceived poverty, Euro-Americans instead saw 'tradition,' valuable precisely because of its difference from 'modern development' and identifiable in such things as thatched rather than tin roofs, cloth sails rather than outboard engines, and in the toys that children fashioned from palm leaves and twigs in contrast to the store-bought motorcars carried by tourist children. On occasion, Mafia residents peppered me with questions regarding the seemingly odd habits of Euro-American tourists. For example, Bi Sharifa wanted to know why light-skinned Europeans would want to lie in the sun and make their skins dark, while on Mafia people themselves wished for lighter skin (a legacy of both Arab and European prejudices). Why, Idi Mohammed asked, do Europeans always want things to be quiet? Don't they like music? An elderly woman near Mlola forest on Mafia's main island quizzed me as to why *Wazungu* (Europeans) would want to hike out to the rocky, windy coastline where there are no people, a place where she admitted she found no beauty. And, why, Ibrahim Abdallah asked, did two young German men camp on Chole's shores several years back and stay there for a week - living completely naked? According to Ibrahim, they even went to fetch water at the main well next to the mosque, right in the middle of a cluster of houses, without wearing any clothes.

I tried to explain as best I could why so many Euro-Americans, myself included, might be tired of urban noise and environmental pollution at 'home' and instead seek 'nature', quiet, and peacefulness in places like Mafia. Even though I knew full well that many Chole residents experienced the island's 'peacefulness' as boredom, such explanations were politely received (indeed, many Chole residents were themselves ambivalent about urban spaces such as Dar es Salaam). Yet, my attempts to explain the Euro-American symbolism which posited nature and tradition as antithetical to modernity (and which led to the presumed desire of the German nudists to be 'natural' with the 'natives') was both more difficult and more embarrassing to convey. Indeed, I was never able adequately to explain why Euro-Americans feared that Mafia might be 'ruined'. Some Swahili-speakers along other parts of the coast did fear a certain kind of moral ruin relating to tourism. In Zanzibar, for example, adults worried about the rise of the 'beach boy' subculture associated with tourists and marked by Rasta dreadlocks, sunglasses, reggae music, drugs and sexual relationships with tourists. However, such concerns were very different from the ideas of 'ruin' expressed by Euro-Americans.

I once broached this issue with Mzee Bakari, perhaps the most philosophical person I knew on Chole. Yet, even beginning the conversation was difficult. The concepts of both 'culture' and 'nature' are difficult to translate into Swahili[6]. Indeed, Mzee Bakari was puzzled by my suggestion that Euro-Americans feared that Mafia's 'culture' would be ruined and argued this was clearly incorrect. Although this might be partially attributed to the historically cosmopolitan outlook of the coast (making the idea of culture contact bringing 'ruin' seem particularly far-fetched), he suggested a more basic consideration. In his view, 'development' (*maendeleo*) clearly enhanced 'culture' rather than ruined it. This was so because greater material prosperity allowed people to decorate their homes or to perform ritual ceremonies in closer accordance with *mila*, in ways which were becoming increasingly rare because of growing poverty on Chole.

During the mid-1990s, misunderstandings stemming from different conceptions of 'development' also arose during the building of Chole's community-based 'eco-tourism' camp. Here, I will offer one example of the consternation the camp caused among the handful of Euro-American expatriates living on Mafia, all of whom were either conservationists or involved in Utende's tourism industry. Mafia's tiny expatriate community was distressed by the expansion in the network of footpaths linking Chole's budding camp to its waterfront as well as other parts of the island. Camp workers had carefully lined the paths with coral rock, painted brilliantly white with limestone. Euro-American expatriates, however, complained that the rocks (a cliche of hotel development along the Tanzanian coast) were 'tasteless' and they derided the aesthetic sensibilities of Chole's *Wazungu* developers for failing to adopt the low-key sensibilities suitable for 'eco-tourism'. I later learned, however, that the white rocks, like the flowers planted along the paths near the waterfront, were not the design of Chole's absentee tour operators, but had been undertaken for very different reasons by Chole residents involved in the camp. One camp worker, Fuadi Hassani, commented cheerfully to me one morning as he painted even more rocks brilliantly white, that they were once again creating a *barabara* (avenue) on Chole. The sandy path from the waterfront to the camp, in fact, lay upon the remains of a coral stone boulevard built by an ambitious Arab administrator in Chole Town in the late 1880s. (Ironically, even in that era, the boulevard had been derided for its 'modernist' pretensions by German geographer Oscar Baumann who visited in 1895). For Chole residents in the contemporary period, the coral-lined paths of the camp, ephemeral as they were, signalled their hopes for a revival of prosperity and *maendeleo* on Mafia.

In sum, Euro-Americans on Mafia drew upon conflicting symbolic traditions in their discussions of 'development'. While modernist sensibilities suggested the need to 'develop' places like Mafia, Euro-Americans also expressed an equally modernist desire to preserve the non-modern, symbolically located in 'nature' and 'culture' and seemingly poised on the verge of ruin. Euro-American worries that development signalled the demise of non-modern spaces, however, failed to acknowledge that the modern world was not simply a European creation, but had emerged in the power-laden colonial interaction between Europe and regions like East Africa and, consequently, had equally long histories in places like Mafia. Such viewpoints also failed to acknowledge that Mafia residents possessed their own perspectives on development, not simply as recipients, but as social actors and commentators in their own right. Indeed, Euro-Americans, who generally perceived themselves as more 'modern' than Mafia residents, were quick to presume that they knew best the benefits - as well as the pitfalls - of development. And, finally, Euro-American perspectives on development also served to obscure international social inequalities. Developmentalist viewpoints naturalized economic inequalities between regions by depicting poorer countries as needing only the right policies and a little donor support to 'evolve' towards greater prosperity, while anti-development positions failed to consider whether the fascination with 'tradition' masked, and hence served to make palatable, the harsh realities of poverty.

Conclusion

Some academics have depicted development as an intrinsically Euro-centric and oppressive discourse (Escobar 1995). Others have countered that development carries no intrinsic meaning and has been defined in various ways, including as a language of entitlement by Africans in colonial and post-colonial contexts (Cooper and Packard 1997, Peters 2000). My research supports the latter perspective. Although Mafia residents desire 'development,' it is a form of development reworked according to their own viewpoints. At the same time, however, residents' redefinition of development should not be interpreted as a simple act of 'resistance'.[7] I argue that such interpretations continue to occur within broader contexts of power in which 'development' serves as a language of social class operating across both national and international terrains and one that continues to marginalize Mafia residents[7].

Despite the strong association between development and a narrative of modernity which assumes that world history operates in progressive fashion towards ever increasing prosperity, it is clear that modernist assumptions are historically inaccurate. In sub-Saharan Africa, development has not readily materialized in the post-independence period, nor has the future been one of growing well-being. As James Ferguson has pointed out for urban Zambians, the high expectations for 'modernity' in the post-independence era have instead been met with the disillusionment of increasing economic and political marginalization, a condition widely shared across sub-Saharan Africa (1999).[8] Indeed, a few

Chole residents used millennial Islamic ideas of 'the coming end of the world' or *aheri zamani* to make sense of the current economic hardships they experience. A concept diametrically opposed to that of 'progress', *aheri zamani* is premised on the belief that residents' ancestors possessed a better life and that with the passage of time the world is gradually breaking down before it comes to an end. For Mzee Bakari, for example, the conditions of the mid-1990s - the growing worthlessness of money due to currency devaluations, the shoddiness of contemporary goods made in China and India, the decreasing fertility of the soil and seas, and the growing impoverishment of Mafia's residents in an era of Structural Adjustment Programmes - all readily accorded with the degrading lifestyles predicted by *aheri zamani*. In comparison, modernist narratives of development, which had foretold of coming prosperity, appeared to be hollow promises.

In sum, this paper has related the differing interpretations and uses of 'development' among actors within the Mafia Island Marine Park to their particular socioeconomic and historical locations. It has pointed to the intertwined relationship between development and narratives of 'modernity' while also offering the possibility of non-modernist interpretations. Ultimately, this analysis suggests the possibility of jettisoning modernist conceptions of development altogether and replacing such ideas with an attention to social class which can more readily make sense of dynamics within places like the Mafia Island Marine Park. In contrast to the concept of development, class is inherently political, points to arenas of debate and contention, and draws attention to inequalities between groups. Although theories of class (like development) carry questionable historical baggage, I believe it is possible to retheorize class to incorporate issues of cultural symbolism and identity as well as material realities in ways that cut across local, national and international terrains[9]. In the end, the concept of class may prove far better suited to helping us understand the growing social inequalities of what many are describing as a 'globalizing' era.

Notes

[1] All names in this article are pseudonyms.

[2] This interpretation is partially based on similar gender critiques offered

by Fatuma Fadhili on other occasions.

[3] Surprisingly, the stereotypes of coastal inhabitants common among government officials closely mirror those promulgated by colonial-era Christian missionaries, who presumably transmitted such beliefs through missionary schools and their post-independence offshoots. Although tensions were also exacerbated by the historical role of coastal inhabitants in the slave trade.

[4] See also Saleh (this volume) for a discussion of the centrality of corruption, i.e. 'going with the times' (*kwenda na wakati*), in contemporary social discourses in neighbouring Zanzibar.

[5] For an in-depth discussion of tourism within the park and its relationship to residents' ability – or not – to 'get ahead', see Walley 1999.

[6] I used an awkward litany of concepts (*mila, desturi, utamaduni*) to signify culture, as well as the term *mazingira*, literally 'surroundings' which is commonly used to translate environment. However, these terms do not carry the symbolic connotations of 'nature' and 'culture' in European and American thought

[7] In the 1980s, 'resistance' emerged as a central concept within the social sciences (Scott 1985 and Ong 1987 being two prominent examples). However, for an apt critique of the tendency to 'romanticize' resistance, see L. Abu Lughod 1990. Analysis of the potentially contradictory outcome of such reforms is beyond the scope of this paper; however, see Walley 1999.

[8] Analysis of the potentially contradictory outcome of such reforms is beyond the scope of this paper; however, see Walley 1999.

[9] Unfortunately, there is insufficient space to fully consider this issue here. Class as a concept has also been subject to the same 'modernist' teleological assumptions evident in development, i.e. that class struggle is inherent to historical progression, that such struggle is necessarily violent, that one class is historically anointed for leadership, that class is readily determined by material factors (rather than cultural, symbolic or other ones), and that class is the dominant form of identity (rather than cross-cut by other identities). The problems associated with Marxist analyses are painfully clear from neighbouring Zanzibar's own turbulent history. In recent years, however, there have been numerous attempts to rethink theories of class and capitalism which seek to address these issues (for example, Joyce 1995, Gibson-Graham 1996, Gibson-Graham et al 2000, 2001, Mitchell 1998). One important direction to take such newer formulations, I believe, is to consider how class dynamics operate across regional, national and international boundaries.

Bibliography

Abu Lughod, Janet, 1989. *Before European Hegemony: The World System 1250-1350*. Oxford: Oxford University Press.

Abu Lughod, Lila, 1990. 'The Romance of Resistance: Tracing Transformations of Power Through Bedouin Women', *American Ethnologist*, 17: 41-55.

Baumann, Oscar, 1895 [1957]. 'Mafia Island', *Tanganyika Notes and Records*, 46: 1-24.

Caplan, Pat, 1992. 'Socialism from Above: The View from Below,' in Peter G. Forster and Sam Maghimbi (eds.) *The Tanzanian Peasantry*. Aldershot: Avebury.

Chaudhuri, Kirti N., 1985. *Trade and Civilization in the Indian Ocean: An Economic History from the Rise of Islam to 1750*. Cambridge: Cambridge University Press.

Cooper, Frederick and Packard, Randall, 1997. *International Development and the Social Sciences*. Berkeley: University of California Press.

Cowen, Michael and Shenton, Robert. 1996. *Doctrines of Development*. New York: Routledge.

Donham, Donald, 1999. *Marxist Modern: An Ethnographic History of the Ethiopian Revolution*. Berkeley: University of California Press.

Escobar, Arturo, 1995. *Encountering Development*. Princeton: Princeton University Press.

Ferguson, James, 1994. *The Anti-Politics Machine: 'Development,' Depoliticization, and Bureaucratic Power in Lesotho*. Minneapolis: University of Minnesota Press.

——, 1999. *Expectations of Modernity*. Berkeley: University of California Press.

Finnemore, Martha, 1997. 'Redefining Development at the World Bank,' in Randall Packard and Frederick Cooper (eds.) *International Development and the Social Sciences*. Berkeley: University of California Press.

Gibson-Graham, J.K., 1996. *The End of Capitalism (as we knew it)*. Oxford: Blackwell.

Gibson-Graham, J.K., Resnick, Stephen A. and Wolff, Richard D. (eds.), 2000. *Class and its Others*. Minneapolis: University of Minnesota Press.

——, 2001. *Re/Presenting Class: Essays in Postmodern Marxism*. Durham: Duke University Press.

Iliffe, John, 1979. *A Modern History of Tanganyika*. Cambridge: Cambridge University Press.

Joyce, Patrick (ed.), 1995. *Class*. Oxford: Oxford University Press.

Mitchell, Timothy, 1998. 'Fixing the Economy', *Cultural Studies*, 12: 82-101.

Ong, Aihwa, 1987. *Spirits of Resistance and Capitalist Discipline: Factory Women in Malaysia*. Albany: State University of New York Press.

Peters, Pauline, 2000. 'Encountering Participation and Knowledge in Development Sites,' in Pauline Peters (ed.) *Development Encounters: Sites of Participation and Knowledge*. Cambridge: Harvard Institute for International Development.

Pigg, Stacey Leigh, 1996. 'The Credible and the Credulous: The Question of Villagers' Beliefs in Nepal,' *Cultural Anthropology*, 11(2): 160-201.

Rofel, Lisa, 1999. *Other Modernities: Gendered Yearnings in China After Socialism*. Berkeley: University of California Press.

Scott, James, 1985. *Weapons of the Weak: Everyday Forms of Peasant Resistance*. New Haven: Yale University Press.

Sheriff, Abdul, 1987. *Slaves, Spices and Ivory in Zanzibar*. London: James Currey.

Shivji, Issa, 1976. *Class Struggles in Tanzania*. London: Heinemann.

Snyder, Katherine, 2001. 'Being of "One Heart": Power and Politics among the Iraqw of Tanzania,' *Africa*, 71 (1): 128-148.

Sunseri, Thaddeus, 1993. 'Slave Ransoming in German East Africa, 1885-1922,' *The International Journal of African Historical Studies*, 26 (3): 481-511.

Walley, Christine, 1999. 'Making Waves: Struggles over the Environment, Development and Participation in the Mafia Island Marine Park, Tanzania,' unpublished Ph.D. dissertation, New York University.

CHAPTER 6

THE MONETIZATION OF MATRIMONIAL PRESTATIONS IN THE COMORIAN GREAT MARRIAGE

Francoise Le Guennec-Coppens
(Translated by Pat Caplan)

Introduction

Comorian society presents numerous cultural and social traits which identify it as part of the Swahili world. One finds the same population mixture as in other Swahili societies, such as the presence of an indigenous African people alongside those of Persian/Shirazi and Arab (especially from the Hadhramaut and Oman) origin. To this immigrant and integrated population which formed traditional Comorian society, were added African peoples – brought by slavery and trade – who are still excluded from the traditional hierarchical system.

The Muslim religion is another important factor in classifying the society of the Great Comoros with other Swahili societies because it is upon Islam, its law and its institutions, that the common ideology of these different societies is based.

Even so, if religion guarantees social cohesion in all these Swahili societies, there are also culturally specific elements which have resisted the dominant Islamic-Arab culture and remain very significant in spite of acculturation. Such is the case of the 'Great Marriage' (*grand mariage*) which, because of its very specificity in the Great Comoros, provides a good illustration of the diversity and cultural pluralism of Swahili societies.

The Comorian Great Marriage or Anda

In the way that it mobilises the energy of the whole community, and the importance it plays in the lives of individuals, this remains even today the central point in social life and one of the most active and significant of Comorian customs. Through it can be discerned the social organization, the structures of power, and the traditional economic system. While it forms a veritable institution, it also constitutes, in Marcel Mauss's sense (1950: 147), a 'total social fact' because it is imposed on individuals by the force of the community which obliges people to understand its importance, should they seek to deny it.

The fact of its existence in a completely Muslim country also demonstrates the ambivalence of a form of social organization which at one and the same time demonstrates Islamic cultural traits oriented towards patriliny and cultural and social traits oriented towards matriliny. Patriliny is revealed in the payment of money from groom to bride (*mahari*), the permitting of polygyny, and the unilateral right of divorce held by the husband. If not unique among the Swahili, matriliny, while less apparent than formerly, still exists in the preference accorded to matrilateral cross-cousin marriage, in the importance given to the marriage of girls, especially the eldest, and above all in the rigorous uxorilocality practised in the Great Comoros (Le Guennec-Coppens 1987).

Traditional power structures reveal themselves in the system of age grades which divide male society into two categories: that of the *wanamji* (children of the city) and that of the *wandruwazima* (accomplished men) (Le Guennec-Coppens 1994, 1998). The passage from one to the other is less one from adolescence to adulthood, than movement into the socially prestigious rank of a man who has accomplished his Great Marriage. Without taking account of either age or experience, it accords to a man the notability and prestige which is translated into various kinds of precedence accorded by the community or even the whole country. A Great Marriage also brings him an important power which is that of speaking in public, a right which is monopolized by the *mdrumzima*. The *anda* is thus the means *par excellence* of social mobility because it is the only way for a man to assume the status of a notable and to acquire the symbolic powers linked to it. In many cases today, it has become the means of acquiring other powers, political power in particular, which is a source of not only symbolic but also material benefits. The young man, in performing his Great Marriage, enters into the good graces of the notables which can bring him useful support; this is often decisive in obtaining non-traditional political or administrative positions.

The status of women is also defined in relation to their Great Marriage; however, their position is based upon that of their father, their brother or their husband to be. Further, when they are themselves married in an *anda* they become *mwana wa anda* (child of the *anda)*; they acquire prestige and can henceforth participate fully in the social life of women. Marrying off a daughter (or at least the eldest) in this way permits a woman to pass into the class of mothers (*wazaze*) of the Great Marriage. Later, on the occasion of the marriage of her grand-daughter, she will enter the class of grandmothers, the *makoko,* who are much respected and have authority over other women (Mroudjae 1989: 132).

The Great Marriage also provides evidence of an economic system, or more precisely, a complex network in which it is difficult to follow all the meanderings and connections. In fact, the prestations, exchanges, gifts, counter-gifts and presents are not only the affair of the families concerned, but also involve the whole community. This may range from the village to the entire country in the case of a family which plays a very important political and social role as in the recent case of the marriage of the son of the Great Mufti of the Comoros. The gifts and money offered by the fiance to his fiancee are brought together not only by the immediately interested parties, but also by his family, his friends and his *hirimu* (age grade). And to these gifts, the family and the whole group of the fiancee respond with counter-gifts. Thus every gift is written in a notebook and becomes the object of a counter-gift of at least equal value.

Since multiple ceremonies are spread out over up to a dozen years without following a strict chronology, there will be a situation of continuous exchanges between families and social groups of interested parties (see Appendix) from the time when the engagement (*mwafaka*) is concluded up to the time of the marriage itself. In principle in this system of exchange no-one should be wronged or injured, even if it seems that the groom's party invests more than that of the bride. In effect, the groom, if not his family, can end up getting his money back on the occasion of the Great

Marriage of a member of his family or one of his friends. All these gifts, which he gave for his own Great Marriage, will be progressively restored to him because he will inevitably receive part of the goods which each *mnamji* accumulates in his turn to celebrate his own marriage. Furthermore, on account of his rank he will be invited not only to all the customary ceremonies of his own community but also to those of neighbouring villages. Thus the celebration in his village or in his area of up to four Great Marriages each year represents for the *mdrumzima* invitations to numerous feasts lasting entire weeks (Rouveyran 1968: 118).

Furthermore, if he knows how to manage the expenses of his marriage and he has not contracted debts, a man can benefit from a sort of life annuity since henceforth his material participation in all customary activity is almost non-existent. One notable said that his investment brought him an income of at least 20,000 Comorian francs (300 French francs) each month, which is half the salary of a government official. If on the other hand, the man married in this way has received more than he gave out in his own marriage, he has to repay his debts before being able to profit economically from his status as a notable.

For the bride, the *anda* is also a source of material and economic benefit: she receives a house built by her father, brothers and maternal uncle which remains her property no matter what happens subsequently. She also receives furniture, jewels, clothes, cosmetics, household goods etc. Sometimes some of the goods, such as furniture bought on credit, are sold after the marriage since they have served to preserve the honour of the family by forming part of the display of riches (which are sometimes feigned). The newly married bride participates also in the repayment of the debts contracted by the family in order for her marriage to be as grand as possible. Often it is the money received from her groom's family in the course of various prestations which serves to reimburse the expenses already spent. As for the jewels received by the bride, according to tradition, part of them can be put back into circulation if she marries off her brother[1] who, in his turn, should offer the jewels to his future spouse (*bwara, upamkono*).

Matrimonial prestations thus play (or used to play) a role as a form of collective exchange at the heart of the community. At the same time they served to pay the entry fee by each *mnamji* in his turn to enter the class of 'accomplished men' (*wandruwazima*).

Today the traditional functions of ceremonial prestations have somewhat changed, especially in the capital Moroni, where they appear rather to elevate some people at the expense of others by making public the superior wealth (or at least the appearance of it) of the family and the extent of its social network. Indeed, by the financial excesses which it imposes today, the Great Marriage gives the impression more of personal social and material success than the good functioning of society.

The monetization of the Great Marriage and its consequences

What astonishes, surprises and intrigues when one attends for the first time no matter which ceremony of the Great Marriage, is its spectacular and ostentatious aspect. In fact, each of the numerous ceremonies is the vehicle for the exchange of presents, but above all of money which can mount up to millions of Comorian francs[2]. There has been an incredible inflation of expenses in the last few years, which can be partly explained by the increase in monetary resources. Formerly, when there was spending on the occasion of marriage ceremonies, it was at the level of slaughter of cattle (some of which were veritable massacres). As a result, the economic consequences were not very important because the herd could be restocked quite easily. It was only after 1960, when migration increased, that financial capital made its appearance and money became the main vehicle of the *anda*. Henceforth, everything had to be bought, and most things imported (suits, shoes, beauty products, cosmetics, etc.). Even the livestock and food products which were formerly part of the exchanges are now compensated for in money.

Since there is very little industry, and agriculture and fishing pays little, most of the money which circulates comes in part from the salaries of government officials (when they are paid!) and from commercial exchanges. But it comes above all from remittances, in the form of cash, gold and equipment, sent by numerous Comorian migrants[3], 'whose main motivation is the desperate quest for income in order to accomplish an extravagant Great Marriage' (Jaffar 1994: 15). In fact, the Comorians do not invest in their country of migration. Their life and their savings are almost exclusively oriented towards the Comoros where their future prospects lie. For example, on his return to his native country, a

Comorian who had spent all his working life as a soldier in France used up all his savings in carrying out his Great Marriage, the sole means of having an honourable place in his community.

It is in the urban milieu, particularly in Moroni, where money circulates the most, that one finds these new forms of matrimonial prestations which attract attention by the sometimes exorbitant inflation in the sums of money which are exchanged in each ceremony. Currently honour is acquired by means of money and the elevation in status of the families of the bride and groom by the proclamation of monetary sums received or given during the course of different ceremonies of the marriage. While traditionally the Great Marriage was a collective effort bringing honour to the individual and his or her social and familial network, today it has taken on the appearance of an intense economic competition in which candidates for the Great Marriage believe themselves obliged to outbid their neighbours in order not to lose face. Thus even the most critical people, intellectuals for example, have to accommodate themselves to the custom of the Great Marriage in its present form given the fact that they cannot do otherwise without going down in public estimation.

Women, especially the older ones, the *mama,* are the most eager to participate in these aims of the Great Marriage, because they cannot lay claim to any other position in the new hierarchies of professional or political status, and thus have only the Great Marriage to exist socially. In order to prove their worth, they participate financially to the maximum in the ceremonies while being in an almost permanent state of anxiety about whether they can quickly find money when the celebration of several marriages follow each other in rapid succession[4]. Furthermore, they always try to outbid each other: if one of their friends gives 100,000 Comorian francs to pay for a song (*jimbo*) they will give twice as much, considering that even if they do not gain from it financially, they will at least gain in prestige (*sheo*).

Younger women who have paid jobs in 'modern' occupations and would like to acquire a position based on rules other than those of the Great Marriage often give way to pressure, especially from their mothers, to have a Great Marriage in order to emerge from their status as children and acquire social recognition. They are therefore obliged to follow the norms imposed by their elders at the price of considerable sacrifice in their daily lives. For example, one young salaried woman, who is in receipt of only 30,000 francs monthly on which to live, donated a whole month's salary in order to make a public gift in a Great Marriage, hoping in that way to equal the richest (Mroudjae 1989: 20). Others try to limit going to such events with pious excuses such as the illness or the death of a distant kinsman or woman in order to avoid participating with a rather inadequate gift in a ceremony which is awash with money. But women who are involved in the system cannot but fulfill their duty and, if they cannot participate physically in the ceremony to which they are indebted, they must nonetheless produce the money which they owe under threat of being disgraced. A repayment must be made on the occasion of an identical ceremony to that in which the debt was contracted. If, for the *sigaretti* of the marriage of her brother, Madame X received 30,000 Comorian francs from Madame Y, Madame X must pay back at least the same sum to Madame Y when the latter organises the *sigaretti* of her brother's wedding.

It is in this way, willing or not, that women are the most penalised by monetization. For example, in order to marry off her eldest daughter in a Great Marriage, a woman, from her daughter's earliest age, will go and participate financially in every marriage, giving in each ceremony a sum of money which will be written down in a note-book. At the time of the marriage of her own daughter, all the sums which she has 'invested' will be returned to her; the risk of not getting reimbursed is nil, since the honour of other women is at stake. But she can also become severely indebted (some women can have six notebooks of debts to pay back) despite her participation over a period of years in the prestations for other marriages. Even so, for this woman, such debts are also synonymous with the greatness of her prestige since their magnitude is the proof of the importance of her social network and her fame.

In sum, then, because of the excessive monetization of the Great Marriage, the exchanges can be summed up as 'money which goes out and comes in, which waits outside or inside, which circulates in all senses' (Mouradje 1989: 136). According to an estimate made during the course of a marriage celebrated in 1989, it appeared that more than 75 million Comorian francs (US$ 12,500) circulated in this way between the families and the social groups of the bride and of the groom. This money was not actually spent, because, at least in part, it is always the same money exchanged in the cycle of prestations.

Monetization has thus brought about, especially in the urban milieu, excesses which have created new models based on cash, on individual and family pride, on a spurious prestige, and which are contrary to the rational development of the individual in his or her community. Indeed, the Great Marriage, the main cause of indebtedness, is one of the heaviest burdens on families and operates to the detriment of economic development. Money acquired or saved is either hoarded to meet the expenses linked to the celebration of a Great Marriage in the family, or else it participates in the circulation of prestations and counter-prestations of different Great Marriages because 'prestige costs a lot' (Rouveyran 1968: 114). In both of these cases, capital is immobilised instead of being utilised, even temporarily, in productive investment.

It is particularly people of moderate fortune or modest social status who try at all costs to accomplish a Great Marriage, because, not having any other means to elevate themselves, they have everything to gain. They have to submit themselves if they want to enter into the circle of those who can speak and be heard in public, decide matters and give directions in the village. From this point of view, the rewards of the Great Marriage can be viewed as one of the root causes of this monetization of prestations, translated today by imitating the practices of those who are socially superior.

Monetization has also created other values which tend to substitute for those of the lineages and traditional status classes by transforming positions acquired by the *anda*. Whereas previously the Great Marriage was reserved for the important lineages, today all individuals, whatever their social category, can do it if they have the means. Nobility of birth, previously necessary, now has less significance than wealth: the son of a prince who will have spent less on his Great Marriage than some *parvenu* will occupy an inferior place in the hierarchy to the latter. Furthermore, the norms of matrimonial alliance, which formerly decreed that there should be endogamy within the lineage or at least within the same status group and territory, are no longer strictly respected since wealth can now compensate for modesty of status.

In this way, while the greatness of the *mdrumzima*, his influence and the respect in which he is held still depend on numerous factors such as social rank, personal qualities, or wealth (Le Guennec-Coppens 1998), they also depend to a greater and greater extent upon the prestige gained through the splendour of his marriage and thus the importance of the spending undertaken.

Finally, the *anda* formerly only concerned the eldest girl and the eldest boy. Their marriage mobilised the whole family which thus accomplished its social duties jointly. It was enough that one had 'put one's walking stick on the threshold' (*ukada mbuda mwangoni*), that is to say, that a person had made a Great Marriage, in order that the prestige and honour would redound on the whole family. Today it is on the number of Great Marriages and their ostentatious display that the prestige of the family is judged because, regardless of inferior status, money has become the main social marker. Families which have the means find it worthwhile and socially gratifying to marry off not only their eldest daughter but all their daughters in a Great Marriage, and, if possible, their sons as well.

Conclusion

In terms of appearances, the fundamentals of the institution of the Great Marriage are the same, but their form has changed: matrimonial prestations are always the expression of social ties, but today their number has become greater and their cost has reached astronomical proportions. Further, the Great Marriage still has the same function - access to the highest status - but its realization demands much more in the way of financial means.

Seen in this light, it appears that the expenses concomitant upon a Great Marriage still have a function which is social rather than economic. As Rouveyran said 'It is really a form of *potlach*' (1968: 122), since one finds the distribution of riches to numerous participants on whom is imposed the obligation to reciprocate under threat of losing their honour. In the Great Marriage, one challenges by honouring and one competes by distributing as much as possible.

Nonetheless, in spite of its materialist appearances, the spirit which animates the Great Marriage still rests on respect for traditional social values because, as an informant said, 'With the Great Marriage, it is either honour or dishonour. If you make a mess of your Great Marriage, it will follow you for the rest of your life'. In fact, it is essential not to make a mistake, in spite of the excessive expenses imposed by the ritual exchanges of the *anda* which treat money with a logic different from that of the strictly monetary. In order to have the place of their choice in the society, each one is ready to spend a fortune in order to enjoy *sheo* (honour) and the right to speak and to take decisions in the community. If the importance and the cost of prestations were to be diminished, might there not be a risk of opening the door of social success to everyone?

Appendix: Exchange on the occasion of a Great Marriage

The tables presented below do not claim to be exhaustive since supplementary prestations, which were formerly free (for example the taking off of the turban and shoes of the groom when he enters the nuptial house for the first time) are not all mentioned. These tables aim to summarize the system of prestations and counter-prestations which put each person into a situation of indebtedness in relation to his or her social group. They also give an idea of the size and number of exchanges made on the occasion of a Great Marriage between two families at the heart of the community and its social groups.

shama	a women's association
mdraya	town district
majilisi	a ceremonial gathering of men, and the place where it is held.
mji pl. *miji*	grouping of men according to the age grade system

MWAFAKA WA ANDA (engagement)

Family of fiancée	Gifts	Family of fiancé
fiancée ←	*Bwara* (pounds)	← his sister
family ←	*Zigelegele* (ululation)	←his sister
fiancée ←	*Marapvo* (for accompanying)	← his sister
her mother's *shama* ←	*Jimbo* (songs)	← his sister
family →	*Hari* (sweat)	→ his sister

DZOROZO (period, which can last several years, between the engagement and the marriage; period of consolidation of relations between the families)

Family of fiancée	Gifts	Family of fiancé
fiancée ←	*gauni* (dresses)	← fiancé
fiancée →	*kandu* (gowns)	→ fiancé
fiancée →	*meza* (tables)	→ fiancé
fiancée ←	*gauni* (dresses)	← fiancé
fiancée →	*kofia* (cap)	→ fiancé
family ↔	*chai* (tea)	↔ family
her mother ↔	*hari* (sweat)	↔ his sister

MAJILISI YA ZINDRU (period during which the dates of the marriage are fixed)

Family of fiancée	Gifts	Family of fiancé
family →	*cherezo* (incense-burner)	→ fiancé
zikombe za kafe (coffee cups)		
family ↓ →	*jimbo* (songs)	his sister + his sister's relatives and her friends ↓ his sister's *shama*
family + her mother's friends ↓ →	*gato* (cake)	family + his sister's friends ↓ his sister (notebook)
family ←	*karwa* (transport)	← his sister
karamu madjilisi (feast of *majilisi*)		
		family ↓ invitees to *majilisi*

93

ZINDRU (the things, start of marriage ceremonies)

Family of fiancée	Gifts	Family of fiancé
	mtwalaan (invitations)	
her mother's relatives ↓ →	*ubuwa mtwalaan* (opening of invitations)	his sister ↓ his sister's *shama* and *mdraya*
	jimbo la shama + *jimbo la mdraya* (songs of the *shama* and of the *mdraya*)	his sister's relatives and friends ↓ his sister + his sister's *shama* and *mdraya*
	ulauliya (greetings)	his sister + his sister's *shama* ↓ invited *shama*
	uhula le jimbo (buying the songs)	his sister's relatives and friends ↓ invited *shama*
her mother ↓ her mother's *shama* and *mdraya*	*ubuwa mtwalaan* (opening of invitations)	
her mother's relatives and friends ↓ her mother + her mother's *shama* and *mdraya*	*jimbo la shama* + *jimbo la mdraya* (songs by the associations of the town district)	
her mother + her mother's *shama* ↓ invited *shama*	*ulauliya* (greetings)	
her mother's relatives and friends ↓ invited *shama*	*uhula le jimbo* (buying the songs)	

Family of fiancée	Gifts	Family of fiancé
jaliko (invitations)		
her mother's friends and close relatives ↓ her mother (notebook)	*tibu* (a perfume)	
her mother's friends and close relatives ↓ →	*sigaretti* (or *msi*) (cigarettes or chewing tobacco)	his sister's *shama* and *mdraya* + his family + his sister's friends ↓ → his sister (4 notebooks)
her mother →	*hari* (sweat)	→ his sister + his sister's *shama*
her mother →	*shileo* (betel)	→ his sister + his sisters-in-law
her mother + family →	*jimbo* (songs)	→ his sister's *shama*
her mother ↓ town districts	*fedha ya mji* (money for the town)	
hupvea zindru (sending the objects)		
her mother's sisters-in-law ←	*shileo* (betel)	← his sister ↓ his sister's *shama*
	fedha ya mji (money for the town)	his sister ↓ town districts
meza ya zindru (the table with objects)		
fiancée ←	*mahari* (dowry)	← fiancé
her mother ←	*pambo* (packaging)	← fiancé
her mother's *shama* ←	*zigelegele* (ululation)	← fiancé
her mother ←	*mapeza ya wapambe* (money for the beauticians)	← fiancé
her mother's *shama* ←	*mapeza ya meza* (money for the table)	← fiancé

Family of fiancée	Gifts	Family of fiancé
	fedha ya miskiti ya jumaa (money for Friday mosque)	← fiancé ↓ Friday mosque
	fedha ya hemeza	guests at the meza ↓ fiancé (notebook)
family →	*zindru* (things)	→ fiancé
her mother ←	*sinia* (tray)	← his sister
the women who carry the *zindru* ←	*karwa* (transport)	← his sister
marapvoo ya zindru (transporting the things)		
her mother's *shama* ←	*jimbo* (songs)	← his sister
her mother's *shama* ←	*fedha ya wapambe* (money for the beauticians)	← his sister
her mother + her mother's friends →	*hari* (sweat)	→ his sister
her mother →	*jimbo* (songs)	→ his sister's *shama*

HWENDA DAHONI (going into the house).

Family of bride	Gifts	Family of groom
paha mwazi (to rub oneself with blood)		
her father ↓ her father's *mji*		
fule za keso (the young goats of the ceremony)		
		groom ↓ his *hirimu* (age grade)
hulala dahoni ha saya (to sleep in the house at the right time)		
her mother and father →	*diner* (dinner)	→ groom + those close to him
her mother ←	*sabuni* (soap)	← groom

Family of bride	Gifts	Family of groom
huyeleya (to distribute)		
her father → ↓ her father's *mji* and *mdraya*	*mapesa ya jeleyo* (the money which is distributed)	→ his *mji*
her father and mother ↓ her mother's *shama* and *mdraya* + her maternal uncles' *miji*	*koo* (the crust)	
her maternal relatives ↓ her father	*funvu* (contributions)	
her father's friends ↓ her father (notebook)	*funvu*	
Jaliko		
family ↓ her mother's *shama*	*ngoma la mishumaa* (a dance)	

Family of bride	Gifts	Family of groom
ladha ya mwana (the happiness of the bride)		
family + her mother's friends ↓ bride (notebook)	*sihu ya heledawo* (the day of the mats)	
her mother's friends and relatives ↓ her mother (notebook) → bride	*godoro* (mattress)	
her maternal uncles' wives + family + her mother's friends ↓ bride	*daho* (the house)	
her relatives and friends ↓ bride (notebook)	*kado* (presents)	
her mother ↓ her mother's *shama* and *mdraya*	*fedha ya mji* (money for the town)	
	sigaretti (cigarettes)	his sisters' relatives and friends ↓ his sisters (notebook)
	chea (the left-overs)	his sister ↓ his sister's *shama* + *shama* of bride
	chai (tea)	his sister ↓ his sister's *shama*
twarab		
her parents' relatives, friends and acquaintances ↓ →	*jimbo* (songs)	his parents' relatives, friends and acquaintances ↓ his *shama*

Family of bride	Gifts	Family of groom
hwenda dahoni (to enter the house)		
bride ←	*upamkono* (giving the hand)	← groom
her father →	*karwa* (transport)	→ the men who carry the *upamkono*
her father →	*madumbuso* (money for invitations)	→ groom
bride ←	*vao la mwana* (the bride's clothes)	← groom
her mother ←	*vao la mzaze* (the mother's clothes)	← groom
her father ←	*vao la baba* (the father's clothes)	← groom
her mother ←	*masurufu* (the husband's contribution)	← groom
tari la ndzia (the small drums of the lane)		
	uhoza mindu (washing the feet)	his friends and close relatives ↓ groom (notebook)
bride ←	*mbere za masiu* (the rings of the night)	← his sister
bride ←	*fedha ya masiu* (the money of the night)	← his sister

Family of bride	Gifts	Family of groom
utoa mwana ukumbi (display of the bride in the living-room)		
bride ←	*paoni* (pounds)	← his sister
her mother →	*pambo* (packaging)	→ his sister
beauticians ←	*wapambe* (beauticians)	← his sister
her mother's *shama* ←	*jimbo* (songs)	← his sister
those who remove the veil ←	*mapeza ya masia husutu* (money for removing the veil)	← his sister
her mother →	*hari* (sweat)	→ his sister
her mother →	*hari* (sweat)	→ his sister's *shama*
her mother →	*jimbo* (songs)	→ his sister's *shama*
	shileo (betel)	groom ↓ his sister
her family + her friends and acquaintances ↓ bride	*uzuguwa mwa* (removing the bad spells)	his family + his friends and acquaintances ↓ ←
bride ←	*sabuni* (soap)	← groom
her mother, sisters, cousins + her friends ↓ bride	*hishima* (respect)	
her mother →	*makate wa mazazi* (the cakes for the mother)	→ his sister
her mother ←	*karwa* (transport)	← his sister
her mother ←	*mziwa ya keso* (the milk for the ceremony)	← his sister

Notes

[1] In the Comoros, it is the mother who marries off her daughter, but the sister who arranges the brother's marriage

[2] For example, for a *twarab* which took place in July 1992, the *shama* (association) of the groom obtained 1,575,000 Comorian francs

(equivalent to approximately US$4,000); at the same time, the clothes of the bride *(vao la mwana)* offered by the groom comprised one hundred dresses and fifty pairs of shoes, and at her display the bride recived more than five million Comorian francs (approx. US$12,500).

[3] Said Hassan Jaffar (1994) estimates the number of Comorian immigrants in France at around 100,000, while the total population in the Comorian Archipelago is estimated to be 600,000. See also Vivier 1990-1.

[4] In consequence there is a great consumption of sedatives by women.

Bibliography

Benëï, Véronique, 1996. *La dette en Inde: Un fléau social?* Paris: Editions Karthala/Institut Français de Pondichery.

Chouzour, Sultan. 1994. *Le pouvoir de l'honneur.* Paris, Editions Karthala.

Jaffar, Said Hassan, 1994. *La communauté comorienne en France.* Paris, Mémoire de DEA, INALCO.

Le Guennec-Coppens, Françoise, 1987. 'Le manyahuli grand comorien : un système de transmission des biens peu orthodoxe en pays musulman' in M. Gast (ed.) *Hériter en pays musulman - habus, lait vivant, manyahuli.* Paris: éditions du CNRS: 257-269.

Le Guennec-Coppens, Françoise, 1994. 'An Influence from the Mainland: the Age Grade System in Great Comoro' in D. Parkin (ed.) *Continuity and Autonomy in Swahili Communities.* Wien: Institut für Afrikanistik und Ägyptologie der Universität/London, SOAS.

Le Guennec-Coppens, Françoise, 1998. 'Les hommes accomplis' in F. Le Guennec-Coppens and D. Parkin (eds.) *Autorité et pouvoir chez les Swahili.* Paris: Karthala.

Mauss, Marcel, 1950. 'Essai sur le don' in *Sociologie et Anthropologie.* Paris: Presses Universitaires de France,145-279.

Mroudjae, Said Islam Moinaecha et Sophie Blanchy, 1989. *Le statut et la situation de la femme aux Comores.* Report for PNUD.

Rouveyran, Jean-Claude (with the collaboration of Ahmed Djabibi), 1968. 'Le "dola n'kou" ou grand mariage comorien', *Revue Tiers Monde,* L'économie ostentatoire, vol. IX-n°33, pp.95-127.

Vivier, Géraldine, 1991. *La communauté comorienne en France. Cohésion et solidarité en région parisienne*, mémoire de maîtrise-sociologie/démographie, Nanterre: Université Paris X.

CHAPTER 7

POLITICAL VIOLENCE, ETHNICITY AND THE AGRARIAN QUESTION IN ZANZIBAR

Greg Cameron

Introduction

Zanzibar, although a multicultural society, underwent a bloody Revolution in 1964, and has recently experienced violent political confrontations once again, this time between the ruling party CCM (*Chama cha Mapinduzi* – Party of the Revolution) and its opposition rivals in the CUF (Civic United Front). In the wake of the 2000 General Elections on Zanzibar, and their immediate aftermath, which included the crushing of mass demonstrations in January 2001, many people fled to Kenya as refugees. What was this latest manifestation of violence all about? Ethnicity, identity and history have been common motifs in Zanzibar studies. Were age-old communal identities merely suppressed during the colonial and single party period, and the lid blown off with the onset of political liberalization? Or are political identities and subsequent violence reducible to the trajectory of post-revolutionary political economy? Or if identity politics are neither primordial nor purely a process of reduction to political economy, how does one explain a contemporary identity politics so ostensibly rooted in the past?

In this chapter I seek to answer these questions in a number of ways. The first is to explain the historical background to the current situation, and the way in which different versions of history have been used by the contestants to construct a political discourse of ethnic essentialism. The second is to examine notions of political accountability in post-revolutionary Zanzibar in the light of the significant changes which have taken place since the 1964 Revolution: the vagaries of state initiatives in the 1960s and 1970s, the gravitation towards economic liberalization in the 1980s, multiparty democracy in the 1990s, and finally the impact of 'globalization'. An analysis of the governance of the regime during the same period reveals the extent to which continuities with the past, including the rhetoric of ethnic essentialism, are used in contemporary Zanzibar society. The third issue discussed is the economic problems which have intensified on the islands during this period and have resulted in the growth of an organized opposition to the ruling party .

This chapter thus seeks to demonstrate the multiple perceptions and meanings of history and political economy and the identities which are formed by these processes. It does so by seeking voices in the opposition heartland of Pemba, showing that identity politics is much more complex than the orthodox version of the regime allows. Identities are neither primordial nor arbitrary categories. Their construction involves belief, understanding, and the utilization of emotive symbols as well as strategic choice. Identity politics can also serve as a counter to the dominant hegemony, that is, the web of beliefs and institutional and social relations organized by intellectuals. I will first examine the orthodox academic version of the Zanzibar Revolution, questioning some of its myths and claims. I then turn to the agrarian policy of the regime and discuss its failure to modernize the peasant smallholder sector, and its exploitation of the clove-producing island of Pemba. Moving back to the regime's version of politics in the 1980s and 1990s, I will argue that it continued to use a discourse of revolutionary ethnic essentialism to quash rural protest rather than addressing the legitimate aspirations of rural communities. The multiparty period in the 1990s witnessed a desperate effort, in part employing the symbolism of the past, to seek a new dispensation beyond Zanzibari *ujamaa* and the actually existing union with the mainland. Finally, I examine more closely the underlying nature of the protest in Pemba, arguing that it was to a large degree a defensive response to the fragmentation of village life by the forces of underdevelopment.

Rethinking the Zanzibar Revolution

A sign hanging above the entrance to the Zanzibar National Archives states 'The Past Is Never Dead . . . It's Not Even Past'. This succinctly articulates the fact that in the real world, outside of those buildings housing the tomes and documents of 'high history', other social actors choose, consciously or otherwise, to employ historical accounts as tools in the contemporary creation of political identities.

To what extent did Zanzibar's political traditions endure into the post-revolutionary era and what were the post-1964 discontinuities with pre-1964 Zanzibar? Perhaps the greatest paradox of the 1964 Revolution was that the actual seizure of power was undertaken by a hitherto unknown Ugandan, John Okello, who led a force of mainland Africans and Afro-Shirazi Party youth against the Sultan's government (see Okello 1971). Leaders of the revolution downplayed the number of those killed in the terror which followed, but it is commonly accepted that the death toll approximated 10,000, a very high percentage for a population of under 300,000 people. Though spared the brunt of the pogroms which took place on Unguja, Pembans suffered humiliation and public floggings, with many having their beards and heads shaved by Okello's Makonde followers. In 1963, the Arab population of Zanzibar had numbered approximately 50,000 but by the end of 1964, it had fallen by 12-15,000 people through death, deportation, or departure (Clayton 1981). Undoubtedly this period left a legacy of fear and hatred in the hearts and minds of many who lost loved ones and/or property. There were also the 'disappeared' of the subsequent Karume era, victims of a ruthless East German-trained security apparatus.

ASP documents justified the violence as the glorious overthrow of a slave-holding feudal regime by an oppressed African majority[1]. Scholars of Tanzania, though more circumspect, have side-stepped the fact that a democratically elected government was overthrown; they have also downplayed the scale of the killing which for all intents and purposes was directed at one community, much of it on personal grounds or for criminal reasons. Moreover, they ignore the fact that, although many people voted for the ASP, this does not imply that they supported such violence. Coastal scholarship in the leftist tradition, much of it written by radical local and expatriate academics at the University of Dar es Salaam between the mid-1960s and the mid-1970s, thus failed to discern the nature of the 1964 ASP/CCM coalition, subsuming it under the *ujamaa* project or uncritically accepting CCM orthodoxy on the Zanzibar Revolution (e.g. Cliffe and Saul 1972, 1975).

Connerton (1989) argues that images of the past may legitimitize a present social order, sustained by ritual re-enactments of past violence between groups and filtered through eye-witness accounts, oral tradition, museums, and restorations. Though such a process was in motion in Zanzibar, the limited number of concrete memorials suggests that even their reconstructed version of history was not fully elaborated by ASP leaders. This commemorative reticence may have been partly due to the violence that tore apart the fabric of Zanzibari society. There were also attempts to expunge the role of the Ugandan, John Okello, who was 'disappeared' from the official version of the revolution, and replaced by the revolutionary Karume. The CIA's role in the creation of the Union was replaced by the pan-Africanist visions of the founding fathers (none of whom hitherto had ever talked of such a union). The Revolution thus became a sanitized non-event whose symbols were to be employed on an occasional basis, either for mobilizing supporters or intimidating opponents.

The 'transition to socialism'

After the Union with Tanganyika, the pattern of Zanzibari politics during the first 25 years of the ASP/CCM regime must be understood as an intra-party struggle, first with the Left in the 1960s, and then with the Right in the 1980s, neither of which was enthusiastic about the Union. With the dissolution of the *Umma* Party, and the banning for ever of John Okello from the Isles later in 1964, intra-party opposition ceased as the Karume faction prevailed, replacing the principle of election by the principle of nomination. Although a popular song glorifies the Committee of Fourteen (the actual revolutionaries) as being of rural stock, in reality the majority of them were urban dwellers who were embittered by the oppressive class system of the Sultanate. As Adam, Raja and al-Moody note: 'This social background narrowed their political vision enormously so that, once in power, their aspirations hardly strayed beyond the edge of a flourishing palm grove or clove plantations which they coveted' (1984: 11). Thus the

ASP political elite remained parochial, enmeshed as it was within the African mainlander and Unguja Shirazi communities (with some limited support on Pemba).[2]

Anthropologists and other social scientists would also concur that history is not a product of 'what actually happened' in the past, but rather a response to the requirements of the present (Erikssen 1993: 72). Recent works in the African Nationalist tradition bear this out. The events of the 1990s are seen in the light of the events of 1964, with a similar premium on 'ethnic' rather than on 'class' identity. Post-1964 economic performance is either ignored or downplayed. In the twilight of the single party era, the historical line given out by the political class remained constant, shaping the boundaries of discourse around political possibilities and impossibilities. The CCM sought to deny political agency to Zanzibar's polyethnic society, its resilient sub-groups and smaller collectivities. In 1990, Chief Minister Omar Ali Juma's line on the 1964 Revolution echoed that of the ASP in the mid-1960s:

> It is difficult to say who killed who. It was a revolution. It was a class struggle, a proletarian revolution and not a racial or lumpen revolt as emotionally referred to by reactionaries. Therefore it is wrong to point a finger to an individual or to a group of people; there was no race which participated *en masse* in the Revolution... No one can and should defend all that happened during the revolution, particularly brutalities and atrocities... If you keep seeking revenge for what happened to your relatives or friends during the revolution then you will be reminded of slavery, so there will be no end to the comparisons and you will be going around in circles. I am appealing to all Zanzibaris that we should forget and forgive each other for what happened during the Revolution (Juma n.d.: 4).

Multi-partyism

In the wake of the controversial 1995 elections, members of the CCM intelligentsia like Omar Mapuri (1996) and Ted Maliyamkono (2000) have emphasized racial, ethnic and historical factors while neglecting analysis of the regime's post-1964 governance. Maliyamkono, presenting a less jejune argument than Mapuri's line on the 'Arab threat', argues that contemporary political parties on Zanzibar reflect colonial-era ethnic and regional schisms among

107

Arabs and Africans, a trend which he says continued in the 1995 elections. He argues that Pemban Zanzibaris of Middle Eastern descent who historically had voted for the old opposition party, the Zanzibar Nationalist Party (ZNP), are now likely to support the Civic United Front (CUF), the main opposition party. However, there are problems with this line of argument. Certainly voting patterns in the multiparty era have closely resembled the colonial elections, but a closer examination reveals a drop in the popular vote for the regime over the single party period, 1964-1990. The decline in popular support for the ruling party, especially on Pemba, cannot be explained by communal voting traditions; rather, it must take into account the events of the post-colonial period in order to explain the decline in the vote on Pemba for the CCM from 44% in 1963 to about 10 % in 1995. This clear trend makes a mockery of the CCM's apparent sudden popularity in five Pemba constituencies in the 2000 elections.

No doubt this discourse at the level of national politics was helped by an opposition which appeared to be promising to compensate former landowners expropriated by the revolutionary land decrees of the 1960s. Letters from the CUF leader to the former ZNP leader, which were circulated to activist CCM cadres at the village level, no doubt added to the fear that CUF would bring back the Sultanate. Furthermore, when opposition politicians referred to pre-1964 Zanzibar, with its perceived efficient social services and educational systems, as a kind of 'golden age', they were actually ignoring its more negative realities, such as its racial and class oppression. This factor appeared to many supporters of the regime to smack of contempt for the advances made for the masses (*umma*) since the Revolution. Thus CUF's developmentalist discourse about contemporary economic problems and corruption were seen as a veil to cover the very real threat to roll back the achievements of the 1964 Revolution. The coded threats of the political parties kept alive the possibility of deep violence, such as when CUF talked of the possibility of another 'Rwanda' if CCM did not respect the will of Zanzibaris, or sent out mixed signals about its commitment to preserve the union with the mainland. This spectral language from the political class points to the ways in which CCM itself used historical and primordial arguments as blunt weapons: 'The Revolution Continues', 'The Inviolability of the CCM Union', 'The Legacy of Julius Nyerere'.

But as the party in power, the CCM had the means forcefully to impose its image of the past and to threaten Zanzibaris resident on the mainland with expulsion should they break CCM's union (a threat made by the President during the 2000 elections). More generally, threats of instability and violence by the CCM were effectively self-fulfilling prophecies. When the 2000 elections were over, many opposition supporters simply said that they should have stayed with a single party system rather than endure all the turmoil, social division and wastage of resources and personnel wrought by campaigning.

The agrarian question

In this section, I argue that a major reason for the recent disturbances in Zanzibar, and more particularly in Pemba, lies less in ethnic identities, and more in agrarian questions, and particularly the agricultural backwardness of the peasantry, a situation which needs to be contextualized historically. The peasants had already been pushed to the margins in the nineteenth century by the establishment of a clove economy and its plantations. Common to both Isles had been the undermining of rice production in favour of clove production, a trend deepened during British colonial rule. Roads were built with clove plantations in mind, while the expansion of plantations encroached on land that could have been used for food crops, fruit trees, coconuts, and maize. Credit facilities for rice farmers were non-existent and many rice fields degenerated into swamps. Additionally, clove harvests monopolized labour for three months of the year to the detriment of the food crop sector. Peasants increasingly had to cultivate the nutritionally inferior but easily grown cassava. Cooper cites an official remarking on the economic irrationality of over one-third of Pemba's cloves financing the purchases of imported rice (1980: 153). The fact that the *Wahadimu, Wapemba* and *Watumbatu* - the Zanzibar indigenous peasantry - did as well as they did in the face of the lavish support provided to the Arab planters makes one wonder how the peasant economy might have evolved if the British authorities had provided sustained support to peasant agriculture. This pattern was to continue into the post-1964 period.

The dominant version of the history of the Zanzibar Revolution assumes that the peasantry, or at least the Unguja peasants, fully supported the Sultan's deposal and that protest in the countryside dovetailed with the goals of the nationalist leaders. Such a perspective fails to see peasants, whether on Pemba or Unguja, as autonomous political actors neither bound to tradition nor blindly following the events of high politics. A historical perspective focusing upon agency would recognize that peasants had their own issues separate from those of their urban-based leaders, such as during the so-called 'Cow War' (*Vita vya Ng'ombe)* in the 1950s when Unguja peasants rioted over government plans to inoculate their cows (Sheriff 1991). In short, what is not clear from the literature is the relationship between agrarian problems and the events of 1964, and whether the interests of the countryside were addressed post-1964.

During the early post-1964 transition period it was agreed that the regime should undertake the diversification of the small-holder economy and gradually lessen the dependence on cloves in favour of greater food self-sufficiency. What was the agrarian policy during the 'transition to socialism' *(kipindi cha mpito kuelekea ujamaa)* in Zanzibar? Very little is known of the ASP's everyday administration in the countryside, including the relative weight of local environment, economy, ideology, or personalities and how these elements fitted together. Therefore until such time as an oral history project is undertaken and government documents from this period are opened to public scrutiny, one must glean information from scattered statements and documents. My working premise is that the *Wapemba* and *Waunguja* peasantries would have followed the revolutionary programme, but only conditionally. Certainly the ASP land reform, a populist strategy emphasizing the minimization of rural differentiation through allocation of small individual landholdings, gave hope to many former landless squatters, particularly mainland Africans. Some new landholders, however, were disappointed because the redistributed land could not be held as freehold or inherited, but only held for the productive life of the cultivator. Furthermore, for those peasants who followed Islamic precepts, the expropriated land was *haramu* (illegal). Moreover many large land holdings were left intact, and some *Wakubwa* (big people) appear to have received more than their fair share. As for the planters, the Revolution merely hastened the demise of their economically inefficient plantations.

The victorious ASP set up the Zanzibar State Trading Corporation (ZSTC) in 1965, a parastatal that many considered squeezed the peasantry even more than had its colonial predecessor, the CGA (Clove Growers' Association), which was responsible for establishing prices. It was a triumph of the Centre over a countryside which had been institutionally weakened by earlier historical transformations. The pricing policy of the ZSTC was such anathema to producers that the regime enacted the death penalty for smuggling. A key demand of Pemba growers and pickers during the multiparty elections in 1995 and 2000 was the divestiture of the ZSTC in favour of a free market in clove exporting, a demand refused by the political elite largely based in Zanzibar Town. Today, there remain problems: the burning of clove trees, the smuggling of cloves to Kenya, the planting of cassava in place of cloves or merely leaving the trees unpicked while CCM youths try to force owners to pick their trees.

The increasing subsumption of pre-capitalist forms by clove production, without any transformation of the division of labour or improvement in technology, provoked the peasantry to defend its remaining economic autonomy and created a moral discourse of rights around how the central government was expected to develop the *shamba*. De-agrarianization, the reconstitution of economic life around the de-specialization of rural activities and the entry into informal markets, plus widening differentiation throughout Zanzibari society, scrambled previously existing social boundaries in the countryside. Communities, whose livelihoods very much depended on what outsiders did, held a moral view of the actions of the latter as either contributing to the further material decline of the *jamaa* (community) or of alleviating it.

If the divisions in the Zanzibar countryside had no clear sociological coherence, then how does one explain the socially potent mix of economic, racial, and ethnic tensions, articulating with a bifurcated inter-island division? It was the political leaders themselves who sought to disseminate the symbols of the 'other', and draw various 'borderlines', in order to undermine the everyday consciousness of village life for purposes of political mobilization. A weakened CCM turned to the creation of what Appadurai terms 'ethno-scapes' (1995: 208), where human emotion, the volatility of images and the conscious identity-producing activities of the nation-state lent a fundamentally unstable quality to social life. The regime was thus trying to reshape coastal history according to its own imagination.

The origins of Zanzibar's contemporary political crisis derived from the agrarian crisis manifested in Pemba's regional isolation, rather than a reassertion of Arab hegemonic designs on the Isles. Undeniably Arabs were respected more than Africans by Pembans in the realms of culture, race, and religion. Nonetheless the political problems were at their core an attempt by Pemba to reclaim its rightful place in Zanzibar. Even when Pembans talked secession from Zanzibar, it was as a community (*jamaa*), not as 'Arabs'. More fundamentally, Pembans generally expressed secessionist sentiment out of political exasperation and did not realistically want to secede from Unguja.

What then does 'peasantry' mean in contemporary Zanzibar? Peasant life is one of enduring and semi-permanent relationships of mutual interaction and interdependence in a context of market marginalization. In agrarian Zanzibar there was no 'peasant mode of production' to hide in. Rural kinship systems - *tumbo, mlango, familia and udugu* - as they articulated with political practice, were at best a moral community ethos, rather than a 'moral economy of affection'. Household survival was not only premised on intra-community relationships, but also on vertical relationships with party-state networks, both formal and patron-client.

Purveyors of the multiparty system failed to realize the consequences of local villagers passionately opposing one another politically and historically, while simultaneously continuing to be neighbours-as-usual. The new inter-party politics fostered competition over scarce external resources, and injected into these communities a notion of a zero-sum game where the gains of some were at the expense of others. Suddenly politics, not the vagaries of nature itself or a bumbling one-party state, could undermine survival strategies for households. Certainly class formation was underway in the Zanzibar *shamba*. However, intra-community divisions were secondary to the division between the rural areas and the state. Any class, gender, ethnic, or racial divisions within the Zanzibari peasantry were secondary to the prime contradiction between state and society, as well as to that between the two main political parties nationally.

From accommodation to quiet resistance, and finally to protest, emic notions such as the golden age and *udugu* were very anchored in how subordinate groups lived their lives in contemporary Zanzibar. Identity, far from being fixed, was very much negotiated and relative to the nature of the post-revolutionary state. An islander could describe him/herself as a Pemban, Ungujan, Zanzibari, Tanzanian, Swahili, Tumbatu, Shirazi, African, Arab, Comorian, Nyamwezi, Makonde, Chagga, Gunyan, *mkulima* (peasant), *mvuvi* (fisher), *mhuni* (street youth) *mwanamke* (woman), *Mzee* (elder), *kijana* (youth), *Mwaislam* (Muslim), *Mkristo* (Christian), *maskini* (poor person), *tajiri* (rich person) and so on. These self-appellations capture nation, region, race, tribe, religion, class, pan-territoriality, gender, and generation, and through time articulated with structural factors such as colonial data collection techniques, changes in class structure, transnational influences, and the strength of the state. Structures and consciousness were firmly anchored to what went on.

The failure to address the malaise of the mono-cultural clove economy continues to afflict Zanzibar. It is likely that rural-urban migration will continue unabated and that many young people will try to flee to the growing Swahili diaspora. Tourism will grow, its effects deepen and the marginalization of the peasantry will continue apace. Perhaps here we are speaking of the 'peasants' revenge': a failed socialist transition and modernization project, in which peasants in great numbers leave the countryside for the urban informal sector, or engage in acts of smuggling (Bernstein and Byres 2001: 16). In such a situation the state is presented with a potential crisis of surplus expropriation. Indeed the regime's recent stringent anti-smuggling measures against clove growers appear to highlight this crisis of surplus appropriation in the Zanzibar countryside.

In the Zanzibar context, the grafting of an *Ujamaa* political structure onto pre-1964 clove relations ensured the continuing dependence of village communities upon urban political elites. Local village governance and economic autonomy had long been hollowed out by clove capitalism. Consequently the central government stood paramount in the village first in the guise of the *sheha* and later the ASP/CCM *tawi*.

What of social consciousness? Values and identities must be placed in their *historical* context. Classes do cut across racial boundaries and political alignments: 'ethnic identities are images people have of themselves or of others, and to use these skin-deep

113

identities to analyse history is "to write the history of images'" (Sheriff 1991: 7). Although the power of ethnicity as an ideological force in history must be acknowledged, ethnicity has to be explained by history rather than it explaining history (Sheriff and Tominaga 1992: 1). People may come to interpret their own ways of life differently over time; and in fact there may be a number of contradictory modes of behaviour centred around political identity.

The growth of opposition

Van Binsbergen (1999) defines localization as the phenomenon whereby a group of people create a collective identity underpinned by meanings particular to them as a social group. In the process, they raise among themselves both conceptual and interactional boundaries so as to protect the locus of meaning and identity which organizes their experience and justifies their actions. Appadurai (1995) reminds us that locality is ever fragile and that national and global systems are ever-present. In line with post-revolutionary and post-Union political trajectories, subalterns supporting the opposition designated the political class as *Wazanzibara* (*bara* meaning continent and referring to those in the leadership who had first or second generation links to the mainland). In contrast to indigenous *Wazanzibari*, *Wazanzibara* were deemed more loyal to the Union than to Zanzibar itself. For its part, the regime jettisoned the discredited socialist model and instead opted for the time-honoured authoritarianism of its 1964 ethnic coalition. Many *Waunguja* also wished to prevent the new opposition coalition taking a bigger piece of the shrinking economic pie for Pemba to the detriment of their own island of Unguja. There was also a genuine fear in many local communities, especially on Unguja, that the opposition would reverse the gains of the Revolution.

The language of *matabaka* (class) was rare indeed in the villages. However, notions of accountability and justice employed by subaltern groups against ruling groups could follow the contours of social being within 'arenas' organic to the Zanzibar *shamba*, and based on rules, expectations, and values as people lived them. The Zanzibar peasantry was both backward-looking (defending its remaining community institutions as the dream of the Revolution faded) and forward-looking (aspiring to benefit from the post-revolutionary development model); the former was increasingly so as the promised fruits of the Revolution shriveled. Closing ranks, both historically and spatially, against outsiders brought together not only most of the Pemban peasantry against the 'African' CCM, but also the Unguja peasantry who saw the political party of the former as the 'Arab' outsiders. Violence to defend their respective visions was ever possible. The subsequent decline in living standards sparked moral outrage among many peasants. With the expanded legal space and the advent of political pluralism, the national level became the focal point for political protest among dominated groups.

By 1995 there were roughly three strata opposing the CCM on Pemba. First there were supporters who had hitherto believed in *Ujamaa,* but who saw the regime fall short in practice. Many were poorer women, youth, and poor peasants. Second were the sceptics who gave CCM the benefit of the doubt and adopted a wait-and-see attitude. Third were natural enemies such as those who had lost property and people in 1964. Peasant ambivalence towards the regime reflected their experience with the revolutionary project itself: failed health and education services, poor producer prices for cloves, government and party institutions of negligible accountability, inflation, unemployment, and other indices of quality of life. People judged the regime on its own ideological terms through *their* understanding of *Ujamaa* and self-reliance. The 1995 election sparked an open political crisis on the Isles. The 2000 General Elections deepened the social conflict and brought the Union government directly into the political crisis.

Conclusion

Zanzibar's contemporary political crisis was the culmination of the interaction of three major factors, all present by the 1980s. First, the 1964 Revolution and its aftermath alienated that half of the population who had supported the ZNP/ZPPP. Second, ASP's authoritarian and accumulationist approach towards the peasantry saw the countryside stagnate due to poor clove prices and inadequate investment in the small holder sector, especially on Pemba. Third, the CCM state reinforced ASP-like policies, in addition to creating a closer relationship with the mainland that was highly centralized in character. The pursuance of 'revolutionary' politics extended far too long into Zanzibar's contemporary political culture. National policies emanating from these three major factors exacerbated unhealed political wounds from the past, which in turn led to a growing demand for political change.

It is still the case that for both Zanzibari political traditions, the state remains of paramount importance. Even for those rural communities in the camp of the opposition, there is still a consciousness of the gains which came from the early post-colonial period, such as health, education and agricultural extension. These were inserted into the local meaning of what constituted the good life. The emphasis on a strong state stems from the earlier post-independence period when life was improving and development and modernity visible in their communities. This perspective shaped the structures and processes of local life, before it began to be eroded.

Afterword

Since this paper was written, an agreement (*'Muafaka'*) was signed on October 10 2001, after eight months of negotiations between the CCM and the CUF. It is a comprehensive document that includes reform of the Zanzibar Electoral Commission, the introduction of a permanent register of eligible voters, a review of the existing constitution and electoral laws, guarantee of fair coverage of both parties in the publicly-owned media, and payment of compensation to those affected by the January 2001 massacres. CCM refused to accept CUF's demand for a re-run of the 2000 elections but accepted that CUF representatives would have a greater share in governmental institutions. There would also be by-elections in the 16 CUF constituencies which were declared vacant when CUF MPs had been expelled following their boycott of the Zanzibar legislature, the Zanzibar House of Representatives (*Baraza la WaWakilishi*). There would also be an independent inquiry into the massacres. Talks regarding a possible coalition government were to start no later no later than June 2003 and would be held under a ten-person Presidential Commission on Implementation and Monitoring. Donor countries indicated that their aid freeze would end once the Agreement was implemented (Anon 2002).

Whether the *'Muafaka'* represents an enduring solution to the political problem of the Isles and the United Republic remains an open question, given the CCM regime's refusal to fully implement the previous Commonwealth-brokered Agreement of 1999. A cynical interpretation of this latest agreement would be that it represents nothing more than the Zanzibar regime's ongoing efforts to receive international aid, frozen for several years because of the dispute, and thereby alleviate some of the dire economic problems of the Isles. Morever, this internal agreement, as opposed to the internationalized Commonwealth intervention of 1999, contains even less leverage on the Karume regime to share power with the CUF, especially in light of the international community's hands-off approach in the wake of the mismanaged 2000 elections. Assuming that the envisaged reforms are undertaken, one wonders whether the Zanzibari CCM leader, Abeid Karume, will really step down in 2005? While some think this may be unlikely, the CCM has recently shown itself to be less recalcitrant than in the past. It is making some incremental concessions that may see gradual reforms to the political system in the longer term, a process that would not be as suddenly threatening to its grip on power as the Commonwealth Agreement may have been perceived to have been. Whether the majority of Zanzibaris would be willing to wait into the indefinite future for gradual reform under an omnipotent CCM regime is another question altogether. For this reason this most recent agreement represents at best only a rather faint hope that the political crisis will truly be solved by the 2005 General Elections.

Notes

[1] The Afro-Shirazi Party itself set the pace with its Tenth Anniversary publication, (ASP 1974); for a more in-depth pro-ASP line on the Revolution see Mrina and Mattoke 1980. In contradistinction, pro-ZNP works detail a litany of tyrannies committed in the 'Communist'-ruled islands, including the killings of *imams* (mosques leaders) and children by ZRC members (See Kharusi 1969).

[2] ASP's pre-1964 support was growing at the time of the Revolution and peaked in the 1963 election at 44.4% of the popular vote on Pemba and 63.2% on Unguja (See Othman and Mlimuka 1990: 162 –163).

Bibliography

Adam, Mohammed Mlamali, Ahmed Rajab and Omar al-Amoody, 1984, 'End of an affair'. *Africa Now,* February.

Appadurai, Arjun, 1995. 'The Production of Locality'. In Richard Fardon (ed.). *Counterworks: Managing the diversity of knowledge.* London: Routledge: 204-225.

ASP, 1974. *The Afro-Shirazi Party Revolution, 1964-1974.* Zanzibar: ASP.

Bayart, Jean-Francois, 1993. *The State in Africa: The Politics of the Belly.* London: Longman.

Bernstein, Henry and Terry Byres, 2001. 'From Peasant Studies to Agrarian Change', *Journal of Agrarian Change* 1, 1, January: 1-56.

Bulletin of Tanzanian Affairs, 2002. 'Zanzibar: a comprehensive agreement'. (71: 8-15).

Clayton, Anthony, 1981. *The Zanzibar Revolution and Its Aftermath.* London: C. Hurst and Co.

Cliffe, Lionel and John Saul (eds.), 1972. *Socialism in Tanzania: an interdisciplinary reader.* Dar es Salaam: East Africa Publishing House.

———, 1975. *Rural Cooperation in Tanzania.* Dar es Salaam: Tanzania Publishing House.

Connerton, Paul, 1989. *How Societies Remember.* Cambridge: Cambridge University Press.

Cooper, Frederick, 1980. *From Slaves to Squatters: Plantation Labour and Agriculture in Zanzibar and Coastal Kenya, 1890-1925.* New Haven: Yale University Press.

Eriksen, Thomas Hylland, 1993. *Ethnicity and Nationalism,* Pluto Press, London

Juma, Dr. Omar Ali, n.d., *Zanzibar in Perspective A collection of speeches and statements* (no publisher).

Kharusi, Seif, 1969. *The Agony of Zanzibar.* Richmond: Foreign Affairs Publishing Co. Ltd.

Maliyamkono, Ted M. (ed.), 2000. *The Political Plight of Zanzibar*. Dar es Salaam: Tema Publishers.

Mapuri, Omar, 1996. *Zanzibar: The 1964 Revolution Achievements and Prospects*. Dar es Salaam: Tema Publishers.

Mrina, B. and W. T. Mattoke, 1980. *Mapambano ya Ukombozi Zanzibar* (Zanzibar's Liberation Struggle). Dar es Salaam: Tanzania Publishing House.

Mukandala, Rwekaza and Haroub Othman, 1994. *Liberalization and Politics: the 1990 Election in Tanzania*. Dar es Salaam: Dar es Salaam University Press.

Okello, John, 1971. *The Zanzibar Revolution*. Nairobi: East African Literature Bureau.

Othman, Haroub and Aggrey Mlimuka, 1990. 'Political and Constitutional Development of Zanzibar and the Case Studies of the 1985 Zanzibar General Elections' in *Tanzania: Democracy in Transition*, H. Othman, I. Bavu and M. Okema, eds. Dar es Salaam: Dar es Salaam University Press: 150-82.

Sheriff, Abdul and Chizuko Taminage. 'The Shirazi in the History and Politics of Zanzibar'. Paper presented at the International Conference on the History and Culture of Zanzibar, Vol. 1, Zanzibar, December 1992.

Sheriff, A., 1991 'Introduction: A Materialist Approach to Zanzibar's History' in *Zanzibar Under Colonial Rule*, A. Sheriff and E. Ferguson eds. Oxford: James Currey: 1-9.

Van Binsbergen, Wim, 1999. 'Globalization, consumption and development' in *Modernity on a Shoestring*, eds. R. Fardon, W. van Binsbergen and R. van Dijk, London, SOAS: Leiden, EIDOS3-13.

CHAPTER 8

CHANGE, CONTINUITY AND CONTESTATION: THE POLITICS OF MODERN IDENTITIES IN ZANZIBAR

Kjersti Larsen

Introduction

Multiculturalism concerns questions of identity, difference and power which can, as Terence Turner (1994) points out, help us to explore how various multicultural formations are fashioned. Multiculturalism has appeared under specific social, political and economic conditions and forms part of the response of its creators to those conditions. In considering multiculturalism in the context of Zanzibar, it is important to keep in mind that Zanzibari society, culturally and socially, forms part of both the Indian Ocean and the East African mainland. In this paper I will discuss what I call the politics of modern identities in Zanzibar and explore how historical narratives and recollections are interconnected with an explicit identity project[1]. The discussion is based on ethnographic material mainly from Zanzibar Town.

I approach Zanzibar as a complex, yet unified society. However, in political or politicized contexts, questions of identity and belonging are reconstructed along essentialist lines: Arab and African. Within this discourse ethnic categorization rather than citizenship becomes the main focus and the 1964 Revolution (*Mapinduzi,* literally 'turning upside down') becomes a main reference point for understanding on-going changes. Moreover, 'the Revolution' has become a synonym for the problems of multiculturalism and for the particular hierarchical social organization often associated with multicultural states.

In the everyday life of most Zanzibaris, however, the multicultural dimension refers to a much more complex conceptualization based on different places of origin or ancestry rather than religious or other differences[2]. While problems of multiculturalism and identity have often been approached through the concept of 'ethnicity', in my own work from Zanzibar I have preferred to use the vernacular term *'makabila'* rather than the term 'ethnicity'. The main reason behind this choice is that, in my view, the concept of ethnicity can all too easily reify certain patterns of differentiation between groups of people, which is misleading in the context of Zanzibari society.

In order to explore how multicultural formations are created, this paper examines the topic from the viewpoint of difference, life-styles and perceptions of wealth which are important in women's and men's self-reflective identity constructions and conceptualizations. Within this setting, I will discuss a series of events that have occurred over the last five decades. My aim is to examine social and cultural processes in which, may be for the first time, external circumstances and internal reactions to these circumstances have resulted in an unprecedented situation. People find that their cultural values cannot accommodate the challenges brought about by the recent events. Nor can they be explained by so-called modernist approaches to the multiplicity of identities and multicultural societies.

Ethnicity

The concept of 'ethnic groups' (Barth 1969) is often used to form categorical units for the analysis of complex societies in which several groups cohabit, each claiming cultural difference with reference to origin. In many ways an analysis using this Barthian notion in its classical sense could also prove meaningful for the empirical material presented in this paper, because, as Marshall Sahlins argues (1999), following Barth, the epitomizing signs used to mark boundaries are conditions of ethnic cum cultural differences. Given the similarities between interacting peoples, such distinctions cannot easily be established. Furthermore when the perspective of 'ethnic groups' has been applied to the analysis of multicultural societies in recent studies, it has tended to reify a certain pattern of delineation between categories or groups of people and fails to recognize the fact that people usually embody several identities. Moreover, in situations where one form of identity discourse is linked to a dominant ideology, this becomes the main focus of attention. Such situations are often characterized by what Sahlins (1999) calls the 'cunning of cultural reason' or the 'inventiveness of tradition': situations 'whereby instrumental interests adapt and extend traditions to novel situations' (ibid: 414).

I have thus refrained from using the term 'ethnicity' and the concept of 'ethnic groups' in the Zanzibari context because, although people are explicit in their use of the term *kabila* and the various criteria used as signs of differentiation, the boundaries between different *makabila* are complex. Although people differentiate between themselves with reference to places of origin, they simultaneously stress that they are all Zanzibari, and thus different from, for instance, people from mainland Tanzania. 'Tribe', in this context, refers to what people see as their own or their ancestors' place of origin, i.e. a certain locality beyond Zanzibar. However, awareness of tribe and place of origin beyond Zanzibar does not necessarily mean a wish to return to these original localities. Rather the term *kabila* is used in the sense of a cultural identity marker through which people mark out what they perceive as their originality (De Heusch 1997; Sahlins 1999). Most of the time, these differences relate to aesthetics and to what in Zanzibar are referred to as habits (*tabia*) and ways of relating to life and people (*desturi*).

Living within a cosmopolitan and socially stratified society, people have an awareness of different ways of life. Even so, women and men simultaneously emphasize their Zanzibariness by referring to what they see as their particular way of being in the world: hospitality, friendliness, etiquette, aesthetics, the Swahili language and, for the majority of the population, their shared Muslim faith, rather than with being from the same locality. The way Zanzibaris create and recreate differences in daily life has produced interrelated networks and complex sets of relationships, particularly in urban areas (Larsen 1995). Hence, from a Zanzibari point of view the world, as well as their society, is multifaceted with regard to 'ways of life'.

However, in recent political campaigns, racial and ethnic constructions of Arab and African have reappeared, playing on various versions of the 1964 Revolution (see Cameron, this volume). Such representations of society refer to political, social and economic identities, to questions of power, and to perceptions of the right to belong. Furthermore, such versions also evoke recollections of the hierarchical social organization associated with the time before the 1964 Revolution and in so doing, both assert Zanzibari-ness and create anxieties about not being perceived as a legitimate Zanzibari – an anxiety that can also be recollected from the immediate post-Revolutionary period. It is not that these historical versions have suddenly reappeared during the recent political period from 1994 until the present, but rather that they have been intensified and re-formulated.

Furthermore, in the aftermath of the election in 2000, a new distinction, linking notions of location with political identification, came to the fore, that is, a distinction between the 'Zanzibari' and the 'Zanzibara' (Cameron and Saleh, this volume; Wallevik 2001). The term *'bara'* refers to the mainland. Hence, while the term Zanzibari denotes those perceived as loyal to Zanzibar as a separate entity, *Zanzi-bara* denotes those perceived as loyal primarily to the mainland-based government of Tanzania and the 1964 Union between Tanganyika and Zanzibar. In this way, not only does the question of origins relate to the production of social distinctions but also to that of political allegiance.

The local understanding that difference with regard to 'tribe' can be a reason for hostility and revenge is not a recent phenomenon, but a conception kept alive in 'story-telling' about the times before, during and after the Revolution (Myers 2000). In my experience, people have always been reluctant to talk about the days of Revolution and on several occasions when I have tried to discuss this event, they have avoided my questions or told me that it is not something they would like to remember. However, in situations of anger, anxiety or conflict, experiences from and stories about the Revolution are often evoked. Let me give some illustrations.

Case 1: A shooting in Zanzibar Town

One afternoon in 1992 we heard that the police had shot two young boys in the Mchangani area of Zanzibar Town. The reason for this incident was that the police had been chasing the boys, suspecting them of dealing in drugs. In such instances the police are allowed, according to what people said, to shoot at the legs of the suspects in order to make them stop. However, in this instance one person had actually been shot dead as one of the bullets had hit him in the back.

Zainabu, a woman in her early thirties, said that the police, who were mainlanders, had deliberately shot the young man in the back and then claimed that it was an accident. She said: 'It is because he (the boy) was an *Mngazija* (Comorian) that the police from the mainland shot him. Do not think that anything has changed. It is just like during the Revolution. People from the mainland (*bara*) do not like people of Comorian or Arabian origin. We all know that this is the reason why the man was shot'.

Case 2: Fear of attack

One evening Muhammed had taken his wife Halima, his daughters and me for a drive around Zanzibar Town in his pick-up. At one point we reached a neighbourhood on the outskirts of the town and Muhammed drove off the road in order to turn the car round. In so doing, the car came to an area between the houses where there was a gathering of people and we could hear drums. Muhammed's wife, Halima, suddenly said: 'Turn the car, we cannot stop here. It may be dangerous. There are many '*Waswahili*' (people of mainland origin) here. We never know what these people might do when there are many of them together. They will see that we are *Wahindi* (of Indian origin)'.

The two incidents described above indicate how, in certain contexts, historical narratives and recollections lead to a reconstruction of relationships according to essentialist identity categories, that is Arab and African, where 'Arab' includes Comorian and Indian identities. Zainab is too young to have experienced the days of Revolution, but still, being an *Mngazija*, she

125

has time and again heard recollections and stories about what happened during those days and about the harassment and mistreatment of people of Comorian and Arabian origin. Thus despite a dominant public political narrative representing the Revolution as a positive change in Zanzibari society, other narratives presented by Zanzibaris who do not associate themselves with an African background continuously contest this with reference to their own experiences and recollections.

Halima experienced the Revolution and recollects days of fear when suddenly fellow citizens became enemies. These enemies she has termed '*Waswahili*'. Whenever she confronts gatherings of people not known to her, she feels threatened and claims that because she is of Indian origin they will probably wish to harm her. This understanding does not, however, mean that Halima does not have many people of so-called Swahili origin among her friends or that she does not seek out healers and Muslim teachers whom she terms *Waswahili*. However, this is different, she claims, because she knows them and they are 'decent' Zanzibari women and men. Moreover, Halima also shares experiences of hardship with her friends and neighbours belonging to different *makabila*. In their discussions about the Revolution and its aftermath, peoples' daily struggle for food and their loss of control over their lives are themes often touched upon. For example, they talk about the introduction of the 'Forced Marriage Act'[3], which meant that men of so-called African origin could marry women considered to be of Arabian or Asian origin without the consent of either the women or their families. They also mention the confiscation and destruction of homes and neighbourhoods (see Barwani 1997). Yet simultaneously, what often remains as an echo from the various different narratives is an understanding that origin does determine people's character and thus what kind of relationships they may engage in, while the very fact that people are of different origin may represent a threat in itself.

A multicultural society and the problem of multiculturalism

Zanzibar Town, along with other urban centres along the Swahili coast, has at certain historical periods been a highly multicultural and stratified society, with merchants considered as high-ranking citizens and others of lower rank (Sheriff 1987, 1995). As the plantation economy and commerce have played a significant role in the island's economy and the development of its urban centre, socio-economic differentiation has also linked people's perceived places of origin with economic status. Moreover, the presence of slavery as an aspect of socio-economic and political life has also divided Zanzibaris into freeborn and slaves as well as into Arabs, Asians and Africans - a form of stratification which increased during the period of British colonialism[4]. Within this political structure the Arabs were the privileged group, especially Arabs from Oman, while Africans were, in this context, perceived as the less civilized or 'cultured'. People who considered themselves as belonging to the higher strata of society often claimed Arab ancestry although historically such claims may have had little foundation (Fair 2002; Larsen 1995, 1998; Middleton 1992). Moreover, no one would normally admit to being of slave descent[5].

An event that dramatically altered this situation was the Revolution in Zanzibar in 1964, the culmination of a period of political tensions, demonstrations, and violence, also called 'the time of politics' which began in 1957. Although the 1964 Revolution can be described as a struggle between propertied and non-propertied classes, at the time it was largely defined on racial grounds. Many land and property owners, mainly of Arab descent, were killed or fled the island. This event also had dramatic effects on the lives of people of Comorian and Asian descent (Saleh 1995). Moreover, differences based on areas within Zanzibar, such as between the islands of Pemba, Tumbatu and Unguja, were also emphasized as markers.

Following the 1964 Revolution, new prestige and power relationships were inscribed in the lives of Zanzibari women and men. After the Revolution, a socialist government of mainly African descent ruled Zanzibar: Arab-ness became disqualifying, African-ness was qualifying and the more public aspects of Islamic activity and rituals were discouraged and even condemned. Zanzibar was meant to become a state where all people should be defined as Afro-Shirazi. This term was constructed in order to re-write existing identities in terms of different 'tribes' (*makabila*) and to create a nation of Afro-Shirazi people, that is, people perceived as being of mixed African and Persian origin, which would in theory, also include people of Arab and Asian origin[6]. Despite this, Zanzibaris continue to think of themselves in terms of tribes or

127

populations (*makabila*) and also continue to celebrate their religious faith.

Muted discourses on identity and identity formation

Since the 1964 Revolution the official policy has, as mentioned above, been to downplay discourses on 'tribe' and cultural differentiation. Yet difference with regard to tribe and place of origin have continued to be articulated through what might be called muted discourses, for instance, with reference to the spirits (*majini, mashetani*) known to Zanzibaris through the various rituals performed on their behalf (Larsen 1995, 1998, 2000). Zanzibaris hold that spirits, just like humans, belong to different tribes. Furthermore, the various tribes of spirits present in Zanzibar have varied over time and thus correspond more or less to the constellation of people that has constituted Zanzibari society at various historical periods. Spirits known to Zanzibari women and men are, as I have discussed elsewhere, presented and represented as distinct with regard to identity and locality.

An extensive body of literature has discussed the role of various performative contexts such as, for instance, rituals and different speech genres in mediating conflict and resistance, encoding affect, voicing dissent and ordering community and tradition (Abu-Lughod 1990, 1986; Kapchan 1996; Larsen 1995, 1989; Meeker 1979). In Zanzibari society rituals represent an arena in which existing hierarchies and social divisions can be challenged or reinforced, depending on the situation and the goals of the participants (Fair 1997; Larsen 1989, 1995, 1998). Through these performative and discursive contexts, women and men express - verbally and non-verbally - their understandings of ongoing changes concerning life in general, and in political and economic hierarchies. Below, I present two cases illustrating what I see as the connection between possessory spirits and their human hosts' negotiation of social relationships and self-identification. These examples focus on problems of multiculturalism in relation to people's small-scale displacements, replacements, and creativity in daily life and explore what kind of cultural and socio-political criteria are implied when they talk about *makabila* and their life-styles.

Case 3: Bi Khadija's negotiation of identities and relationships

Bi Khadija has four spirits, all belonging to different tribes. She has one Arab, Muslim spirit (*shetani ya ruhani*), who is the kind of spirit perceived as most in accordance with images of being Zanzibari, a good Muslim and 'civilized'. She also has a pagan, Swahili spirit from Pemba (*shetani ya rubamba*), that is, the kind of spirit less in accordance with images of Zanzibariness. Bi Khadija herself never stresses her tribe, however others hold that she is an *Mswahili*, and Bi Khadija herself sometimes says that her grandmother was a slave. Bi Khadija also has a Christian spirit from Ethiopia (*shetani ya habeshia*), a representation which refers to a particular historical period where women of Abyssinian origin were among the Sultan's concubines. In present recollections this story thus confirms and presents a certain relationship between an Arab dynasty and a slave population in Zanzibar (see also Larsen 1998). Finally, she has a Christian spirit from Madagascar (*shetani ya kibuki*). These spirits are associated with the Comorians (*Wangazija*) in Zanzibar Town with whom Bi Khadija has close ties since many of her neighbours and close friends are of Comorian origin. Moreover, Bi Khadija's only daughter married a man of Comorian origin and as such her granddaughter, who is living with her, is partly Comorian and has, like Bi Khadija, a *shetani ya kibuki*.

It thus appears that the spirits who possess Bi Khadija are associated with important relationships in her life. In my experience, it is often the case that the tribes of spirits possessing people are associated with the tribes of humans who, in one way or another, echo aspects of their life history and embrace various facets of their rather flexible Zanzibari identity. Her relationships with the various spirits produce a politics of identity in a changing world.

When possessed by her spirits significant identities are inscribed onto Bi Khadija's body and her historical and social belonging in Zanzibar is highlighted and presented as multifaceted. The distinctions between the various tribes of spirits are expressed through their ways of behaving, speaking and moving as well as through their likes and dislikes, and the particular forms of

129

knowledge and strengths (*nguvu*) associated with them. When a spirit enters and uses the body of someone like Bi Khadija in order to manifest itself in the human world, the tribe of the spirit is recognized by people on the basis of the characteristics described above. Distinct ways of being in the world are, thus, linked to what is considered their places of origin: the identified location of their identity.

All of Bi Khadija's spirits signify central aspects of her identity represented with references to significant localities. Through the spirits Bi Khadija negotiates her present identity as well as her more immediate relationships. Thus, the everyday life politics of modern identities shows that multiculturalism as expressed, for instance, in the context of *mashetani*, actually contests essentialist representations of identity, life-style and belonging.

Case 4: Bwana Saidi Mahmoud

Bwana Saidi Mahmoud is a married man in his fifties with several children and both he and his wife are considered to be of Arabian origin. Many of their relatives live in Oman and Abu-Dhabi, where Bwana Saidi visits them for long periods. Bwana Saidi Mahmoud has three spirits: one is a Christian spirit from Ethiopia (*shetani ya habeshia*), one a pagan spirit from Pemba (*shetani ya rubamba*), and, one a Muslim spirit from Arabia (*shetani ya ruhani*). Bwana Saidi's spirits relate both to his past, that is, his defined origin, and his present life situation. His Muslim, Arab spirit underlines his Zanzibari religious identity and orientation towards Arabian-ness. His Christian, Ethiopian spirit, who in the Zanzibari context is associated with the former Sultanate, is a reminder of his Arab origin, presents links with Oman and the Emirates, and, thus, despite his actual economic position, connections with what is seen as the upper stratum of society. Yet, Bwana Saidi also has a pagan spirit from Pemba. Through his relationship to this spirit, his identity is also grounded in what is perceived as the more African or Bantu facets of Zanzibariness. Hence, he becomes through his various spirits, a true Zanzibari - a person whose identity is multifaceted.

These processes through which identity and belonging are negotiated draw upon imprints and narratives of the past as well as of the meanings of *makabila* and notions of difference inherent in this term. While in the human world issues related to *makabila* are often reduced to political terms, the phenomenon of *mashetani* encompasses all its complexity. When present, the spirits, together with their human hosts, contest any politically defined and simplistic identity construction. Yet paradoxically while such contexts of identity negotiations contest they also perpetuate essentialist images of 'Arabian' and 'African', the reason being that, while humans may not be distinct with regard to identity and locality, spirits still are.

Furthermore, the very same essentialist categories may be evoked in situations of emerging conflicts and economic differentiation. In discussing the phenomenon of multiculturalism in a Zanzibari context, it is thus also important to analyze how recent social stratification processes have been built up.

The politics of modern identity and social stratification

As mentioned above, identity construction and the formation of social relationships have, through time, been influenced by various social, political and economic changes. For instance, under Omani rule the divide between 'Arab' and 'African' was constructed in terms of freeborn and slave, ruler and ruled. British rule further institutionalized distinctions between Zanzibaris according to identification as Arabs, Asians or Africans. The category in which people were placed had, among other things, consequences for what kind of staple food they had access to through government-issued ration cards (see also Crozon 1998; Fair 1994) where Arabs or Asians were privileged compared to people identified as Africans.

The 1964 Revolution[7] reordered the social context in the sense that, for around a quarter of a century, Zanzibar became a socialist state, relatively isolated, with only selective contacts with other socialist countries. In the aftermath of the Revolution, Arabian and Asian identities were politically defined as illegitimate, and the introduction of several Acts and policies meant that to be identified as either was to be politically, economically and socially marginalized (see also Crozon 1998). One of the Acts introduced was, as mentioned above, the Forced Marriages Act that only increased the cleavage between Arab/Asian identity and African identity.

The mid- and late eighties and nineties proved to be a period of further political and economic change in Zanzibar, which eventually resulted in the reintroduction of a multi-party system, the liberalization of the economy and the reopening of private enterprises. Recently, the Zanzibari authorities have focused on tourism as a major means of achieving desired economic growth[8]. Following these changes there have reappeared campaigns in which political visions based on ideas of universal rights and equality are paradoxically expressed in an ideological language of ethnicity and religion[9]. This ideological language seems not to favour socio-cultural diversity or multiculturalism as an integrated part of human relationships and identity construction.

As a result, during recent multiparty elections, many people have explained to me that they refrained from voting. One woman, for instance, told me that her family decided not to vote because it could become dangerous (*hatari*) if neighbours started to ask each other how they had voted. In another case previously good neighbours actually became bitter enemies because they suddenly realized that they were supporting different parties. Although people expressed contentment with regard to the political and economic situation during the 1990s, many would simultaneously argue that, although multi-party systems are good, such a system does not suit their society. Explaining their views they would immediately refer to the 1964 Revolution and claim that in relation to public political issues Zanzibaris would always divide according to 'tribe' and family lines. And, this, they said, would in such matters only lead to hostility and enmity.

Even so, the present political and economic situation in Zanzibar is not the same as it was in the period leading up to the 1964 Revolution. The present political and economic processes of change are causing new systems of stratification to emerge. In discussing these ongoing changes, people participate in a discourse defining what is and what remains, for them, specifically Zanzibari (Fair 1994; Larsen 1998, 2000; Myers 1993). Women and men claim that people these days have less *imani*, a term denoting 'faith' but which extends to honesty and uprightness. They often argue that people no longer value *ujirani* (neighbourliness) or *utani* (literally joking relations i.e. solidarity and reciprocity). In this context discourses on relations of reciprocity and redistribution are contrasted with those of self-interest, capitalism and commodification (Myers 1993; Parkin 1995; Swartz 1991). The recent changes taking place are often interpreted as a return to the previous system of stratification based on perceptions of origin linked with economic and political privileges. Most people do not, however, analyze previous or emerging systems of stratification from a social, political and/or economic position.

Recent economic liberalization policies have led to increased social stratification in urban areas, a situation that has time and again been politically explained with reference not to class and the structures of capitalist and free market economy, but rather with reference to the ethnic identities of wealthy citizens. Political and economic processes enter into an already constituted order where external factors become reshuffled, appearing as if they already form part of the existing social order. These social and cultural processes constitute precisely what Sahlins (1999) calls 'the inventiveness of culture'. Let me exemplify my points by presenting a final case study.

Case 5: Economic success and social vulnerability

Muhammed and his wife Halima are both from Makunduchi in the South Eastern part of Unguja. They are also cousins and of Indian origin (*Wahindi*), more specifically they are *Makumbaro*, a term referring to people of Indian origin living in rural areas who are not part of the wealthy urban elite[10]. In the wake of the 1964 Revolution they moved with their children to Zanzibar Town and settled in one of the neighbourhoods in Ng'ambo. During the 1964 Revolution Muhammed, known as a supporter of ZNP[11], managed to hide. However several of their relatives, regardless of party-political orientation, were harassed or killed while others were hidden and rescued by their Swahili neighbours. Many of their relatives left Zanzibar in order to settle on the mainland or even as far away as England or Canada.

Their neighbourhood is one where there are people belonging to different *makabila* and where economic and political position varies. However, people in their neighbourhood, as in other neighbourhoods in Zanzibar Town, value '*utani*' (joking relations) and, thus, the ability to live together as good neighbours. When I came to know this family in 1984, Muhammed and Halima were living with their six daughters, three sons, one grandson and a grandmother in a typical two-bedroom Swahili house. They had a small shop in the Stone Town and were neither poor nor wealthy, sharing in the everyday life of the neighbourhood: daily discussions in the back-yard during the daytime and on the *baraza* in the afternoon, attendance at weddings and funerals, participation in saving-networks, health concerns, and food-sharing. Among the immediate neighbours were other *Makumbaro* as well as *Wangazija*, *Wapemba*, *Waswahili*, *Wabaluchi* and *Waarabu*.

When I first met the family, two of the older sons were working abroad. In the mid-eighties, when more liberal economic policies were introduced, they returned home and brought with them foreign currency saved while abroad. Together with other Zanzibaris, they began to go to Dubai to buy goods to ship back to Zanzibar. The family became economically very successful during the late 1980s and the 1990s and expanded from one small shop to several shops, then to bigger shops and finally managed to open several hotels just as the tourism boom started.

During this period the father Muhammed died, and two of his five sons came together to act as the joint heads of the family. The five sons got married and all but one married local women of *Makumbaro* origin; the fifth went to India to find a wife. This son, the oldest, was at this point already divorced from his first wife who was his cousin. They had been married off in a hurry in 1972 when the then-President Karume had promulgated the 'Forced Marriage Act', but when it was abolished they, like many others in similar circumstances, divorced. The oldest daughter who, like her brother, had been married during the period of the 'Forced Marriages Act' and then divorced, also re-married later.

In Zanzibar Town it is relatively common for people to marry someone belonging to a different *kabila* although this is more usual in the case of second or third marriages. However, although in the case of people of Indian origin, men will often take a woman of non-Indian origin as their second wife, it is rare for Indian women to marry out of their ethnic group. The few such women I have known, who had married men of non-Indian background in the 1970s and 1980s, were often marginalized by their relatives.

The marriages of Halima's and Muhammed's daughters were discussed intensively within the family, by relatives and people in the neighbourhood. The mother, in compliance with her sons' wishes, decided that the daughters could themselves decide whom they wanted to marry as long as the men were decent and respectable. This decision was made with reference to certain notions of modernity where the choice of partner should be based on love (*mapenzi*) and not on family alliances and the reinforcing of boundaries between different *makabila*.

Both daughters married men belonging to *makabila* other than their own, one husband being of Arabian origin and the other of mixed Indian and Arabian origin. Both sons-in-law became involved in the family-business. This was discussed in the neighbourhood and even joked about. It was said that the men were under the control of their wives. Some would even say that the family had only accepted the men because they knew they would be able to tie them to the family, behaviour, it was said, typical of *Wahindi*. Such remarks turned what the family saw as an attempt to be 'modern' and transgress existing socio-cultural markers into a question of *makabila* – in this case, the ways and habits of people of Indian origin. Thus, it seems that in this example of the dynamics of identity construction, changing understandings and existing notions with respect to the formation of social relationships collide.

As the family became wealthy the members wanted to build a new house in which the mother, the then unmarried daughters and the sons with their wives could all be accommodated comfortably. However, the mother argued that she would never move from their neighbourhood and from the neighbours that she had shared her life with for so many years. Given the mother's decision, the family offered to buy the houses of two neighbours and a plot from the third neighbour. While one neighbour declined the others accepted and so the family was able to build its big house. The neighbours who had not been willing to sell claimed that the family continuously pressurized them to sell, something that was interpreted by them as well as others as a sign of greed and attributed, in this context, to typical *Wahindi* behaviour.

The new house is big and relatively luxurious and thus separates the family from the rest of the neighbourhood. Given their obvious wealth, the house is also well protected with grilles in

135

front of doors and windows and the employment of several guards. Furthermore, while most of the other houses in the neighbourhood are still typical Swahili houses with the *baraza* (verandah) at the front and a room inside where visitors can be entertained without entering the privacy of the back rooms, the new house is perceived as modern. There is no back yard for the neighbours to enter and no *baraza* to sit on in the afternoon or evening. In this house all activities take place indoors, so visiting means that one enters the privacy of the family – at least if the visit is not expected.

The mother in the family became worried that visitors would give them the 'evil eye' (*kijicho*) or leave other kinds of 'medicine' (*dawa*) to destroy their recent prosperity. She would constantly employ various kinds of protection against different forms of witchcraft (*dawa ya uganga*) in order to protect the family - something that she tried to hide from her sons. The latter did not want anyone in the family to be involved in matters that they described as 'destructive superstitious practices' and which they perceived as being in conflict with their aim of being a modern family living a modern life. However, the mother was preoccupied with the envy (*wivu*) the family's recent wealth had created and the importance of preventing it from creating problems. She was convinced that their Indian origin even reinforced such envy. She also told her daughters and grandchildren not to have anything to do with women and children perceived as *Waswahili* in order to protect them from the danger of 'envy'. Explaining what she meant she would briefly refer to the numbers of people of Indian origin that were killed during the days of Revolution and how others lost their homes and property.

The family continued to give *sadaka* (offerings) for the *Idd* celebrations to people in the neighbourhood, in town more generally as well as in Makunduchi. However, they would engage much less than before in more intimate relationships within the neighbourhood. The daughters, who had earlier enjoyed friendships with other girls in the neighbourhood, increasingly stayed at home watching videos and satellite TV or going out shopping together. Neighbours said that they did not want to visit them any more because they had become so arrogant and proud with their wealth. 'They hardly welcome you if you go there and nobody will even ask to use their phone any more' they claimed.

Again, neighbours would say that this was typical of people of Indian origin, that is, being friendly only as long as they need you.

The family, on the other hand, would often say that recently people would come to ask them for things only because they had become wealthy, that they did not have the capacity to engage too much in the lives of others and that people had to take more responsibility for their own lives in the same way as they had done. Moreover, while the mother would still be present during mourning periods and contribute economically to neighbours in need, the other female family members would not do so, except in situations where their next-door neighbours were involved. I often heard complaints from the very same neighbours that nowadays they only received second-hand clothes and leftovers from them and that it was typical for people of Indian origin to be miserly.

Thus over the years, the family as well as their neighbours, have increasingly stressed the family's Indian origin. The women, to a greater extent than the men, have begun to refer to themselves as 'we *Wahindi* ' rather than as before, *Makumbaro*. People from the neighbourhood would talk about the difference between the situation before and after the father died, saying it was sad that he had died so suddenly, and that he had been generous, kind and hospitable and would never have allowed his children to act in such arrogant ways. Now that he was gone the family could act without shame (*haya*). Some neighbours would even claim that they would no longer approach the family to ask for loans or to go to their shops and ask to be allowed to pay at a later stage. They said that, even if in need, they would not ask for food for their children, something they remembered having done when the father was still alive. In such contexts, their father would be talked about as an exceptional man of Indian origin. Thus, in recent times, the life-style of the family and the choices its members have made are not explained in terms of their change of economic position and a changing society, but rather as an expression of their attitudes and character due to their Indian origin.

Conclusion

In its recent history Zanzibar has undergone different political and economic periods: in some ethnicity and communalism have been made part of social organization and the formation of human

137

relationships and in others such social features have been less relevant. I argue that it is essential, in discussing multiculturalism, to investigate local understandings of identity formation and social relations and the effects such understandings have on people's lives. But it is also necessary to relate these issues to ongoing social, political and economic processes in the society (see Larsen 1998, 2000; Myers 2000) in order to grasp how different political initiatives affect social relations and identity formations as, for instance, in the case of the family of Halima and Muhammed.

In times of conflict, people still tend to explain changing relationships and life-styles with reference to the essentialist African and Arabian divide, categories meant to describe political structures in a pre-Revolutionary Zanzibar. The effect of recent politics using the ideologically motivated images of 1964 is, however, to divide people who would otherwise perceive difference of origin as a sign of their very Zanzibariness.

Recently, forms of stratification and ways of life are emerging in which those who have less find that they cannot expect to be cared for by wealthy neighbours or relatives. In order to find ways to understand these perceived changes, many people in unfavourable socio-economic situations accept the available political rhetoric of ethnicity and fill this in with recollections and dominant narratives of the events of the 1964 Revolution. In this situation everything negative is associated with a pre-Revolutionary Zanzibar, while the good society is the post-Revolutionary one. The multicultural dimensions of this society may, in this context, be reified as a particular form of economic and political stratification - a certain pattern of delineation between categories or groups of people (Taylor 1994; Turner 1994). Hence when focusing on difference defined by communalism, it is important to explore how human relationships, identity constructions, conceptualizations of personhood and notions of aesthetics are formed in specific multicultural societies. In Zanzibar Town, discourses on identity taking place in relation to the phenomenon of *mashetani* contrast sharply with the image presented in political rhetoric. Even so, a more visible system of socio-economic stratification also tends to reinforce the messages in the political rhetoric, as illustrated by the story of the family of Halima and Muhammed. Thus, there are several discourses on the problem of multiculturalism in this society: one based on political ideology and the other grounded in people's immediate relationships and everyday-life experiences. However, in voicing their frustrations arising from the present social, political and economic changes, most people follow the political rhetoric. In so doing they may ignore different lived experiences, or define them as exceptions, thereby leaving out the presence and involvement that spirits and 'good' neighbours have in their lives. It is thus essential to move beyond the more or less politicized rhetoric and relate it to ongoing social, political and economic processes and their effects on people's lives, including the way in which complex shifts of meanings affect the formation of human relationships.

Notes

1. I have conducted social anthropological fieldwork in Zanzibar, altogether totalling two years and five months, in the period between 1984 and 2000. My data are based on observation, participation in household-based activities, ritual contexts, conversations, discussions, gossip and semi-formal interviews with women and men holding different positions within households as well as people in different socio-economic positions and belonging to different *makabila*.

2. A person's 'tribe' indicates her or his ancestral place of origin outside Zanzibar such as Arabia, India, the Comoros or various places on the mainland. The term *Waswahili*, which actually means 'people of the coast', is seldom used in a self-descriptive way. To be an *Mswahili* means, in this context, that a person does not know her/his place of origin and, thus, must be of slave origin which, in this society, is still stigmatized in most social contexts.

3. The main aim of the Forced Marriage Act, introduced in 1969, was to create a society in which notions of tribe became irrelevant. It was abolished after the assassination of President Karume in 1972.

4. Although distinctions were never clear-cut, from about 1840 to 1964 three racial groups were officially recognized: Arab, Indian and African.

5. By contrast, in most rural areas, being of Arab descent is not something people would stress. Although people in rural areas are also concerned with questions of *makabila* they would, in contrast to people in urban areas, rarely talk about it or ask about each other's *kabila* (Eide 2000; Middleton 1992; Olsen 1999). Even so, to admit that one's ancestors were slaves is as unusual in rural areas as in urban.

6. Despite the significance of Indian influence on aesthetics and ways of life (Pearson 1998), it has been the delineation of Arab-ness and African-ness that has dominated images of Zanzibari culture.

7.   A body of literature discussing the 1964 Revolution claims that it should be understood as a class struggle rather than one based on racial terms (Babu 1991; Bailey 1973; Clayton 1981; Lofchie 1970; Saleh, 1995, 1996; see also Cameron this volume). It is important, however, to keep in mind that in pre-Revolutionary Zanzibar, perceived tribal affiliation normally coincided with socio-economic position.

8.   After the 1964 Revolution, the new Government made plans for developing the industrial sector. However, for a variety of reasons, including lack of competent personnel and the devaluation of the Tanzanian shilling on the world monetary market, the industrial sector in Zanzibar is still almost non-existent and represents only three per cent of GNP (Le Cour Grandmaison et al. 1998). Clove exports were until recently the basis of the Zanzibar economy, but since the 1980s cloves from other countries such as Indonesia and Madagascar have come to dominate the world market. Agriculture and fishing are the main activities and the majority of the population (approximately 70 per cent) lives in rural areas where these activities are also essential to subsistence.

9.   Expressions of radical Islam remain quite rare in Zanzibar in spite of the fact that almost the entire population is Muslim and Islam is a central dimension in people's lives (Larsen, 1989, 1995, 2000; Middleton 1992; Penrad 1995; Prins 1967).

10.   The ancestors of *Makumbaro* are said to come from the Kumbar caste, i.e. pot-makers from Gujerat.

11.   The Zanzibar Nationalist Party (ZNP) was widely thought to have been supported by those of 'Arab' origin.

Bibliography

Abu-Lughod, Lila, 1986. *Veiled Sentiments: Honour and Poetry in a Bedouin Society.*, Los Angeles: University of California Press.

——, 1990. 'The Romance of Resistance: Tracing Transformations of Power through Bedouin Women', *American Ethnologist* 17: 41-55.

Babu, Abdulrahman M., 1991 'The 1964 Revolution: Lumpen or Vanguard?' in Abdul Sheriff (ed.) *Zanzibar under Colonial Rule.* London: James Currey.

Bailey, Martin, 1973. *The Union of Tanganyika and Zanzibar: a Study in Political Integration.* Eastern African Studies vol. 9, Program of Eastern African Studies, Syracuse University.

Barth, Fredrik, 1969. 'Introduction' in *Ethnic Groups and Boundaries: The Social Organisation of Culture Differences.* Oslo: Scandinavian University Press.

Barwani, Ali Muhsin et al., 1997. *Conflicts and Harmony in Zanzibar (Memoirs)*. Dubai, UAE.

Bloch, Maurice, 1996. 'Internal and External Memory: Different Ways of Being in History', in P. Antze and M. Lambek (eds.). *Tense Past.* London: Routledge.

Clayton, Anthony, 1981. *The Zanzibar Revolution and its Aftermath.* London: C. Hurst & Co.

Cooper, Frederick, 1981. *From Slaves to Squatters: Plantation, Labour and Agriculture in Zanzibar and Coastal Kenya, 1890-1925.* New Haven and London: Yale University Press.

Crozon, Ariel, 1998. Zanzibar en Tanzanie: Une Histoire Politique Mouvementée', in C. Le Cour Grandmaison and A. Crozon (eds.). *Zanzibar Aujourd'hui.* Paris: Karthala.

De Heusch, Luc, 1997. 'L'ethnie: Les vicissitudes d'un concept', *Arch. Europ. Sociol.* XXXVIII (2): 185-206.

Eide, Rachel E., 2000. 'Kvinner i tiden. Om sosial konstruksjon av tid på øya Mafia, Tanzania', unpublished Master's thesis, Institute of Social Anthropology, University of Oslo.

Fair, Laura, 2002. 'Pastimes and Politics: Culture, community and identity in post-abolition urban Zanzibar', 1890-1945. Athens: Ohio University Press.

Goldberg, David T., 1994. *Multiculturalism: A Critical Reader.* Oxford: Blackwell.

Kabeer, Naila, 1991 'Gender Dimensions of Rural Poverty: Analysis from Bangladesh', *Journal of Peasant Studies* 18 (2): 241-262.

——, 1994. *Reversed Realities: Gender Hierarchies in Development Thought.* London: Verso.

Kapchan, Deborah, 1996. *Gender on the Market.* Philadelphia: University of Pennsylvania Press.

Larsen, Kjersti, 1989. 'Unyago - fra jente til kvinne'. Oslo: Oslo Occasional Papers in Social Anthropology, University of Oslo.

——, 1995. 'Where Humans and Spirits Meet: Incorporating Difference and Experiencing Otherness in Zanzibar Town', unpublished Ph.D. thesis, University of Oslo.

——, 1998. 'Spirit Possession as Historical Narrative: The Production of Identity and Locality in Zanzibar Town', in Nadia Lovell (ed.) *Locality and Belonging.* London: Routledge.

141

——, 2001. 'Spirit Possession as Oral History. Negotiating Islam and Social Status', in Biancamaria, Scarcia Amoretti (ed.) *Islam in East Africa: New Sources*. Roma: Herder.

——, forthcoming. 'The Other Side of Nature: Expanding Tourism, Changing Landscapes, and Problems of Privacy in Urban Zanzibar', in V. Broch-Due and R. Scroeder (eds.). *Producing Nature and Poverty in Africa*.

——, forthcoming. 'Dialogues Between Humans and Spirits: Ways of Negotiating Relationships and Moral Order in Zanzibar Town, Zanzibar', in M. Gaenszele and U. Demmer (eds.). *Language and Power in Ritual Performance*. London: Routledge.

Le Cour Grandmaison, C. and Crozon, Ariel, 1998. *Zanzibar Aujourd'hui*. Paris: Karthala.

Lofchie, Michael F., 1970. 'African Protest in a Racially Plural Society', in R.I. Rotberg and Ali Mazrui (eds.) *Protest and Power in Black Africa*. Oxford: Oxford University Press.

Meeker, Michael, 1979. *Literature and Violence in North Arabia*. Cambridge: Cambridge University Press.

Middleton, John, 1992. *The World of the Swahili*. New Haven: Yale University Press.

Myers, Garth A., 1993. 'Reconstructing Ng'ambo: Town planning on the Other Side of Zanzibar', unpublished Ph.D. thesis, University of California.

——, 1994. 'Making the Socialist City of Zanzibar', *The Geographical Review*, 4: 451-64.

——, 1997. 'Sticks and Stones: Colonialism and Zanzibari Housing', *Africa*, 67 (2): 252-272.

——, 2000. 'Narrative representation of Revolutionary Zanzibar', *Journal of Historical Geography*, 26 (3): 429-448.

Nunez, Theron, 1989. 'Tourism Studies in Anthropological Perspective', in V. L. Smith (ed.) *Hosts and Guests: Anthropology of Tourism*. Philadelphia: University of Philadelphia Press.

Olsen, Elisabeth F., 1999. 'Dealing with Conflicts: An Anthropological Study of Joking Relationships Among Women in a Zanzibari Village', unpublished Master's thesis, Department of Social Anthropology, University of Oslo.

Parkin, David, 1995. 'Blank Banners and Islamic Consciousness in Zanzibar', in Anthony Cohen and Nigel Rapport (eds.). *Questions of Consciousness*. London: Routledge.

Pearce, Douglas G., 1989. *Tourist Development*. Harlow: Longman.

Pearson, Michael N., 1998. *Port Cities and Intruders: The Swahili Coast, India, and Portugal in the Early Modern Era*. Baltimore: The Johns Hopkins University Press.

Penrad, Jean-Claude, 1995. 'Zanzibar, Les Cités Swahili: Rivages imaginaires et découverte d'un espace', *Journal des Anthropologies*, 61/62, automme.

Prins, A.J.H., 1967. *The Swahili-speaking Peoples of Zanzibar and the East African Coast* (Revised edition). London: International African Institute.

Saleh, Mohamed A., 1995. 'La Communauté Zanzibari d'Origine Comorienne: Premiers Jalons D'Une Recherche en Cours', *Islam et Sociétés au Sud du Sahara*. Paris: Editions de la Maison des Sciences de L´Homme.

———, 1996. 'Zanzibar et le monde swahili', *Afrique Contemporaine*, 177, 1er trimestre.

Sahlins, Marshall, 1999. 'Two or three things that I know about culture', *Journal of the Royal Anthropological Institute*, 5 (3): 399-421.

Sheriff, Abdul, 1995. 'An Outline of the History of Zanzibar Stone Town', in Abdul Sheriff (ed.) *The History and Conservation of Zanzibar Stone Town*. London: James Currey.

———, 1987. *Slaves, Spices and Ivory in Zanzibar*. London: James Currey .

Swartz, Marc J., 1991.*The Way the World Is: Cultural Process and Social Relations among the Mombasa Swahili*. Berkeley: University of California Press.

Taylor, Charles, 1994. 'The Politics of Recognition', in David T. Goldberg (ed.) *Multiculturalism: A Critical Reader*. Oxford: Blackwell.

Turner, Terence, 1994. 'Anthropology and Multiculturalism: What is Anthropology that Multiculturalism should be Mindful of It?' in David T. Goldberg (ed.) *Multiculturalism. A Critical Reader*. Oxford; Blackwell.

CHAPTER 9

'GOING WITH THE TIMES': CONFLICTING SWAHILI NORMS AND VALUES TODAY

Mohamed Ahmed Saleh

Introduction

Kwenda na wakati (literally 'to go with the times') is a frequently-used phrase which seems to sum up the notion of modernity in Swahili society today. In practice, this concept largely refers to corruption and is thus in total contradiction to those norms and values which have, up to a very recent period, formed the principal moral foundations of Swahili identity and culture: *heshima* (respect), *uaminifu* (honesty), *uadilifu* (ethics) and *ari* (honour). In the present context of Tanzania (of which Zanzibar is an integral part), where corruption is rife, to be 'modern' means being able to deviate from the above-mentioned fundamental principles.

This chapter will attempt to look at the evolution, during the last four decades, of this new concept of modernity in Tanzania, with particular emphasis on Zanzibar. It will highlight the impact of outside influences, such as the socio-political and cultural hegemony of mainland Tanzania, and the impact of structural adjustment programmes, as well as the adoption of alien patterns and modes of life which arrived on the isles with the tourist boom. The chapter considers whether the development of corruption as an important political and socio-economic institution in post-colonial Tanzania is an inevitable part of modernity, or whether people still consider, as in the past, that honesty is the most important social and moral value to define a person's existence and worth.

Zanzibari Swahili identity and culture: norms and values

Geographically and culturally, Zanzibar belongs to that string of islands which extends all along the east African coast, from Lamu to the Comoros, where for many centuries Swahili culture and civilization took shape and flourished. Zanzibar developed into an important melting pot, where migrants from the Arabian peninsula, the Persian Gulf and Indian sub-continent, as well as people from other parts of the globe, were integrated into society. Ultimately, whether they came as invaders or merchants, such people became part of the social, cultural and political life of Zanzibar and assumed a Swahili identity and culture. At the same time, Zanzibar was a multicultural community in which it was possible to identify different ethnic origins in what had become a relatively homogenous Zanzibari Swahili culture. Nonetheless, the traditional values referred to above are among the major components of this culture and played a vital role in merging together the different elements of Zanzibari cosmopolitan society. They are henceforth referred to as 'Swahili values'. Such values also constituted a stabilizing factor by furthering a spirit of tolerance, discouraging discrimination and encouraging mutual understanding in the Swahili communities of Zanzibar (see Saleh 2002).

The above-mentioned Swahili values were the ideals which each Zanzibari family wished to acquire, transmit to its children and be identified with in order to build up its reputation. As an essential source of recognition in the society, these norms and values were never attributed to the possession of money but to morally good conduct. One was never judged by material wealth but by behaviour as well as by wisdom and intellectual contribution to the society. Swahili values were not only abstract concepts elaborated in the Swahili language, but they also constituted the basis of day-to-day life in the society. They were the fundamentals of one's *utu*, which could literally be translated as dignity and integrity, or even more than that, humanity, including gentleness and goodness. Traditional teachings encouraged people to be kind and hospitable; they indicated that a good deed lasts and it is hard to erase its effects.

These major Swahili norms and values connote an attitude of self-restraint. They encourage people to be content with themselves and to avoid acts which could compromise their reputation in society, especially with regard to money. It was a common practice for parents to advise their children to be satisfied with small amounts and to dissuade them from seeking big things by wrong means. The famous Swahili proverb '*Si hoja kitu bora utu*' literally means 'One's dignity and integrity are worth more than material objects'. Traditional teachings encouraged each and everyone in the society to shy away from greed and stressed the limitations of the pleasures of the world. It was widely believed that one's lawful means of livelihood, even if humble, was better than wealth acquired through illicit means.

Swahili values also encompass *imani* (faith, uprightness and integrity). *Imani* presupposes constant effort to surpass one's ego and acquire the capacity of consideration and generosity in the most positive way towards others. It goes even further by encouraging the development of the spirit of sacrifice for others, for small as the sacrifice may be one should never be found lacking in willingness to perform it.

This was why '*mstaarabu*' (a civilized person) was someone who was not only enlightened, self-conscious and cherished his or her *utu* (dignity and integrity), but also someone who would never risk tarnishing his or her image in exchange for material wealth. In this sense corruption in Zanzibari society was considered synonymous with selling one's soul. Although greed and corruption have always existed in all societies, the Swahili communities of Zanzibar had their own system of social control which strongly discouraged such behaviour.

Dominant values were inculcated into members of society during the process of socialization. Islam, the religion of the majority of the population, constituted the backdrop and the major reference point of this process. Starting right from birth socialization was conducted through the observance of different rites of passage as well as religious and moral teachings. Parents had an absolute moral obligation towards God of ensuring the religious education of their children up to the age of puberty. It is only after this age that parents ceased to be accountable for all the deeds of their children, assuming that the latter were brought up in conformity with religious obligations. Those parents who did not properly assume their religious duty towards their children continued to share the responsibility for all the sins the latter might commit in the rest of their lives.

Similarly, the parents had a moral obligation towards society of moulding their children in such a way that they would abide by its code of good conduct. *'Heshima na adabu'* (respect and good manners) are an integral part of this code of conduct. They are not only due to one's parents who, according to moral teachings, come next after God in the hierarchical order, but also should be extended to the rest of society. The Swahili would frequently tell their children that one is not paid for being courteous to parents, courtesy is due to all those senior to you in years and no less to your contemporaries. While it is acknowledged in society that such courteous behaviour could be the source of friendship and happiness, arrogance is considered to be the source of misfortune, for its fruit is enmity. This is why the Swahili say *'Asiyefunzwa na mamaye hufunzwa na ulimwengu'*, which literally means that someone who is not taught good behaviour by his or her mother (parents) will be taught it [the hard way] by the world. A badly brought up person will be cursed by many, and it is widely believed that someone who receives too many curses has no salvation and will end up in damnation.

Conscious of their religious and moral obligations towards God and society, most Zanzibaris would try to encourage their children to hold fast to devotion and bring them up as respected members of the society. They would always look at their religion in a holistic perspective, i.e., as a fundamental element which lights up the soul and envelops the whole personality.

Some of these religious and moral principles are initiated very early in life through different rituals, among which is *kushindiliwa* which takes place at birth and is widely practised throughout the Swahili world (see Saleh 1996). It consists of putting a thumb on the neck of a newborn while repeating to the baby that it is necessary to be humble in life, to resist temptation, jealousy and greed, to practice restraint and not to be jealous or envious of others. In this way, the child is taught the virtues of humility, reserve, moderation and self-restraint.

Through such customary rites and moral teaching children were brought up to understand life in all its complexity and to believe in the universality of the human race. Honour and pride were among the ideals that were highly valued by the society and every member of the society strove to acquire them for they were the major proofs of one's worth. Such ideals were not at variance with the other fundamental values of the society; rather they were complementary, both together vying against shame.

Modernity or cultural degeneration?

Growing up in Zanzibar in the 1960s, I could still recall parents, especially mothers, being very much preoccupied with making sure that their children did not play with *wahuni*. The latter is the plural of *mhuni*, which, according to John Middleton (1992: 192), means vagabond. However, in reality the term also connotes bad manners, the result of not being brought up properly, and failing to respect the norms and values of the society. Today, when I talk with friends with whom I grew up in Zanzibar, we sometimes wonder who was the *mhuni* among us then, and nobody can come up with an answer, for none of us was a *mhuni*. This kind of societal pressure was part of traditional efforts at avoiding shame by assuring a decent upbringing of children with resultant good manners. Today, it might sound nostalgic to say that for many Zanzibaris the pre-*kwenda na wakati* period is the one when the fundamental values of the society had their place and were well respected, and when people were very conscious of their honour and would never have dared under any circumstances to compromise their integrity and dignity for the purpose of gaining money or other material benefits.

But times have changed. The foregoing discussion relates to a period when Zanzibar was an important political, economic and cultural centre with its own elite who could influence ideas and provide moral leadership to the society. Zanzibar was one of the important centres of religious and secular learning in East Africa. Zanzibari religious scholars studied in Zanzibar, the Hadhramaut (Yemen), El Azhar (Egypt), as well as in Medina (Saudi Arabia). Some of them even taught in those centres. Other secular Zanzibari scholars were trained in Makerere University (Uganda) and in various Indian, British and American universities. Such scholars established important exchange networks with other centres of learning. Thus up to the early 1960s Zanzibar was in the forefront of intellectual production in the region, in both religious and secular terms. A significant amount of Swahili literature was produced and Zanzibari authors were famous not only in East Africa but also in all the rest of the Swahili-speaking world. From the founding of the first Gazette of East Africa in 1892 more than forty journals were produced there. Zanzibari Radio programmes were very popular inside and outside the borders of the islands. This was the time when the old saying *'If you play the flute in Zanzibar, all Africa as far as the Lakes dances'* (Ingrams 1942: 10) was often repeated.

During the last four decades Zanzibari Swahili society has been going through rapid political, social and cultural changes, which make one wonder whether the new trends are leading to modernity and cultural transformation or the degeneration of traditional norms and values. Today, the spirit of *ari* (honour) is challenged by the new spirit of *kwenda na wakati*.

The Revolution in Zanzibar, and the subsequent union between Zanzibar and Tanganyika into the United Republic of Tanzania, meant a transfer of the centre of gravity from Zanzibar to Dar es Salaam (see Cameron and Larsen, this volume). Furthermore, the post-revolutionary policies of Zanzibar were not at all favourable to members of the Zanzibari elite. A substantial number of them had to flee the country to avoid persecution and some were even killed, leaving an important vacuum which could not be filled. This situation was further exacerbated in the aftermath of the Revolution by the absence, to date, of any form of mass media or literary or intellectual production free of the ruling party political ideology in Zanzibar[1].

Deprived of their major sources of inspiration, Zanzibaris were subsequently forced to look to the mainland from where their rulers derived their ideas. Gradually the mainland's political and cultural hegemony started to be imposed over the islands, initially through their Zanzibari protégés in power who served as their transmission agents and ultimately, through their control to this day of the social, cultural and political institutions of Zanzibar. The rulers have absolute control over the mass media and the educational curriculum. In this instance, then, *kwenda na wakati* means adapting to the mainland's way of life in many respects, including language, to which I now turn.

One can see in the daily usage of Zanzibari Swahili that it is being increasingly influenced by mainland speech patterns. Paradoxically, while the Zanzibari dialect *'Kiunguja'* was the origin of standard Swahili, today the Zanzibaris do not have any control over its development. The Swahili spoken in Pemba (*'Kipemba'*) had a distinct and particular character which is now disappearing and being replaced by the Swahili spoken on the mainland, particularly in Dar es Salaam. What is most shocking for many Zanzibaris is the imposition of new words without taking into consideration their cultural sensibilities. For instance, the word *kusimikwa* 'to be erected', which was used by priests inside the church, is now being forced into the language as part of accepted vocabulary. For the Swahili of Zanzibar this word has clear sexual connotations and cannot be used in public discourse. They cannot understand why they should substitute existing words such as *kutawadhishwa* or *kuapishwa* by *kusimikwa*. Their general feeling therefore is that their language is being corrupted.

Previously social change in Swahili societies had been in terms of material and technological innovations or the adoption and transformation of new cultural elements to suit the needs of the society without destroying its fundamental ideals. Zanzibaris were always in tune with what was going on in the rest of the world. For instance, Zanzibari tailors and dress-makers would adopt new fashions from places such as the Middle East, Europe or America, and give them a local Zanzibari touch. Nevertheless, all this was possible and took place when Zanzibar was still the metropolis of the region and the Zanzibaris had their social and cultural destiny in their hands. Being a maritime civilization, nurtured by overseas contacts, the Swahili have always been exposed to different aspects of modernity throughout their history. They have constantly adapted to new social, economic and political realities, a factor which enabled them to overcome the problems posed by different waves of invaders. *Kwenda na wakati*, in the sense of changing with the times, thus has overtones of *déjà vu* for 'modernity', and is not at all a new phenomenon in Zanzibar, or in Swahili coastal societies more generally. Such an argument has some rationality, but only to a limited extent, for the prevailing situation is more complex than any previous ones in history. In spite of the different changes which have taken place in Swahili communities throughout history, most of the traditional norms and values which formed the core of their identity and culture survived. One of the most important concerned money with which the Swahili had a particular relationship.

There were a lot of taboos surrounding money relationships and no-one wanted to give the impression that she or he was being bought. Until a few years ago, one had to be very careful when it came to giving money to someone in Zanzibar. People would not accept it if they thought that they were being bribed or paid for their hospitality or generosity. I recall an incident in which a European woman who had been a guest in a Zanzibari family for several weeks thought that she could pay back her hosts' hospitality in money, and consequently she provoked a big crisis. The host family were very hurt thinking that their guest was trying to insult them. They threw the money in her face and told her that if she wanted to pay she should have gone to a hotel. Today the situation is totally different.

Kwenda na wakati is a newly introduced concept which has developed in Tanzania during the last two decades. Its use has gone in parallel with the rapid development of corruption in the society. Tanzania is on the list of the most corrupt nations in the world. In 1999 it was ranked seventh (after Cameroon, Nigeria, Indonesia, Azerbaijan, Uzbekistan and Honduras) (Odhiambo 1999). Economic recession, which led to the introduction of Structural Adjustment Programmes (SAP), the rapid development of tourism and new patterns of consumerism have all had a tremendous impact on society. The new wants as well as the ordinary necessities of daily life have transformed Zanzibaris from people once well known for their hospitality to people who are profit-oriented and interested in money. Over a very short period of less than two decades many of the taboos related to money have ceased to be observed. An important breach, which is effectively a generational conflict, has developed between the older people who would like to preserve the fundamental values of the society and the younger ones who are struggling to assure their day-to-day survival through any means possible.

The Zanzibari diaspora: repository of traditional norms and values?

Post-revolutionary policies deprived Zanzibar of most of its elite - including intellectuals - and the current difficult political and economic situation in the country has forced many Zanzibaris to look for a better life outside the islands. The most common destinations of Zanzibari emigrants are the Gulf countries, Europe (especially U.K), Canada and the USA.

It is a common phenomenon among emigrant populations to re-emphasize their traditional cultural values wherever they go and the Zanzibaris living in the diaspora are no exception. They continue to maintain their Zanzibari identity. They identify themselves with Zanzibar, and maintain their social and cultural networks. They make efforts to reproduce their Zanzibari patterns of life: they have their *baraza* (meetings) and *taarab* groups (see Musau this volume), speak Swahili with their children, and maintain and transmit to their children other aspects of Zanzibari culture, such as cuisine and personal adornment. They regularly exchange information on Zanzibar, including cassettes of political meetings, *taarab* or weddings. They meet to recite prayers in case of the death of a friend or a relative back home. They also send back home remittances, on which a substantial number of urban families depend for their livelihood. The remittance economy has helped sustain the local economy and may even be said to have thereby avoided further social explosions in the country.

Furthermore, this assertion of Zanzibari identity has profound political implications. As Mazrui and Shariff note

> Identity is in fact a process by which power and status are negotiated, disinheritance and oppression legitimised, and liberation struggles waged. Intellectual debates on the identity of a particular people, therefore are seldom free of political underpinnings revolving around struggles of dominance and liberation of subjection and autonomy (1994: 5).

The Zanzibaris from the diaspora constitute an important political force in the defence of the identity of their islands and in the struggle for the restoration of democratic rights there. From the early 1980s, for the first time in the history of the country, Zanzibaris in the diaspora and those remaining in Zanzibar have managed to work together to make sure that their country remains on the world map.

Hence, Zanzibaris in the diaspora, particularly the ones who left before the major economic crisis which started at the end of the 1970s and continues to date, are still living out the traditions and values which once were part of the Zanzibari way of life and a source of pride. They see themselves as the repository of their ancestral traditions and cultures.

It would be interesting to examine the extent to which the spirit of *kwenda na wakati* has transformed traditional norms and values in Zanzibari Swahili society and whether the same norms and values have managed to survive without being totally destroyed in the countries of the diaspora.

Notes

1. *Nuru,* the government weekly, and *Jukwaa,* which is owned by a businessman who is a staunch ally of the ruling party, are the only local newspapers published in Zanzibar.

Bibliography

Ingrams, W.H., 1942. *Arabia and the Isles.* London, John Murray.

Mazrui, Alamin and Shariff, Ibrahim Noor, 1994. *The Swahili: Idiom and Identity of an African People.* Trenton, New Jersey: Africa World Press, Inc.

Middleton, John, 1992. *The World of the Swahili: An African Mercantile Civilization.* New Haven and London. Yale University Press.

Odhiambo, Nicodemus, 1999. Panafrican News Agency, 30 October.

Othman, Haroub, 1994. 'Zanzibar's political history: the past haunts the present', *Change* (Dar es Salaam), 2, 4/5: 20-27.

Saleh, Mohamed Ahmed, 1996. 'Zanzibar et le monde Swahili', *Afrique contemporaine.* Paris, Trimestriel N° 177, janvier - mars, La documentation Française: 17-29.

——, 1997. 'Zanzibari Diaspora: Identity and Nationalism', *Western Indian Ocean: A Cultural Corridor.* Stockholm: Department of Social Anthropology, Stockholm University.

——, 1997. 'Kiswahili : Patience, humilité et dépassement moral', *Dire la Tolérance.* Paris, UNESCO – Praxiling: 65-66.

——, 2002. 'Tolerance: The Principal Foundation of the Cosmopolitan Society of Zanzibar', *Cultures of the World Journal* (Barcelona), March.

CHAPTER 10

POLITICAL POETRY AMONG THE SWAHILI: THE KIMONDO VERSES FROM LAMU

Assibi A. Amidu

Introduction: The Swahili coast and political poetry

The Swahili coast is no stranger to the use of poetry in politics. Poetry was used in the past by the Swahili legendary hero Fumo Liyongo to taunt his half brother, Daudi Mringwari, a factor which probably hastened Liyongo's assassination (Harries 1962: 48-71). It was used by Muyaka Bin Haji al-Ghassaniy in the early nineteenth century to mock as well as to warn both the Mazrui rulers of his time and Seyyid Said, the Sultan of Oman and nominal ruler of the East Coast, to keep thier hands off Swahili lands and islands (Hichens 1940). It was used during preparations for war between Mombasa and the Lamu-Pate axis around 1819 as a psychological and satirical tool to unnerve the enemy. It was used again in 1834 before the battle between the Mombasa-Pate axis and the people of Lamu (ibid: 6-32).

Poetry was used on other occasions too as a corrective tool for society or individuals. During the reign of Seyyid Barghash, Sultan of Zanzibar and the Swahili Coast, poetry was used by a determined Suud bin Said al-Maamiry to ridicule and prepare the way for the final downfall of Muhammad bin Abdallah, the Al-Akida or Commandant of Fort Jesus at Mombasa (see Hinawy 1970 for details)[1].

Thus the *mashindano* or poetic contests along the Swahili coast are as old as the age of the poetry itself and continue to the present day (Harries 1966; Nassir 1974; Chiraghdin 1974: 7-9). In the twentieth century, several poetic works which discuss political themes have emerged with overtones and meanings praising a ruling group or party. Poems of direct engagement in politics are, for example, the *Ngonjera za Ukuta* of Mnyampala (1970, 1971) which even formed part of the school curriculum in Tanzania and were intended to further the ideology of *Ujamaa* of the ruling TANU (later CCM) in the country.

But the Kimondo is different from these poems. It is a cry to battle very much like the contests between Muyaka and the people of Lamu in times of war. The verses make it clear that the political process is viewed as a form of war which liberates individuals from want, unemployment, illiteracy and disease. Elections are seen as a battle to bring progress and the good life to as many people as possible without sacrificing too many of the old ways.

The Kimondo verse form arose in Lamu, specifically, the Lamu East Constituency of Kenya, during the general election of 1974 and by-election of 1975 which pitted Bw. Mzamil Omar Mzamil against Bw. Abubakar Madhubuti, the incumbent MP, in a struggle for the Lamu parliamentary seat in the National Assembly in Nairobi, the capital city of Kenya[2]. We might thus say that the modern electoral system of Kenya gave birth to the Kimondo.

Before 1992, Kenya was a one-party state and every Kenyan of voting age was automatically a member of the Kenya African National Union (KANU), the national party. In other words, the State and the Party were one and the same. In the Lamu East Constituency of 1975, each candidate for election had his own sub-party within KANU. Bw. Mzamil O. Mzamil's sub-party was called *SAA* (The Clock), while Bw. Abubakar Madhubuti's sub-party was called *NDEGE* (The Aeroplane). In 1975, Bw. Madhubuti was the MP who had been defeated in the 1974 elections, and Bw. Mzamil had been elected MP in that year.

The by-election of 1975 in Lamu East brought to the fore important questions which were troubling the people their. These included: 'What exactly is democracy? Can democracy thrive under a one party state? Can the electorate influence the pattern of change in the society within such a system?' Some of the answers have been stated elsewhere (Amidu 1993: 36-39), and remain valid in the multi-party system of today. Democracy, for the people of Lamu East, is the right to select the person best suited for the job of representing the interests of the constituents. Democracy can thrive in a one party state, but only at the constituency level because the Lamu people have the vote and are free to decide who should represent them in Parliament. The Lamu voters affirm that they can influence affairs in their district if they make use of the ballot box to elect men or women of wisdom and vision who can bring about qualitative changes. On the other hand, they also confront the problem of vote buying and selling in the district. As a result, they are aware of the dangers of succumbing to intimidation, greed or the attraction of wealth (Amidu 1993: 41-43, 51-53). These are some of the views expressed by Lamuans in the Kimondo and they are equally relevant for the Swahili everywhere in East Africa today under multi-party 'dictatorships'[3].

The introduction of *Kimondo* verses into Lamu politics

While the contestants in Lamu East were busy sizing each other up and doing everything they could to put their messages across to the electorate, their supporters decided to get involved in the contest in a new way on the side of their candidates. They felt that it was not enough merely to follow their favoured candidate around, shout slogans and organize support from podiums and pulpits, or from the sidelines. Rather it was time to employ an old strategy in a new context, namely the use of poetry to carry the message of the candidates standing in the elections. For the first time in modern politics in East Africa, we find an indigenous tradition mixing with the modern electoral process.

Apart from the contestants for office, therefore, we have the shadow contestants in the form of the poets who pit their skills against each other, who vie for the laurels of being the best composers of verse in support of their candidates. Candidates also compete to find the best communicators in Lamu, namely those who can carry burning political issues to the general body of the electorate in an easy to understand medium. In this saga, there will be more than one loser or victor at the end of the day since whichever candidate wins, the victory is not just for the politician, but also for the poets who threw their weight behind him and the supporters who voted for him. For, in the end, the poetic works immortalize the politics and personalities of the day. In Lamu East, the poet-supporter is also on trial, as it were. He is standing for elections as a shadow candidate. Indeed, he is defending a particular political view and establishment. For this reason, he requires all the literary and political skills of his traditional art in order to win the contest.

Aggression and pacifism in a Swahili democracy

The Kimondo verses are aggressive verses in the satirical genre. The term *kimondo* itself means a shooting star with a blinding flash. Its aim is to blind the enemy, and expose his or her weaknesses, lay bare failings to public scrutiny so as to allow an electorate to make an informed choice. Mahmud A. Abdulqadir, who invented the Kimondo form of Lamu East, tells us about the effects of the verses when they were first intoned in public, and later transferred to the tape recorder[4].

349. *Tulipotoa Kimondo,*   When we came out with the Kimondo,
    chalikuwa na kishindo!   there was pandemonium everywhere!
    Nguo wakapinda pindo   They folded the loose ends of their
    ndiani wakakimbia.   gowns and ran helter-skelter about the
        streets!

350. *Wakajifunga masombo*   Then they girded themselves and
    na kushindana kwa nyimbo.   tried to compete with us in song.
    Wakitoa vina kombo,   But their rhymes were defective,
    wala hazikwelekea!   and not well written at all!

Political opposition always sends panic through the camp of its opponents. This is particularly so if the opposition hammers home the weaknesses of the other side and presents a viable alternative agenda to the electorate. But the mark of a good challenger and his supporters is the ability to recover from a set-back, take up the gauntlet and bring the political contest alive. This is exactly what the NDEGE group did when the Kimondo was first released by the SAA group in the form of Kimondo no. 2[5]. They did not think of ways to harm their opponents or send in thugs to beat them up, even though they were alleged to have lots of thugs at their disposal. Rather the NDEGE group went to work and produced the Madhubuti Kimondo. This recourse to words rather than blows to disagree with the SAA group is evidence of political maturity.

Swahili tradition demands that a poetic challenge should be answered in poetry and not by brute force or even plain language, hence in responding positively to the challenge from the SAA camp, the NDEGE group shows that it understands and respects Swahili rules of debate and discussion. These rules are understood and respected by all members of the society, more so than the new rules of multi-party or one party democracies which are often incomprehensible to the majority of people. If democracy is couched in familiar terms through a medium with which voters are familiar, they are most likely to make a success of it than all the preaching from abroad in support of democracy can achieve.

In Kimondo number 2, the poet, Mahmud Ahmed Abdulqadir, alias MAU, challenges his opponents on the NDEGE side as follows:

355. *Na hini ndiyo bahari!*   The battlefield is now like the sea!
    lete yenu manowari   so bring out your warships,
    ya nyimbo na mashairi   of songs and poetry,
    tusafirini pamoya.   and let us set sail together!

356. *Farasi na nyangwa hizi,*   Or with horses on the plains of battle,
    na wangie tubarizi.   let them come in for a convention.
    Kiwa kweli ni wajuzi,   If truly they have the muse in them
    watu watashuhudia.   people will testify to it then.

For the people of Lamu East, politics is seen as a type of war or battle for a better tomorrow. The imagery of battleships and horses in the poems above represents the contest between candidates and between their supporters alike. There is a constant tussle to win the hearts and minds of the electorate and only the skilful politician, like the skilful poet, can win. The spectators of the battle for a life better than the *status quo* are the voters, and only they can judge who the best and most qualified candidate is for Parliament, in the same way that they judge who the best poet is at the end of the contest.

In such a context there arises the question of whether a political contest has to be acrimonious and violent. Kimondo

161

answers this question by saying that a political war should be filled with debates and not violence. One of the key elements of democracy is debate, devoid of fear and intimidation. We find this theme repeated in Kimondo No. 2. For example, it says to its opponents on the NDEGE side:

357. *Na wasongee karibu,*   They should, therefore, come around,
     na wasifanye ghadhabu.   without any reluctance or anger.
     Twambiane na kujibu,   Let us pour out questions and answers,
     mambo yote moya moya.   and tackle each issue one by one.

358. *Ndooni na silaha,*   Come with your weapons,
     na dawa ya majaraha.   and medicaments for your wounds.
     Haya sasa si izaha   These weapons are not offerings
     chama mepanda ngamia.   or like a person riding on a camel!

359. *Silaha nilotamka,*   The weapons I am talking about
     ni ala za kuandika.   are writing tools.
     Musije kufanya shaka,   Be not, therefore, apprehensive,
     nyingine mukadhania.   and think that I mean something else.

360. *Kulla mmoya anene,*   Let each person speak out,
     maneno tujibizane.   and also answer the other's queries.
     Na wananchi waone   And let the citizens see
     nani atakaokwea!   who will triumph over the other!

Politics should not divide a people, it should rather be an opportunity for healthy exchanges of views and opinions, opportunities for discussion, a process of communal education and a common search for the answers which will decide the future of the group. In this regard, the Kimondo No. 2 exhorts its opponents in the NDEGE camp as follows:

361. *Sambi haya kwa hasira*   I am not saying this in anger,
     wala kutaka kukera.   or with intent to provoke you.
     Nimezidiwa na ghera,   I am filled with competitive zeal,
     ndiyo nikasema haya.   that is why I say these things.

362. *Na kuvunda urafiki,*   To break up bonds of friendship,

mimi kabisa sitaki.	is what I do not want to do at all.
Kikisa kiwingu hiki,	When this little cloud blows over,
tutarudi mazoea.	we shall return to our routine ways.

Political elections come and go, but the people remain as members of the same community, of the same culture, of the same heritage with the same destiny. It is, therefore, only fools who allow politics to divide them, because the politics of yesterday must give way to the daily routines of living.

The Kimondo verses served in this way to enlighten the people of Lamu East about the essentials of democracy. For all who wish to see progress and prosperity in Lamu, a healthy debate between peoples with differing views is the best step in the right direction. For, after all, the candidates and their supporters must remember that they will wake up the day after the elections to face each other as they used to do before. On this important subject, the Kimondo No. 2 of the SAA camp says finally:

409. *Siasa ni muungano,*	Politics is a unifying force,
si michafu minong'ono!	not just evil and mischievous prattle!
Siasa si matukano!	Politics is not a slanging-match!
Ni kumwangalia ndia.	It is for keeping a person on the track!

410. *Siasa ni kuvutana,*	Politics is a forum for debate,
yalo mazuri kunena.	where constructive criticisms are voiced.
Lakini kutukanana	But the hurling of invectives
moyo hughairi nia	merely distracts the mind from the issues.

We find the same kind of sentiments expressed by the opposition in another poem, the Madhubuti Kimondo, although not as extensively as in the Kimondo No. 2. Three stanzas from the NDEGE verses will do as illustrations:

102. *Kwa haya niliyotunga,*	For these verses I have strung here,
uko mwenye kunipinga,	there is somebody who will disagree with me,
kuwa mimi nimepanga.	and say that I have invented these claims.
Haya hakututendea.	That he never in fact did these things for us.

103. *Nduu zangu kikutubu*
     alofanya Mahabubu,
     nyingi mutaona tabu
     kwa yote kusikia.

     Brothers and sisters, if I tell you
     what he has done, our Beloved one,
     so many things, you will be overwhelmed
     on hearing all of the accounts.

104. *Wacha mambo ya siasa.*
     Mara moya yatakwisa.
     Sisi huyo kumkosa,
     ndugu zangu twaumia.

     Put politics aside.
     These are soon over and done with.
     If we lose this fellow,
     dear brothers, we shall be hurting
     ourselves.

In the verses above, we see that the NDEGE side is also aware that political electioneering comes and goes and the people or electorate must get on with their lives as best they can while waiting for a better tomorrow. Lastly, we learn that without tolerance, no amount of free elections and no multi-party system will heal the wounds of their societies, or unite them for the greater challenges of development and progress, and the preservation of their heritage.

Democracy is about sacrifice, not about greed

Very often in Africa, the electorate expects its leaders to make sacrifices, without at the same time being willing to make sacrifices itself. In the Kimondo verses, we learn that the first lesson of democracy is that the supporters of candidates must think not about what they can reap from the success of their candidate but what they can do to help their candidate fulfil his or her promises. As noted above, when the Kimondo was first produced by the SAA group in the 1974 December elections, the NDEGE group responded in the true fashion of a *mashindano* 'competition'. But it was noticed that one of the composers of the NDEGE verses, Said al-Hajj of Pate, included a thinly veiled reference to possible future rewards for his efforts in composing the verses for Bw. Abubakar Madhubuti as is seen in the following verse:

36. *Initoke ya hatari ya bunduki na mapanga.*
    Bwana hoyo mashuhuri babake aliounga,

lo lote akahitari mzee cha kunihonga,
hakuna wa kumpinga. Mjumbe ni Madhubuti

36. May many dangerous things be kept from me such as guns and
swords!
This reputable person who has been moulded by his father,
whatever he chooses for an old man like me as a present,
I say there is no one to oppose him. Madhubuti is the MP.

In response to this disguised soliciting for payment in return for
support, the SAA's poet lost no time in writing tauntingly as
follows:

351. *Sisi hwandika kwa dhati.*   We on the other hand write diligently.
Nao hutunga noti!   They, however, write mere words (notes).
Kuna kubwa tofauti   There is a big difference
katika haya mawili.   between these two compositions!

352. *Zetu hutoka nyoyoni,*   Our verses come from the heart,
na zao nda ulimini!   but theirs are only from the mouth!
Zetu sisi nda imani,   Ours are grounded in faith,
zao ni chambo huvia!   theirs are like baits - they attract profit!

353. *Sisi hufanya ni ghera,*   For us it is a matter of honour,
wao wataka ijara!   but they write for a fee!
Wakikosa ni hasara   If they get no payment, it is a loss
kubwa imezowangia.   which is too great for them to bear!

Politics is about sacrifice and not about making money. When the
followers of a candidate begin to hope for rewards, they encourage
their candidate to abandon the principles upon which he or she is
voted into office and to embrace the path of corruption in order to
satisfy the greed of those who assisted him to get into office.

Consider also the following episode in which a group, which
was formerly a supporter of the SAA camp, decided to cross the
floor to the NDEGE camp:

183. *Kuna watu maalumu*   There are particular individuals
ambao twawafahamu.   who are known to us.

Walikuwa makhasimu	They were inveterate enemies
wa yeye huyu mbaya.	of this bad fellow.

184. *Watu hawa twakumbuka* — These individuals, we remember,
ni wao waliotoka — were those who came forward
bendera wakaishika — to bear the flag aloft
mwaka sitini tisia. — in the year sixty-nine.

185. *Walisimama imara* — They stood firm,
kwa nguvu nyingi na ghera — in complete solidarity and with patriotism

wakampa zao kura — and cast their votes
Mzamilu kwa umoya. — unanimously for Mzamilu.

186. *Walikuwa ni mashina* — They were the roots
yaliyo imara sana. — which were very firmly grounded.
Ghafula tukawaona — But we saw all of a sudden
muda wametukimbia. — that they had deserted our ranks!

Why did the stalwarts of the SAA sub-party of KANU desert the party they worked so hard to nurture and bring to fruition? The answer follows below:

187. *Tukauliza habari* — We, therefore, made enquiries,
tukajua zote siri — and discovered the full secret,
zilowapa maamiri — that which induced these stalwarts
upande ule kungia. — to defect to the other side.

188. *Nami hapa tabaini* — And here I shall explain it all to you,
niwape wao undani — and give you inside information,
niseme sababu gani — and why and wherefore
wao walifanya haya. — they behaved in this manner.

189. *Huyu mtu aliona* — This man saw that
hawa watu wa maana — these were formidable personalities
yeye wampinga sana. — who opposed him strongly.
Lazima kuwavamia. — He must take the sting out of them.

190. *Hapo kawatambalia*   Then he wormed his way up to them,
    taratibu kawendea   stealthily he went to them and coaxed them
    mkononi wakangia   till they were firmly in his grasp
    kwa tamaa kuwatia.   by awakening in them the passion of greed.

191. *Hapo wakaungamana,*   After this they came to an agreement,
    wao pamoja na bwana   they together with him as leader,
    kwa wote wakaagana   all of them made a pact
    wame ni shauri moya.   so that they were of one mind.

192. *Na shauri walilokata*   The essence of their deliberation
    ni manopoli kupata   was to gain a monopoly
    ya kununua mafuta   for the sale of fuel oil,
    na zote zilosalia.   and all its by-products.

In the above verses, we see how the desire to become rich quickly entices people who start out with great principles to abandon the course of honesty, integrity and accountability for quick gains and so become in the end corrupted. It is clear from the above that what is wrong is not the type of political system in place but the corruptibility of the leaders of the Swahili themselves. The resources of the state or district are not safe so long as men and women, allegedly of high moral principles, are willing to throw caution to the winds in order to join the ranks of the affluent.

One of the stalwarts of the SAA sub-party of Lamu refused to defect with the others, at least for a while. What happened to him after he saw his friends 'prosper' in the camp of Bw. Madhubuti?

204. *Na yule alosalia*   And even he who remained on our side,
    naye metukimbia!   has now deserted us!
    Meandama ile ndia,   He has followed the same corrupt path
    ya watu kumi na moya.   as the eleven previous ones.

And what was the reason for the latest defection to the NDEGE camp? The answer is as follows:

205. *Na sababu afuate*   And his reason for teaming up with them
    yeye ataka apate   is that he wants to gain

| *manopoli ya boriti* | a monopoly over the sale of beams |
| *iwe ni yake mmoya.* | as his exclusive preserve. |

A modern society thrives on business entrepreneurs, on investments and the exploitation of natural resources. But when the people who go into business do not wish to share the profits with anyone else, but rather want to be the sole magnates in the society, the seeds for unscrupulous politics and corruption are thereby sown. Mnyampala (1965: 18) rightly understood the corrupting influence of greed when he wrote, *'Tamaa ni wayowayo haina moyo kuchoka'* (Greed is fickle, it never makes the heart content).

Conceptions of leadership among the Swahili of Lamu

An MP is elected by his or her constituents to fulfil the agenda that was approved by the majority of the electorate, whether this involves expansion of the health services, job creation ventures, attracting investors to the constituency, improving food production, drawing the attention of the government to the conditions in schools and the salaries of teachers, etc. In addition, the MP has parliamentary business to deal with, especially if he or she is a member of various sub-committees of Parliament. Now, consider, in this regard, the following episode which was considered by a section of the Lamu electorate as evidence of a lack of leadership skills and the inhumanity of their MP, Bw. Abubakar Madhubuti. The verses are taken from Kimondo No. 2:

21. *Siku alipofariki*
    mwenzetu Abdurazaki,
    walitoka halaiki
    kwake wakamwendea.

    On the day on which he died
    our companion Abdulrazak,
    people left here
    to go and see him.

22. *Kaambiwa tafadhali,*
    tu maiti sipitali.
    Fanya ala kuli hali
    upate kututolea.

    He was told 'Please,
    we have a corpse at the hospital.
    Do everything in your power
    to get the body released to us.

23. *Fanya haraka kabisa*

    Please, act with the utmost speed

tusije tukamkosa.	lest we should fail to get him.
Twataka rudi Mombasa;	For, we want to return to Mombasa;
huko tutamzikia.	and there we shall bury him'.

The verses above reveal that the electorate expects from their MP that, on top of all his official duties, he should be approachable and available to listen to the views and complaints of his constituents even in matters like recovering the body of a dead member of the constituency. There is no evidence in the above verses that the constituents had first been to the hospital and had been turned away! They made their way straight to their MP and looked to him to help them get the body of the deceased Abdulrazak out of the morgue and transported to Mombasa.

What was Bw. Madhubuti's reaction to the request from the delegation from Lamu to reclaim the body of the dead member of the community from the hospital? The Kimondo No. 2 tells us about this as follows:

24. *Akawajibu umati,*	He answered the delegation,
kawambia, Hiki kiti	and told them, 'This seat of mine
si cha kutowa maiti	is not for doing an undertaker's job
cha Bungeni nilongia.	here in Parliament where I am!'

25. *Kisa hilo kutamuka,*	After saying this,
papo hapo kazunguka;	he turned round there and then;
na bila ya kusikitika,	and without any tinge of pity,
mlango kawafungia.	he shut the door in their face.

26. *Akangia zake ndani,*	And he went inside,
kawaata milangoni,	and left them at the door,
hao jamaa wageni,	these poor strangers,
ruhuma kutoingia	without showing any remorse.

Bw. Madhubuti did not drop everything he was doing, as is expected of modern political leaders, to follow the delegation from Lamu to the hospital to see that the goal of the delegation was fulfilled. He did not understand that in modern democracies he was the servant of the people of Lamu East and their interests and welfare come first before his own. This cost him dearly at the general election of 1974, and the subsequent by-election of 1975. Observe, therefore, that the expectations of the electorate can stretch the patience of their leaders to the limit. Bw. Madhubuti refused to go along with the wishes of the delegation from Lamu East, and he was accused of being insensitive to the needs of the electorate. But he should have known that these expectations and demands are part of the paradox of leadership facing any leader in East Africa today. A leader must satisfy the needs of members of his constituency in addition to fulfilling the mandate given to him by them to bring progress and prosperity to the constituency. He is a social and economic, as well as a political leader. Yet such kinds of expectation almost invariably also lead elected leaders down the road of corruption and influence peddling.

There is also the problem of bureaucracy to contend with. In a working democracy, one should not need an MP to reclaim a body from the morgue. Yet it is clear that the bureaucracy and corruption in Kenya's hospitals compelled the Lamu people to seek assistance from their MP, quite apart from the prestige and fanfare that goes with having your MP take the lead on such occasions. Whatever it is, in terms of priorities, it would appear that, for the Swahili, accompanying delegations to visit the sick in hospital, assisting in matters to do with death, are just as important as assisting in matters to do with the health and well-being of the living.

Are you wondering, perhaps, about what happened to the late Abdulrazak? A good Samaritan came along and resolved the problems facing the Lamu delegation. The following verses say how it happened:

27. *Na walipokosea budi,*　　Having no alternative left to them,
　　wakawa sasa hurudi,　　they set out to return home,
　　kawaadhini Wadudi　　while calling on the One God
　　haja yao kutimia.　　to help them fulfil their mission.

28. *Walipokuwa ndiani,*　　While they were on their way,
　　wasema shauri gani,　　wondering what next to do,
　　katoka mwenye imani,　　a righteous man appeared,
　　akawa nao pamoya.　　and at once sympathized with them.

29. *Wala hakuwafahamu*　　And he did not recognize

kuwa ni watu wa Lamu.	that they were people from Lamu.
Lakini Mola Karimu	But God, the Generous One
imani alimtia.	gave him courage and faith.

30.	*Kawaonea huruma,*	He sympathized with their plight,
	akasimama kwa hima	and took the matter up urgently
	mpaka mambo kukoma,	until everything was done for them,
	shida kawatatulia.	and their problems were resolved.

The success of the good Samaritan contrasts with the poor leadership skills of Bw. Madhubuti. It is the kind of poor performance that every leader dreads.

Multi-partyism today

On the political front today in Lamu, it is still persons with money who dominate the scene. The KANU party chairman of Lamu district is Bw. Tahir Sheikh Said, a very rich business man who is locked in a struggle for power in Lamu district with Bw. Shariff Nassir, the Minister in the Office of the President and KANU party chairman for Mombasa. Both are leaders of the Swahili of the coast, and both, incidentally, come from Mombasa. But they are busy washing their dirty linen in public (Kwena 2000). For example, Hon. Minister Bw. Shariff Nassir is reported in *The Nation* (30 October 2000) to have claimed that Bw. Said is 'trying to use his wealth "to re-introduce servitude" in Lamu District'. The Malindi MP, Bwana Abubakar Badaway, supporting the Hon. Minister Nassir is said to have 'accused Mr. Said of practising divisive politics while using his massive wealth to buy positions of influence in the Lamu KANU hierarchy' (ibid). These are exactly the kinds of allegation that the Lamu East electorate had levelled at Bw. Abubakar Madhubuti of the NDEGE sub-party of KANU in 1975, and the same allegations persist today in Lamu, even though the actors and times are different. Our study shows that neither a one party nor a multi-party system dampens the enthusiasm of the Swahili of Lamu East for political combat, accusations, or debate.

Conclusion

We conclude, therefore, by saying that, at least as far as can be inferred from the Kimondo verses, for the people of Lamu East, and their politicians, it is not the type of political system that makes democracy work better. Rather, the verses suggest that what is required is a culture of democracy which guides people in the selection of candidates who will represent or govern them and provides guidelines for participating in the debates about the manner in which they are governed. However, given a level playing field, according to SAA poets, the electorate can make a choice, and the poet can assist them in arriving at their decision. Politics, therefore, may appear frightening, even chaotic, but for the Swahili of Lamu East, it is a contest of skills, wit, oratory, intelligence, as well as of leadership 'on sea as well as on land', i.e. in happy times and in difficult times.

In this regard, the Swahili have their heritage of poetry, an art much loved by almost every one who is a Swahili person. By exploiting this traditional medium of communication, interaction and democratic debate, as the Lamu East people have demonstrated, it should be possible for constructive discussions to take place among the Swahili of the coast. It should also be possible for open and participatory democracy to happen in the Swahili territories without violence. Acrimonious as some of these debates sometimes are, they provide a guarantee against abuse of power, safeguard for freedom of speech and of the person among the Swahili, and keep the elected leaders on their guard. The electorate is always watching and, sooner or later, they hold the leaders accountable for their stewardship at the polls. Multi-party or one party democracy has not changed the Swahili penchant for a good debate and a political fight, at least in the Lamu District of Kenya.

Notes

1 Fort Jesus in Mombasa was the seat of administration of the Northern Swahili coast from the time of the Portuguese up to the partition of Africa into colonial territories of Western Europe.

2. Lamu on the Kenya coast is a very important cradle of Swahili literature. It was at its height during the third of the five literary periods of written Swahili literature (Amidu 1995: 116-117). The main centre during

the first period in the seventeenth century was Pate, during the second it was Mombasa, in the fourth it was Pemba, and in the fifth, it was Zanzibar. Others might argue that the place in the second period should be taken by Lamu. In reality, secular verse flourished in both Lamu and Mombasa at about the same time, but Mombasa verse was undoubtedly the more celebrated of the two cities, especially in the person of Muyaka Bin Haji al-Ghassaniy (Knappert 1979; Hichens 1940; Harries 1962; Allen 1971; Amidu 1990, 1995).

3. A multi-party dictatorship is one in which the same ruling party always wins because of the benefits of incumbency, including its ability to manipulate ballot boxes, change the constitution in its favour, intimidate and jail its opponents, divide the ranks of the opposition, etc.

4. The verses – and the numbers referring to them -- are drawn from Amidu (1990). Some changes in the original translations also appear in this paper.

5. The Lamuans called one poem 'Kimondo No. 2' while the other remained unnamed; I have called it 'Madhubuti Kimondo' after the other candidate.

Bibliography

Allen, John W.T., 1971. *Tendi*. London: Heinemann.

Amidu, Assibi. A., 1990. *Kimwondo: A Kiswahili Electoral Contest*. Vienna: Afro-Pub.

——, 1993. 'Lessons from Kimwondo: An Aspect of Kiswahili Culture' *Nordic Journal of African Studies* 2, 1: 34-56.

——, 1995. 'Kiswahili: People, Language, Literature, and Lingua Franca'. *Nordic Journal of African Studies* 4, 1: 104-125.

Chiraghdin, Shihabudin. 1974. 'Utangulizi wa Mhariri'. in A. Nassir, *Malenga wa Mvita: Diwani ya Ustadh Bhalo*. Nairobi: Oxford University Press: 3-24.

Harries, Lyndon. J., 1962. *Swahili Poetry*. Oxford: Oxford University Press.

——, (ed), 1966. *Poems from Kenya*. Madison: University of Wisconsin Press.

Hichens, William, 1940. *Diwani ya Muyaka Bin Haji Al-Ghassaniy*. Johannesburg: University of Witwatersrand Press.

Hinawy, Mbarak. A., 1970 [1950]. *Al-Akida and Fort Jesus, Mombasa*. Nairobi: East African Literature Bureau.

Knappert, Jan, 1979. *Four Centuries of Swahili Verse: A Literary History and Anthology.* London: Heinemann.

Kwena, Edmund, 2000. 'Nassir Is a Liability, Says Tycoon'. *The Nation* (Nairobi), October 30, 2000. Retrieved February 2, 2001, http://allafrica.com/stories/printable/200010310151.html. See also 'Nassir Hits at Coast Tycoon'. 2000, October 30, 2000. *The Nation* (Nairobi). Retrieved February 2, 2001, http://allafrica.com/stories/printable/200010300385.html

Mnyampala, Mathias. E., 1965. *Waadhi wa Ushairi.* Dar es Salaam: East Africa Literature Bureau.

——, 1970. *Ngonjera za Ukuta: Kitabu cha kwanza.* Dar es Salaam: Oxford University Press.

——, 1971. *Ngonjera za Ukuta: Kitabu cha pili.* Dar es Salaam: Oxford University Press.

Nassir, Ahmad, 1974. *Malenga wa Mvita: Diwani ya Ustadh Bhalo.* Nairobi: Oxford University Press.

CHAPTER 11

TAARAB SONGS AS A REFLECTION OF THE CHANGING SOCIO-POLITICAL REALITY OF THE SWAHILI

Paul M. Musau

Introduction

The aim of this paper is to discuss how *taarab*, a variety of Swahili music, has responded to the social and political pressures that have in modern times come to bear on the Swahili people. It specifically shows how the changing times have affected this variety of Swahili music in content, performance and style. It argues that *taarab* as a music genre is struggling to reflect new realities. The paper also argues that, as *taarab* music changes, the boundaries of the performer and audience shift constantly, reflecting multiple identities. However, before the changes that are affecting *taarab* music are discussed, it is necessary to define two terms that are repeatedly used in this paper: these are, 'modernity' and 'the Swahili'.

Modernity

Modernization refers to the overall societal process by which societies change technologically, socially, politically, economically and culturally. Taylor (2001: 2) states that cultural theories of modernity tend to describe the transition to modernity in terms of a loss of traditional beliefs and allegiances. This loss may be seen as coming about as a result of institutional changes. For example, mobility and urbanization are understood to erode the beliefs and reference points of relatively static rural society. Or the loss may be supposed to arise from the increasing prevalence of modern scientific reason. Such change may be positively valued, or it may be judged a disaster by those for whom the traditional reference points were valuable and for whom scientific reason is too narrow.

However, 'modernity' as a construct is not without controversy. It has been criticized as too abstract because it creates the impression that the present is discontinuous with the past (Hooker 2001: 2). Oommen (2001: 1) argues that the underlying assumption behind the tradition-modernity dichotomy is the proposition that there is a wide variety of traditional societies and that a series of 'izations', for example, industrialization, urbanization, bureaucratization, will eventually bring about a single global or world society. He shows that the idea of unilinear movement from tradition to modernity is untenable, and instead suggests multiple traditions and multiple modernities (ibid: 5), arguing that the notions of unilinear globalization and singular globality are also untenable. He reasons as follows: (a) displacement whether cultural or otherwise is never total and invariably partial, (b) the process of displacement differs across societies and (c) accretion of alien elements into societies is necessarily selective. He concludes that the current notion of a monolithic globality and modernity should be examined with great care.

Modernity in this paper will simply refer to social and political events of the present or the recent past that have affected or are affecting the Swahili and will be used in a culturally neutral sense. For convenience, and in order to delimit the period of reference, the paper will refer to a period of thirty years, roughly between 1970 and 2001.

The Swahili

Allen (1993: 11) states that there can be few peoples whose identity is as elusive as that of the Swahili. He explains that they cannot be defined as a tribe or group held together by links of blood or marriage but rather as a highly permeable population whose commonalities are cultural in nature. Allen contends that the Swahili can be identified by both *lugha* (language) and *mila na desturi* (customs and tradition), for example, *harusi, mapishi, sherehe* (weddings, cooking, ceremonies), *mavazi* (clothing) and *tabia* (mannerisms) (ibid: 252). Allen then goes on to define a Swahili as a person who has made his or her home in or around one of the traditional Muslim settlements (*miji* or *majengo*) of the East African Coast or their modern counterparts in the interior whose lifestyle conforms to that of the sub-cultures of the former and who has adopted the Swahili language as his/her preferred language (ibid: 15).

Now, the Swahili as defined here and particularly those who live on the East African Coast belong to particular geopolitical entities and are also very much members of the changing world. They are therefore not exempt from those intra-state and global socio-cultural, economic, and political pressures that have been brought to bear on African countries in general. The remaining part of this paper will therefore discuss the extent to which Swahili music, as represented by *taarab*, can be seen as a reflection of the changing world of the Swahili. In other words, the paper examines how Swahili music has been responding to modernity. By extension, this paper also shows how Swahili culture has been affected by contemporary events.

Taarab

Taarab comes from the Arabic *tariba* and means 'to be agitated' or 'to be moved' (Graham 1992: 155). Bakari characterizes it as involving *raha* (pleasure) or *kifurahishacho roho* (that which brings pleasure to the heart) (1994: 4). As a type of music, it refers to both the performance by a group of persons or the event, as well as the music. Sources such as Bakari (1995: 5), Graham (1992: 133), and King'ei (1992: 34) associate the origin of *taarab* in East Africa with the ruling family of Zanzibar towards the end of the nineteenth century. These sources claim that in the 1870s Sultan Barghash sent a Zanzibari by the name of Mohammed Ibrahim to Cairo to learn more about this form of music. Although initially sung in Arabic, in the 1920s the first African orchestras started singing in Kiswahili. It was then that this upper class music became more widely popular (Graham 1992: 155). One of the most famous and dynamic *taarab* singers was Siti Binti Saad of Zanzibar who traversed the length and breadth of East Africa in the nineteen thirties and forties entertaining people; she even visited Bombay in India to record her music. Her biography has been written by Shaaban Robert, one of the best known Swahili writers (Robert 1967).

Taarab as it is traditionally understood is rhythmic poetry which is sung with Arabic or at times Indian melodies. The soloist often sings unaccompanied except for occasions when the chorus may cut in to sing a refrain (King'ei 1992: 36). Conventionally, *taarab* is performed mainly at weddings and other social gatherings (Senoga–Zake 1986: 55).

However over the years *taarabu* has been changing. As Graham (1992: 155) explains, '*taarab* like so many complex and living things refuses to be thrust into neat bags'. This is because it is open to the incorporation of new styles, themes and instruments[1]. The complex nature of *taarab* is also reiterated by Khamis (2001: 5) who says that it is characterized by variability, openness, versatility and adaptability. In the following sections, the paper shows the changes that have occurred to *taarab* music in terms of instruments, performance themes and language use.

Innovations in Taarab music

a) *Instruments*

According to Euba (1999: 69) and Graham (1992: 55), the instruments used in the 1930s and 1940s in playing *taarab* were mainly Arab: *Oud* or *Udi* in Swahili (a kind of lute), *Ganun* (a plucked box, zither or psaltery), *dumbak* (a drum with a leather head), a Middle Eastern fiddle, tambourine (*kitari* in Swahili), ney and rattle. In recent times, however, a number of new instruments originating from the West have been added. These include the violin, electric guitar, accordion, keyboard, cello, trumpet and saxophone.

The introduction of new instruments, and particularly the electronic ones, has not been received well by some members of the Swahili community. One of them, Bakari (1999: 7), expresses her discontent:

Watribu mashuhuri wa taarab mara nyingi wamekuwa wakijaribu kuwahadharisha wasanii wenzao wa taarab wajaribu kuepuka kuigiza ala zisizo za taarab katika sanaa hii hususan vyombo vya electronic. Kwa maoni yao vyombo vya electronic hupunguza utamu wa muziki wa taarab.

La aghasi, ni kwamba vyombo hivi vikiachiliwa kuchukua nafasi kubwa; hatima yake vitapelelekea kuiua kabisa taarab (Bakari 1999: 7).

Many prominent *taarab* singers have often tried to warn their colleagues to avoid instruments that are not sutiable for playing *taarab*. In their view, these electronic instruments reduce the pleasure of *taarab* music. The truth is that if these instruments continue to be used, they will eventually dominate and in the final analysis will kill *taarab*.

This writer ends her essay with a stern warning:

> *...taarab taarab lazima ilindwe, ienziwe isivurugwe kwa kuchanganywa na ngoma nyengine na ipewe uwezo wa kushika nafasi yake kama mama wa muziki wa mwambao* (Bakari 1999: 10).

> ...the real *taarab* must be protected and respected so that it is not mixed up with any other type of music and so that it is given the ability and potential to play its role as the mother of coastal music.

These views are echoed by Khamis (2000: 3) who feels that this new variety of music is so different that a name other than *taarab* should be found for it.

But while one body of opinion argues that 'real *taarab*' is defined by its traditional instruments, another contends that nothing in the world, *taarab* included, remains stagnant:

> '*u-kale*' *lazima utakwenda na 'wa-kale' wake, na kinachochukua nafasi ni 'wa-sasa' na 'u-sasa' wao ambao nao zama zao zitakwisha na wataonekana si lolote* (Issa 1999: 4).

> 'the old ways' will go away with 'the old' and in its place will be 'the new' and 'modernity', the latter will also end and will be deemed to be nothing'.

This latter body of opinion does not in fact see the form of *taarab* played by traditional instruments and the one which includes 'modern instruments' as mutually exclusive, but rather as complementary and mutually enriching:

> *Hawa wote wanapiga taarab kwa mitindo ya kisasa, bali hili halijawafanya wasanii na mashabiki wa taarab asilia kuweka ala zao chini na kuwaachia vijana wafanye watakavyo. ...kuna ushirikiano mkubwa baina ya vikundi vyote hivyo, kwani kila*

179

upande haukosi kitu cha kujifunza kutoka upande mwingine (Issa 1994: 4).

All of these people play *taarab* by using new styles, but this does not make the traditional musicians and their fans lay down their instruments and leave the young people to do as they wish. ... there is great co-operation between the two groups, because each side has something to learn from the other.

Thus the debate as to what constitutes 'real *taarab*' clearly shows the changes through which this variety of Swahili music is going.

b) *Performance*

It is not only the introduction of new instruments that has brought discontent to some of the *taarab* fans; its general performance has also changed with time, leading to more complaints. As King'ei (1992: 37) and Euba (1999: 67–70) note, *taarab* is traditionally and essentially a non-participatory form of entertainment. Bakari (1999: 4) lucidly describes the non-participatory nature of *taarab*:

> *Taarab kwa asili ni burudani ya kukaa juu ya viti na kusikiliza mashairi bulbul yakiimbwa kwa mahadhi yanayofuatana na muziki nyororo unaopigwa kwa ufundi kabisa na watribu kwa kutumia ala kama vile fidla, oud, ganun, nei, matari, mandolin, msondo (bongos) n.k. Kwa wale waliopenda kuicheza taarab wakicheza kwa kwenda mrama hapo juu ya viti na kugongana mabega, yaani bega la kulia linamgonga mwenziwe bega la kushoto na kinyume chake* (Bakari 1994: 4).

Traditionally, *taarab* is an entertainment where the listener sits and listens to beautiful poetry in continuous melodies and soft music which is played with artistry by experts who use instruments like the fiddle, ganun, ney, tambourines, mandolin, drums etc. Those who would like to dance only do so with their shoulders as they sway from left to right and vice-versa.

This lack of vigorous activity conventionally seems to be compensated for by the use of highly figurative language which keeps the listeners busy as they try to decipher the meaning behind the deep imagery. This 'passivity' is occasionally broken by clapping or when the participants stand up to give cash gifts to the singer (King'ei 1992: 37; Bakari 1994: 4).

However, with the introduction of new instruments, the non-participatory nature of *taarab* is also changing. The introduction of what has come to be known as 'modern *taarab*' (Bakari 1999: 8), has included not only new instruments but also dancing rhythms. Graebner (1999) explains that a Zanzibari *taarab* group known as East African Melody plays modern *taarab*, which for the first time is '*taarab* to dance to'. In fact Mahmoud confirms that in Zanzibar modern *taarab* features in the major disco in town. Other groups that perform modern *taarab* are to be found in other coastal towns such as Dar es Salaam, where Muungano Cultural Troupe and Tanzania One Theatre Group feature, among others.

Taarab music is also being blended with new music styles from other parts of the world. In one song, 'Malika' (Asha Abdo Suleiman), a well known *taarab* singer resident in Kenya and familiar in most coastal towns of East Africa, adapts a prominent *lambada* style in her song entitled, '*Wewe wajidai*' (you boast)[2]. Another *taarab* singer Malkiya Rukia has incorporated rap music into her two songs, namely, '*Penzi kwetu*' (love between us) and '*Leo nataka tamka*' (today I would like to declare)[3]. In the first song (given below), each stanza is sung in the conventional *taarab* manner by a soloist and then repeated in rap, either by the soloist or by another singer:

Naona mwafurahika na vingi vyenu vicheko
Mkiyapika majungu moto na moshi wa meko
Bure mtahadhirika mtajipiga viboko
Mbona mnajisumbua, mnajishtuka
Msivunje yenu miiko.

Anipenda nampenda hatuna mabadiliko
Japo kuwa mwatuvunja penzi kwetu bado liko
(Malkiya Rukia 1999-casette)

I see you are happy with lots of laughter
Cooking many pots, fire and smoke from the fire place (gossiping)
You will come to naught, you will harm yourselves
Why do you bother, you surprise yourself do not break your taboos.

He loves me and I love him, there is no change

Although you undermine us, love between us still persists.

The two *taarab* songs referred to here were sung in 1999[4]. They are evidence of the way *taarab* can be modified or adjusted to cater for a felt need especially that of young people or tourists for whom *lambada* or rap may be popular. They may also be a way of popularizing *taarab* outside the Swahili domain. Whatever their motivation, such songs attest to the external influences that are being exerted on *taarab* music and by extension Swahili culture.

c) *Themes*

Although everyday concerns, foremost among them love, continue to dominate the themes of *taarab*, this type of music is also sensitive to the changing socio-political environment. Some of the songs in the recent past have discussed music copyright matters ('Face to face' – Malika 1992[5]. Others describe the merits of birth control ('*Uzazi wa Mpango*' (birth control) (Tanzania One Theatre (1994)[6]. In others, the rights of the individual in society are championed ('*Kuonewa Sitaki*' – I don't want to be oppressed – Malika)[7]. The theme of individual rights, including for example the right of a young girl to go to school, is poignantly captured by the Maendeleo Musical Club from Zanzibar in a song entitled '*Mtoto wa Shule*' (a school pupil)[8]. In this dialogic poem, a daughter is involved in an argument with her father who wishes to marry her off to an older man although she is still keen on completing her education. The girl complains of the breach of her right to education and her right to marry a person of her choice:

Mtoto:	*Baba niko na huzuni kuhusu ndoa yangu*
Baba:	*Hasa ni kitu gani cha kukuudhi mwanangu*
Mtoto:	*Umri wangu ni duni, sijaweza kuwa kwangu*
	[..]
	Na hasa niko shuleni sijesha masomo yangu
Baba:	*Utamaliza nyumbani, kaahidi mkwe wangu*
	[..]
Mtoto:	*Nimeonewa jamani kuukosa uhuru wangu*
Baba:	*Hayo semea pembeni, sivunji kauli yangu*
Mtoto:	*Mtu wa miaka sitini juwa ni mzee kwangu*
Baba:	*Bali jingine sioni, kulinda heshima yangu*

(Maendeleo Musical Club-1979-cassette)

Child:	Father I am worried about my marriage
Father:	What is it that is actually worrying you, my child?
Child:	I am still young, and I cannot manage married life
	[...]
	In particular I am still at school; I have not completed my studies
Father:	You will complete at home, my in-law has promised
	[...]
Child:	I am oppressed, I have no freedom
Father:	That is irrelevant, I will not break my word
Child:	A man of sixty years -- he is too old for me
Father:	I see no alternative; I must defend my dignity

This poem captures the dilemma of a society caught between conventional and emerging values and one in which the values of the older generations are being challenged by the younger. The questioning of values and practices that were in the past thought to be sacrosanct occurs in another poem, '*Ukewenza*' (polygamy) by the same musical group[9]. In this poem a woman rejects polygamy, a common practice among the Swahili. She declares:

> *...ukewenza utesi singoji nakimbia*
> *[....................................]*
> *Sikubali , sikubali kabisa kuonewa,*
> *Nitajikaza kweli kweli ibaki kuzidiwa.*
> (Maendeleo Musical Club 1979 cassette)

> Polygamy is like a brawl, I will not get involved
> I will run away.
> [...]
> I refuse, I refuse to be mistreated
> I will fight to the best of my ability.

The composition of *taarab* music has also not shied away from other topical issues like the AIDS pandemic. In a poem quoted by Fargion (1995: 130), the composer/singer prays to God to intervene so that a cure for this dreaded disease can be found:

Mola tujialie dawa	God, help us get medicine
Ukimwi tuondoa	So that we can exterminate AIDS
Maradhi alosakili.	It is a terrible disease

183

Mola tujalie dawa	God help us get medicine
Maradhi haya mabaya	This disease is bad
Mola tujialie dawa	God help us get medicine (Fargion 1995: 130)

This theme also features in another poem entitled *'Asali kuwa sumu'* (What is sweet has become poisonous)[10]. In the chorus of this song, the listener is warned that what might appear pleasurable could in the end become fatal:

> *Katikati ya asali, tamu limekuwa chungu*
> *Hiyo kwetu ni hatari, vitamu kuwa haramu*
> (Dar Nyota Theatre 1998-cassette)

> In the midst of honey, sweetness has become bitter
> This is a danger to us, when pleasure becomes forbidden

Taarab music has also responded to the political happenings of the day. Some have paid tribute to prominent political figures ('Mandela' – Malika)[11]. Others espouse partisan political orientations or support the policies of the ruling party or elite (*'Kura ni mlolongo'* – voting is by the queuing method – Juma 1988)[12]. Some seek to glorify individual leaders (*Heko Mtukufu Moi* – thank you honorable Moi – Shukrani Musical Group 1987 (quoted in King'ei 1992: 120)[13] or take the opportunity to rationalize the existing social order. Yet others are critical and in fact condemn the manner in which politicians conduct themselves during political campaigns and elections:

Mwalikitumia khila	You used tricks
Sasa hamba lahaula	And swore lies
Na mmekuwa hutanda	Now you curse your luck
Pesa zenu tumekula	And have become desperate
Na voti hatukuwapa	We have eaten (taken) your money
	But we did not vote for you
	(King'ei 1992: 117, quoted from Mukimbo 1978)

In this song by Lamu women, the rampant practice of bribing voters by politicians in Kenya is exposed and ridiculed. It is a song that aptly captures the problems that beset the nascent democracies of Africa.

d) *Language use*

Taarab songs are deeply metaphorical and are often tricky to understand. Although a song may be entitled '*fundi*' (expert e.g. tailor), '*mtwangio*' (pestle or that which pounds), '*papai*' (paw paw), the literal translation is not always intended. Hidden in these metaphors are messages of love, sexuality, praise, hate, vilification, exaltation, persuasion and even derision.

Although such deep imagery continues to be used in *taarab*, in recent years there appears to be a relative shift from obscurity to openness and indeed to obscenity. This is happening particularly in a subcategory of *taarab* called '*mipasho*' which is characterized by vulgarity and a non-euphemistic way of telling things (Bakari 1999: 8). The use of plain language in themes that would traditionally be conveyed in metaphors has elicited criticism from some *taarab* commentators:

> *Kwa upande wa lugha inayotumika, tunakuta mashairi bado ni pungufu kwa pande mbili: kwanza lugha iko wazi sana katika nyimbo zinazohitajiwa kufichwa. Watu wa rika zote wanayafahamu yaliyokusudiwa hata kama umri wao hauruhusu kulingana na mila zetu. Kwa kuwa jamii yetu ni yenye tabia ya kuheshimiana, kustahiana na kuoneana aibu, siyo jambo zuri kwa mtoto na mzazi kusikiliza pamoja baadhi ya nyimbo hizo* (Khamis, 2000: 4).

> In respect of language use, we find that poems are still defective in two ways. Firstly, the language is employed too directly in songs which [in the past] would have been couched in metaphors. People of all ages immediately understand what is intended although, according to our customs, their age does not permit them [to partake of the meaning]. Since our society is built on respect and reverence for one another, it is not appropriate for a child and a parent, or a person and his or her in-law to listen to some of these songs together.

The use of plain language, as opposed to metaphorical language, is one of the recent changes that has characterized *taarab*, and this has been attributed by some critics to 'transcultural influence' (Khamis 2001: 8).

e) *Code-Switching between Swahili and English*

The language of *taarab* reflects the linguistic situation in East Africa, where Swahili is the lingua franca, but where English is the language of prestige. In their songs, some *taarab* singers dot their songs with English words. Such use of two or more languages in an utterance is called code-switching. In the following chorus by Malika (1993) titled 'Mr. Mahmoud', code-switching between Swahili and English is clearly evident:

> Hello, hello, hello, I love you Mr. Mahmoud
> *Usiku kuwaza sana,*
> *kukicha silali tena*
> I love you Mr. Mahmoud.
> (Malika 1993- cassette)

> Hello, hello, I love you Mr. Mahmoud
> I think a lot about you at night,
> I sleep not till morning
> I love you Mr. Mahmoud

Khamis (2001: 15-16) gives many similar examples in which English is interspersed with Swahili in *taarab*, and where in some cases whole stanzas are rendered in English. In other cases it is not surprising to find a song with an English title such as 'love letter', 'double face' and 'promise me' or a song in which Swahili words have been inflected by the use of English morphemes, for example, *'mavitu'* (things) and *'majambos'* (matters) (Khamis 2000: 5). Whereas in the past code-switching would have been restricted to Swahili and Arabic, English is now becoming a common feature. This influence has an effect on the prosody of a *taarab* song; instead of strictly sticking to the metered rhymes, there now appears to be a tendency towards free versification.

Taarab beyond the Swahili domain

If traditionally, *taarab* was performed mainly in weddings or in ceremonies that had to do with Swahili culture, contemporary *taarab* is now going beyond these confines. While retaining its traditional role, the performance of *taarab* is now held in hotels, guest houses, tourist resorts and night clubs (King'ei 1992: 40)[14]. It also features prominently as part of the entertainment for national days and in election campaigns and political rallies by different candidates and political parties (ibid.).

Taarab is also played on radio and performed on TV in Kenya and Tanzania. The Kenya Broadcasting Cooperation radio, for instance, has at least two half-hour weekly programmes that are dedicated to *taarab* music. This music also features on the newly established FM radio stations in Kenya and Tanzania.

Taarab has therefore moved outside the confines of Swahili communities and as, King'ei (ibid: 44) correctly observes, it has been appropriated by large segments of the Kenyan and Tanzanian populations. Just to illustrate this, the famous *taarab* singer Malika, in 1998, sang *vidonge* (tablets)[15]. This song became very popular in Kenya and was played in *matatu* (shared taxis), bars and discos. This writer is also aware that at one time it was used by students in one of the local universities as a rallying call in their demonstration.

Although many of the well known *taarab* singers are still from the Swahili community, their constituency has grown beyond the Swahili settlements on the East African coast and the offshore islands. It is also significant to note that some *taarab* singers are now travelling and performing outside East Africa in places like the United Arab Emirates and Europe (see Saleh, this volume)[16]. Equally important is the fact that with the emergence of the revolution in information technology, a lot of information on *taarab* (for example various groups and their songs) has been posted on the internet as a marketing strategy and a tourist attraction to various destinations in East Africa.

Accounting for change in Taarab music

The performance of *taarab* outside its traditional Swahili domain could partly explain the changes in its character that have already been highlighted. As the number of consumers of this music grows, the music is also likely to change to accommodate the tastes of the emerging clientele. As Harrow (1994: 11) argues about literature in general, when an inherited model cannot serve the needs of the text, the text struggles to free itself, and in the struggle succeeds in elaborating something new.

The innovations in *taarab* music could also be seen as cultural change that is motivated by both internal and external factors. Merriam (1964: 313, quoting Barnett 1953) suggests that cultural change can be brought about by both internal and external incentives to innovation. Internal incentives include 'credit wants', which refer to the desire of some individuals to bring credit to themselves by initiating change; 'creative wants', in which individuals have the drive to creativity; 'relief and avoidance wants', prompted by the desire to change existing conditions because the individual experiences physical or mental discomfort; and 'the desire for quantitative variation', in which changes occur in society because existing mechanisms in the society do not provide enough of something that is valued.

Internal and external motivation for change as outlined here may not necessarily be mutually exclusive in so far as *taarab* music is concerned. For example, a *taarab* singer may incorporate new instruments, a new singing and dancing style or even new themes because of both internal and external motivation. In other words, change may come about as an innovation to satisfy a felt need in a society or may be introduced because of external influence. Separating these two types of motivation is likely to be very tricky.

Changing music and Swahili identity

What does the changing music of the Swahili suggest about their cultural identity? Kellner (1992: 141) and Goonatilake (1995: 232) have proposed a dynamic framework within which cultural change can be interpreted. They argue that in the world today the individual self is encroached upon dynamically by many shifting cultures because of globalization. Instead of having just one culture, the 'Lebanonization' of the mind of an individual occurs, with multiple frames of reference for action corresponding to each sub-culture. Instead of having one fixed and stable identity which is a function of predefined social roles, an individual has multiple selves and identities (ibid). Identity thus becomes mobile, multiple and self-reflexive (Kellner 1992: 141).

Changing Swahili culture as reflected by *taarab* music could be analyzed following this dynamic framework. Accordingly, a *taarab* singer, or by extension a Swahili person, could be said to have multiple identities. At one time he or she could have the identity of the 'traditional Swahili area'; at another time that of belonging to a larger geopolitical entity (e.g. Kenya, Zanzibar, Tanzania), while on another occasion he or she could have yet other identities. The culture of the Swahili could thus be seen as a dynamic one with multiple identities, where there is an interpenetration of the 'local', 'national' and 'global' domains.

Conclusion

This paper has looked at *taarab* music as a reflection of the changing socio-political reality of the Swahili. It shows that *taarab* music has been changing in order to accommodate new socio-political realities that have come to bear on the Swahili. The music has incorporated new instruments, new music styles and new ways of performing. Thematically, the music has also been adjusting to express topical issues, whether in politics, health matters, intellectual property rights or individual freedoms and rights. In conclusion, it is argued that a dynamic framework that sees cultural identity as mobile and multiple could be profitably applied to *taarab* music, Swahili culture, and hence Swahili identities.

Notes

1. It is possible to show different types of *taarab*. Fargion (1995: 125-131), for example, identifies three types of *taarab* in Zanzibar namely:

   a) an 'ideal' modeled on Egyptian forms of urban secular music,

   b) a counter–style '*Kidumbak*', developed by people of African descent,

   c) '*taarab ya wanawake*' (women's *taarab*).

Said Ahmed Khamis (2001: 5) indicates that *taarab* can also be stylistically categorised according to countries and regions in which it is created and performed, hence Mombasa *taarab*, Zanzibar *taarab*, Dar es Salaam *taarab*, Dubai *taarab* etc.

In this paper only distinctions that have a bearing on the aim of the paper are mentioned.

2. *Lambada* is an Afro-Brazilian dance of love which was very popular in Europe in 1989. Couples dance in extremely close proximity to one another in a tight embrace accompanied by Afro-Brazilian–Caribbean rhythms <http://genres.artsdirect.com/lambada.html> 25 July 2001.

3. Errol Henderson <http://www.nbnfront.org/html/fvwin98/errol/1/html> explains that hip- hop, or rap music, began in the early 1970s. The first synthesis of self-conscious poetry and music can be traced, most directly, to Black American nationalist poets.

4. Malkiya Rukia (1999), '*Penzi kwetu*', '*Leo nataka tamka*' Cassette, Nairobi.

5. *The Standard*, 12 March 1992, p.20.

6. Tanzania One Theatre, (1994) Cassette, Dar es Salaam.

7. Malika (Asha Suleiman, Abdo) (1994) '*Kuonewa Sitaki*', Cassette, Nairobi.

8. Maendeleo Musical Club (1979) '*Mtoto wa shule*', Casette, Dar es Salaam.

9. ____. '*Ukewenza*', Cassette.

10. Nyota Theatre (1998) '*Asali kuwa sumu*' Cassette, Dar es Salaam.

11. Malika (Asha Suleiman Abdo) (1994) 'Mandela'- Cassette, Nairobi.

12. Maulidi Juma (1988) '*Kura ni Mlolongo*', Recorded by Kenya Broadcasting Corporation. This song was sung in 1988, the year of an election in Kenya in which the ruling party waived the secret ballot and imposed an unpopular 'queue-voting' method. The *taarab* singers were hired to popularize the move.

13. Shukrani Musical Club 1987, Cassette, quoted in King'ei 1992: 120.

14. For instance, Zein al Abbaddin Ahmed, one of the composers of Zein Musical Party, has in the past signed contracts and performed regularly to entertain tourists on the south coast of Kenya (*Sunday Nation*, 23 January, 1994).

15. Malika (Asha Suleiman, Abdo) (1998) 'Vidonge' Cassette Nairobi.

16. *Sunday Nation*, 23 January, 1994.

Bibliography

Allen, James de Vere, 1993. *Swahili Origins: Swahili Culture and the Shungwaya Phenomenon*. London, James Curry.

Bakari, Amina Mussa, 1999. 'Taarab au Nini?' *Jua*, Juzuu 1 & 2, 4-10.

Euba, Ekin, 1999. 'African Traditional Musical Instruments in Neo-African Idioms and Contexts'. DjeDje, Jacquiline (ed.) *A Celebration of African Music*. Los Angeles: Regents of the University of California: 68-75.

Fargion, Janet Topp, 1995. 'Nyota Alfajiri - The Zanzibari Chakachaka'. *Swahili Forum II, Afrikanistische Arbeitspapieren*, 42: 125-131.

Goonatilake, Susantha, 1995. 'The Self wandering between cultural localization and globalization' in Pieterse, Jan Nederveen and Bhikhu Parekh (eds.), *The Decolonization of Imagination*. London and New Jersey, Zed Books: 224 –239.

Graebner, Werner, 1999. quoted by Mahmoud, Yusuf 'Taarab Music of Zanzibar' in <http://www.zanzibar.org/ziff>. 20 July 2001.

Graham, Ronnie, 1992 *The World of African Music vol. 2.* London, Pluto Press and Research Associates.

Harrow, Kenneth, 1994. *Threshold of Change in African Literature.* Portsmouth, Heinemann.

Herndon, Marcia, 1992. 'Song', Bauman, Richard (ed.) *Folklore, Cultural Performances, and Popular Entertainment.* New York, Oxford University Press, 159 –166.

Hooker, Richard, 1996. 'Crisis of Modernity' <http://www.wsu.edu/udee/Glossary/MODERN.HTM> 2 August 2001.

Issa, Salim Vuai, 1999. 'Ipi taarab halisi? Mambo yote yamebadilika', *Jua*, Juzuu, 4, 3-6.

Kellner, Douglas, 1992. 'Popular Culture and the Construction of Postmodern Identities' in Lash, Scott and Friedman, Jonathan (eds.), *Modernity and Identity.* Oxford: Blackwell.

Khamis, Hassan Abdulla, 2000. 'Hii ni ngoma ya kutafutiwa jina', *Jua*, Toleo la 4, Na. 2, 3-7.

Khamis, Said. Ahmed, 2001. 'Taarab: globalization and local influences', Unpublished paper presented at the University of Bayreuth.

King'ei, Geoffrey, 1992. 'Language, Culture and Communication: The Role of Swahili. Taarab songs in Kenya, 1963 –1990' Unpublished Ph.D thesis, Howard University.

Merriam, Alan, 1964. *The Anthropology of Music.* Evanston, Northwestern University Press.

Oommen, Thomas, 2001 'Recognizing Multiple Modernities: A Prelude to Understanding Globalization', <http://members.com/tripodcom/ncssjnu/oommen.html.> 15 July 2001.

Robert, Shaaban, 1967. *Wasifu wa Siti binti Saad, Mwimbaji wa Unguja.* London, Nelson.

Senoga – Zake, George 1986. *The Folk Music of Kenya.* Nairobi, Uzima Press.

Taylor, Charles, 2001. 'Two Theories of Modernity,' <www.uchicago.edu/research/jul-pub-cult/backissues/pc27/07–TaylorX.html.> 5 August 2001.

CHAPTER 12

MODERNITY OR ADAPTABILITY? THE INCORPORATION OF FOREIGN WORDS INTO SWAHILI POETRY

José Arturo Saavedra.

Introduction

Their geographical situation on the Coast of East Africa has given the Swahili people the opportunity of having contact with cultures from all over the Indian Ocean. Over the course of centuries, constant migrations from the Middle East, Persia and the Indian subcontinent have made the Swahili familiar with alien customs and practices, while borrowed technology, for example in navigation, has led to the inclusion of vocabulary loans from the most diverse languages (Le Guennec-Coppens 1997). All these elements, combined with the African features already belonging to the Swahili, have contributed to the making of a unique mixed culture.

Poetry is one of the most studied aspects of Swahili literature. The interesting and abundant scholarship in this literary genre is due to the latter's peculiar characteristics deriving from an old and rich oral tradition which began using Arabic script several centuries before European colonization. Since its beginnings, Swahili poetry has incorporated foreign elements from Arabia, India and Persia. It adapted the Arabic script to the phonetic needs of Swahili and developed local topics with their own culturally-specific flavour.

In the twentieth century, new means of communication such as the press and radio have diminished the use of poetry for instruction or as a way of diffusing information. However, until two or three decades ago the public recitation of *tenzi* (narrative poetry) was still frequent (Kessel 1980: vii) as was the production of poetry about remarkable events which had impacted on the community (Lienhardt 1968). Furthermore, the composition of poems about political and social concerns is still a common occurrence in the main newspapers of East Africa.

The aim of this paper is to analyze words of foreign origin – specifically from the English and German languages - which are included in some historical *tenzi* written before and on the eve of the European colonization at the turn of the twentieth century[1]. The poems were written between 1891 and 1907, years when the Germans were consolidating their rule in East Africa, and they depict this dramatic period in a remarkable way. They not only contain information on local history and culture but also show the use of terms of English and German origin. This poetry surely mirrors the process of incorporation of foreign words by people themselves when they were in contact with the Europeans for commercial and political reasons. The use of personal and geographical names, of administrative and bureaucratic terms, and terms for modern armaments compelled the poets to adapt words whose phonetics barely resembled those of Swahili and made their writing in Arabic script difficult. The impossibility of finding equivalents in Swahili or Arabic forced the poets to create neologisms in order to be able to include them in the rhyme and metre of the verses. This adaptation of poetry to new historical contexts represents a response to the overwhelming changes brought about by the establishment of European rule in East Africa. The poets had to work out how new ways of keeping poetry as a means of instruction and communication for the community and even those who composed under European patronage aimed for this goal.

This does not mean that, in this process, modernization took the place of tradition. Rather, it reveals the adaptability of a culture which, since its origins, has always incorporated from abroad the elements required to face new or unexpected situations, combining them with those which already existed. In other words, the 'traditional' culture is not abandoned but enriched with loans and borrowings from the new cultures which interacted with the Swahili. Thus, this paper deals with the appropriation and absorption of words and the accommodation of language to new demands produced by the context of the colonial struggle.

In order to explain this idea adequately I will briefly review the scholarship which has analyzed this process of adaptation of prosodic and literary features in Swahili poetry in order to show how the flexible nature of this poetry has contributed to the incorporation of foreign loans. Then I summarize the historical *tenzi* and the context in which this genre was developed. Finally, I give some examples taken from several poems written between 1880 and 1907, and analyze the kind of words which have been adapted.

Swahili prosody and its social function

The study of Swahili poetry has passed through several stages, from the formal study of its prosody (Abedi 1954, Hichens 1963, Allen 1967) to the analysis of its contents and its social function (Harries 1962, Knappert 1979, Massamba 1983, Shariff 1983, 1988). Specifically in the case of poetry, there have been debates related to the 'modern and traditional' tendencies. Some have considered pre-colonial poetry as feudalistic, not African but Arabic, and its prosodic rules as 'old fashioned', 'obsolete' and 'anachronistic' (Mulokozi and Kahigi 1979). Other scholars have asserted that this is genuine Swahili poetry with its own characteristics and originality (Shariff 1988, Mazrui and Shariff 1994). Further scholarship has dealt with methodological aspects of the study of poetry manuscripts and also with new interpretations of their contents (Biersteker and Plane 1989, Biersteker 1996). Additionally, several historians have used parts of the historical *tenzi* as sources or references for illustrating the political context of the events narrated in these works (Jackson 1970, Kieran 1970, Glassman 1995). Thus, we are now far from the days when pre-colonial Swahili poetry was considered only in so far as its religious content made it suitable as material for the study of East African Islam, as Knappert once asserted (1971: 5).

Swahili poetry is a good example of how this culture adapted foreign elements in order to create a genuine indigenous literature with a unique form of prosody. The most remarkable adaptations are:

1. The adaptation of Arabic script to the Swahili language. There is no certainty about the date when the script was adopted and when Swahili was written down for the first time (Omar and Frankl 1994: 263). However, literacy has existed in East Africa since the first Muslim migrations to the area in the eleventh century (Pouwels 1987: 16).

2. The adaptation of Arabic literary forms to Swahili. The most remarkable example is the *Hamziya* written in 1652. This is actually a translation of a famous Islamic poem *Umm-al Kura* (The Mother of the Cities) written in Egypt during the thirteenth century. The poet Sayyidi Aidarusi adjusted the rhyme and structure of the stanzas to Swahili creating the basis for its own prosody (Hichens 1963: 127, Harries 1962: 5).

3. The creation of the *utenzi* (singular of *tenzi*) form and its transformation from religious and epic poetry, whose themes were initially taken from Arabia, to a form of secular and religious poetry, with local themes on history, philosophy and moral reflections. According to Knappert Swahili epic poetry is entirely an original invention of the Swahili 'because there is not a similar genre in Arabic literature' (Knappert 1979: xix).

The historical *utenzi* genre has its origins in epic poetry which had links with 'the battle day literature' of pre-Islamic times as well as a substantial element of Muslim historiography. These stories, combining verse and prose and mainly centred on the *Jihad* (holy wars) engaged in by the first followers of the prophet Mohammed, were written in Arabia (Rosenthal 1952: 43-60). The Swahili Epics dropped the prose parts, constructing the narrative discourse with the use of poetry alone. Some epics were clearly based on real historical facts. The *Chuo cha Herikali*, also known as the *Utenzi wa Tambuka*, is the oldest *utenzi* poem preserved. The manuscript is dated 1728 but we do not know who wrote it or its place of origin either (Knappert 1967: 143-4). The historical facts narrated in the *utenzi* have been reshaped in order to exalt the role of Muhammad. For the Muslim community this poem was much more than a 'simplistic' religious legend. It represented a depiction of facts that no one would question as false. Epic poetry thus fulfilled the role of teaching young people the most precious Muslim values exemplified by the life of the Prophet and the heroes who fought against the unfaithful. Thus the production of the *utenzi* genre was initially linked with religious instruction and with Muslim celebrations such as the *Maulidi*.

The importance that Swahili people give to poetry as a tool of communication has been evident since the oral tradition of Fumo Liyongo which mentioned ability in composition as one of the attributes of this hero. According to Pouwels, people who were recognized in the Swahili towns as *wazee* (notables) included those who enjoyed the reputation of having poetical skills as well as being famous for leading their *mitaa* (quarters) in dancing competitions (Pouwels 1987: 84-5). The confrontation between distinguished poets using *mashairi ya kujibizana* (dialogue poetry – see also Amidu, this volume) was extended not only to local rivalries but also played a role in wars between Swahili states such as Mombasa and Lamu. Zahid bin Mngumi, the famous Lamu leader who led his people to a memorable victory against their enemies in the battle of Shela, was also an accomplished poet who exchanged his verses with the no less famous Muyaka bin Haji (Biersteker and Shariff 1995: 59-60, 66, 68). Muyaka not only composed poems to discourage the people of Lamu from fighting the Mombasa forces, but he is also remembered as the most important poet to support the independence of Mombasa, creating passionate poems against the pretensions of the Omani Busaidis who sought to control the whole coast of East Africa (Abdulaziz 1979).

The social function of this poetry would not be possible without its flexible prosody and the morphological characteristics of the Swahili language that has made it such an appropriate vehicle for the expression of narrative and religious and philosophical ideas. Ibrahim Noor Shariff has shown that Swahili prosody does not restrict the expression of ideas since prosodic rules, that is, the patterns for a proper composition with rhyme and metre, are easy to acquire for two reasons. In the case of rhyme it is because in Swahili, as in many other Bantu languages, 'All the verbs, nouns and adjectives end with a vowel, and some of those words of foreign origin that do not end with a vowel are given a vowel ending as they are assimilated into the language' (Shariff 1983: 85). This situation ensures that the rhyme is easy to obtain because there are many syllables with the same letters and there are plenty of options when an ending sound is required (Shariff 1983: 86). As to the aspect of metre, Shariff reminds us of another distinctive feature: 'Most Swahili sentences and phrases can be shortened or lengthened without losing the meaning, therefore, meter is also easily obtainable' (Shariff 1983: 88-9).[2]

Furthermore, Shariff adds to all these reflections another interesting argument. He contends that in the specific case of narrative poetry, the content is more important than a strict application of the prosodic rules. He gives as examples references to ancient poems such as the *Kibuzi*, whose topic is the Portuguese invasion of East Africa in the sixteenth century. This poem was passed down orally from generation to generation using very irregular metre and rhyme, however 'the survival of such poems by word of mouth attests to the fact that it is ultimately the content that ensures a poem's survival through the centuries' (Shariff 1983: 80).

Yet Shariff also alerts us to the fact that this flexibility should not be considered so wide as to ignore the entire prosodic framework. All poetry must possess enough concordance with the rhyme and metre in order to avoid a defect called *guni*, since all the prosodic forms are sung or chanted when performed in the peculiar way of Swahili poetry. There are several defined tunes for each prosodic form and an excessive amount of *guni* in a poem would make its recitation impossible (Shariff 1983: 94-6, Allen 1971: 29-41).

In spite of this limitation, Swahili poetry has incorporated words of alien origin and, like the Swahili language itself, poetry enriched its vocabulary from an early stage with loans from Portuguese, Farsi and Hindi. Since the beginning of the nineteenth century it has also added loans from French, English, and German. The political presence of these European powers in the area and the establishment of colonies by the British and German empires represented a series of changes and transformations in all aspects of Swahili culture and society.

In the case of the interaction between colonizers and colonized people, nothing reflects better the way in which these contacts and encounters between these cultures took place than the literary production of the Swahili poets. Among the materials, such as the first prose accounts and oral narratives directly transcribed into Roman script, the historical poetry written during this turbulent period gives hints of how the new vocabulary was incorporated and also indicates the fields from which these words came, mainly the military and administrative ones.

Incorporation of foreign words into Swahili vocabulary and the appearance of historical poetry

The incorporation of foreign words into Swahili began with the adaptation of numerous Arabic words due to the influence of Islam, migrations from the Middle East and the political rule of the Busaidi Sultanate in Zanzibar. Until recently the high rate of vocabulary of Arabic influence has led to the mistaken and biased idea of considering Swahili as a pidgin of Arabic or as a hybrid, and it created a debate about the Africanness or Arabness of this language (Mazrui and Shariff 1994: 67-9).

From the end of the fifteenth century to the beginning of the eighteenth, the Portuguese presence left an important stock of vocabulary that is still present in contemporary Swahili, such as *bendera* (flag), *bomba* (pump), *meza* (table), *boriti* (beam), and others that appear to be no longer in use, such as *amari* (cable) and *almari* (chest of drawers) (Johnson 1939: 10, 33, 38, 70).

In the case of the English language the earliest references that we have include the word *marekani* or *merikani* (American), an allusion to the cotton cloth arriving in Zanzibar from Massachusetts on the first visits of American ships to East Africa between 1832 and 1834 (Whiteley 1969: 45). In the case of poetry, according to Knappert, the earliest example appears in a poem composed at the beginning of the nineteenth century by Sheikh Swadi bin Ali of Lamu, apparently a *wimbo* song:

Haifai kutoyuwa yangu hali	You ought to know my condition:
Nili hai kwako siweki badali	I am alive, I love no one but you,
Gudi bai yanisiki mai dali	Good-bye, I am sick my darling

As we can see the last line is entirely composed using words that are derived from English. Knappert also adds another fascinating verse, an anonymous poem about drinkers and alcoholic beverages. I have modified the translation where appropriate (Knappert 1979: 34):

Wa wapi wanyao biya	Where are the drinkers of beer,
Wisiki na champeni.	Whisky and champagne?

Sipiriti inangiya	Spirit is entering
kwa rahisi madukani	In shops with ease.
sitimu ni mara moya	Drunkenness is instantaneous,
mara hamutambuwani	Suddenly you no longer recognize
	each other.

Unfortunately, Knappert does not explain how the English word 'steam' is associated with 'drunkenness' and indeed, we have to trust his word that this poetry was composed at the beginning of the nineteenth century[3]. It is likely that at that time, poems with English words may have been isolated cases. For instance, a careful review of the works of Muyaka reveals the strong presence of Kimvita, the predominant regional dialect of Mombasa, and the absence of words of Anglo-Saxon origin (Abdulaziz 1979). In a similar way, the famous poem of *Al-Inkishafi*, composed around 1820 in Pate by Sayyid Abdallah bin Nasir, is mainly written in Kiamu dialect (Mulokozi 1999: 63-77) and we do not find any alien words other than those from an Arabic and Islamic context, except those deriving from Portuguese.

Another example is found in the *Utenzi wa Mwana Kupona* composed in 1858 by Mwana Kupona binti Mshamu from Pate. This poem consists of advice from a mother to her daughter about the duties of the wife in the household. It is also a very good indicator of the culture and society of the *waungwana* (patrician) class at that time (Mulokozi 1999: 101-6). While an important part of the vocabulary contained in the poem is focused on ornaments, perfumes, furniture, cosmetics and dressing, all of them with clear Oriental allusions, we do not find any word derived from English and German in the composition. In the case of all three of the afore-mentioned poems, it is evident that the composers lived in a social context where the impact of the economic and political activities of British and Germans was not yet significant. Additionally, the philosophical and didactic contents of both *Al-Inkishafi* and *Mwana Kupona* would have made unlikely the possibility of including foreign words which at that time were used only in diplomatic and commercial spheres.

In the case of Muyaka, his patriotic verses do not make reference to the unsuccessful establishment of a British protectorate in Mombasa, as a desperate action of the Mazrui *liwali* (governor) for preserving the autonomy of the city against the claims of the Omani Sultan Sayyid Said. Between 1824 and 1826 the British consul Owen, acting on his own initiative, arranged a protectorate in Mombasa without the consent of his Government. However, the British decided finally to support Said's claims of overlordship over the East African coast (Abdulaziz 1979: 140) and so we are left to wonder how the Mombasa poet would have adapted English administrative words or personal names to the peculiar characteristics of the Kimvita dialect[4].

During the second half of the nineteenth century, the increasing political interests of the British and the Germans in the area, together with the arrival of Christian missionaries interested in learning Swahili, created new and multiple contacts between Swahili scholars and poets with missionaries and European functionaries. Without any doubt this collaboration gave Swahili scholars familiarity with foreign names. We read in a poem written by Mwalimu Sikuja, a famous Mombasan poet and preserver of the work of Muyaka, the name *Wiliyamu* with reference to the Rev. William Taylor, one of the first collectors of Swahili poetry (Abdulaziz 1979: 2 -3).

Unfortunately, not all the contacts between African and Europeans were friendly or constructive. In several parts of the coast there was armed opposition to the implementation of the colonial regime. Between 1884 and 1905 there were several struggles in Witu, Mombasa, the Mrima coast, Zanzibar and Kilwa, in which the Swahili elite *(Waungwana)* confronted British and German forces. In the middle of this struggle, foreign words related to the military – weapons, battleships, uniforms, military ranks and so on – together with a political and administrative vocabulary, became popular not only among the *ulama* (intellectual class) but also among the common people who witnessed the impressive technological power of the European armies. The historical *tenzi* which narrated these dramatic events were the depositories of a new vocabulary adapting to Swahili the phonetics and morphology of these alien words.

As already stated, the early *tenzi* were on religious themes but later we find secular ones, immersed in local contexts. The first historical narrative poem that has been preserved is the *Utenzi wa Al Akida*, written around 1880, before the European regime was yet consolidated. It deals with an episode in the local political history of Mombasa, and is, as far as I know, the first *utenzi* to include English words in its verses. This *utenzi* is about the history of the *Akida* Muhammad bin Abdallah bin Mbarak Bakhashweini, an official of Hadrami origin who between 1870 and 1872 was *liwali* or governor of Mombasa appointed by Sultan Bargash. Later, he was relieved of his posts of *liwali* and *akida* (commander in chief) of the Hadrami garrison in Fort Jesus, due to the intrigues of his enemies. In 1874 Sultan Bargash demanded that the *Akida* leave the Fort but he refused to do that, resisting for several months and supported by his Hadrami soldiers. He finally surrendered in January of 1875 after a siege by Omani troops backed by British battleships (Hinawy 1950: 22-32, Berg 1971: 98-9, 123-4).

The *Utenzi wa Al-Akida* is mainly concerned with the refusal of the *Akida* to abandon the fort and his armed opposition to the Omani and British forces. The poet Abdallah bin Masud, composer of this work, narrates in ninety-nine stanzas events from the moment when the Sultan's *Waziri* (minister) Muhammad bin Suleiman al-Busaidi arrives in Mombasa and receives the complaints of the elders about the tyrannical behaviour of the *Akida*. The involvement of the British in the incident was not only in the field of military assistance. They were also mediators in the dispute and there is documented evidence that the *Akida* himself asked for this intervention in a letter that he sent to the acting consul Prideaux (Berg 1971: 127). Thus, the British military attacks and the negotiation of the English commander are included in the poetic narrative. In the following verses we find a number of foreign words (Hinawy 1950, pp 86-7):

(83) *Akanena Admeri*	The Admiral considered
Sasa ni lipi shauri	What was the best advice
La kusema Zinjibari	To give advice in Zanzibar
Ambalo limelekeya	About what should be done
(84) *Tatengeneza manuwari*	I will order gunboats there
Itambae na bahari	by sea
Uwovo amekhitari	He (the *Akida*) has chosen to
Lazima kumtendeya	rebel
	And must suffer for it.
(94) *Wakateremka pwani*	They went down to the shore,
Wakaingiya melini	And went on board,
Wakifika Ungujani	When they reached Zanzibar
Akamwambiya tuliya	he told him not to worry

Here we find three adaptations that do not present problems of metre or rhyme for the Swahili poet. *Admeri* is the most adapted word compared with its original spelling (Admiral) in English. *Manuwari* (also *manowari* or *menowari*) is probably the most frequent foreign adaptation found in all the historical *tenzi* written about the wars of European conquest and the establishment of colonial rule in East Africa. It corresponds to the term 'man-of-war' attached to the nineteenth century frigate whose powerful batteries devastated many Swahili towns at those times. It is complemented with the word *Meli*, which appears in the poem with the suffix's locative. According to Johnson this word was specifically applied to the steamship which carried goods, cargo or passengers. It derives its name from the word 'mail' probably because it was the most longed-for item contained in the cargo of these ships (Johnson 1939: 274).

It may be noted that in this *utenzi* there are synonyms taken from the Arabic. One example is the word *Merikebu* (also *marikabu*) that appears in the poem (stanzas 12 and 93); that term, adapted to Swahili, was used to denominate ships of foreign construction as distinct from the native vessel *chombo* (Johnson 1939: 275).

Adaptation and use of foreign words in historical poetry, 1891 to 1907

To find other early examples of the adaptation of foreign vocabulary to Swahili poetry we need also to consider that written on the Mrima and southern coasts of Tanganyika during the German wars of conquest of this territory. We also find interesting examples in Zanzibar when the British protectorate was completely established and when its political decisions affected the autonomy of the Sultanate.

Hemedi bin Abdallah el Buhry, poet, *mganga* (healer) and fighter against the Germans, wrote around 1891 the first poetic account of the coastal wars in the *Utenzi wa Vita vya Wadachi Kutamalaki Mrima* (el Buhry 1968). This depicts the first incursions of the Germans onto the northern coast of Tanganyika and the armed opposition of the leader Abushiri bin Salim al Harti, who fought them from 1888 until his execution on December 15th 1889. The *utenzi* of Hemedi shows the rich vocabulary of the Kimrima dialect with many words of Arabic origin that help him to describe

203

in detail all the events of the war. The abundant prayers to God and the depiction of the rites of divination and preparation of charms against the invaders scarcely present an opportunity for including alien words from European languages in the poem. Even for the names of the German officials, Hemedi prefers to use the nicknames that probably were used by the ingenious Swahili. Thus, Captain Emil von Zelewski is called *Nyundo* (hammer) (stanza 164), Herman von Wissman receives the name of *Kitambara* (napkin, small piece of cloth) (stanza 165), and General von Trotha was given the nickname *Muhogo Mchungu* (bitter cassava) (stanza 167). In other cases, however, Hemedi is compelled to adapt European names into Swahili: Dr. Bümmler is *Bima*, Lieutenant Conradin von Perbandt is known as *Bwana Lauti* (stanza 169), the Baron von St. Paul is *Hambaroni* (stanza 501) and General Lloyd Matthews, Chief Commander of the Sultan's army, is called *Mushti Mafiyu* (Mister Matthews) (stanzas 325 and 327) (el Buhry 1968: 84).

As to military terms, Hemedi mainly uses the words derived from Arabic to denominate weapons: *kombora* (bomb), *mzinga* (cannon), *risasi* (bullet), *bunduki* (rifle, gun), *baruti* (gunpowder). In the case of European ships the poet uses the word *dukhani* for steamer (instead of *meli*)[5] (stanzas 170, 315 and 318) but he does use *manuwari* (stanzas 129, 171, 241) probably since this battleship with its powerful cannons was so well known that everyone was familiar with the term.

Hemedi also composed a series of epic poems in the pure classic style of the Swahili literary traditions. One of them is the *Utenzi wa Abdirrahmani na Sufiyani* that recounts the story of one of the most popular heroes of early Islam. Abdirramani was son of Abu Bakari, one of the friends and companions of the Prophet Muhammad. Abdirramani, after a life of sin and pillage, regrets his behaviour and decides to come back to the Islamic faith. However, the hero is compelled to confront his father in law, Sufiyani, who was his comrade in assaulting and killing travellers. Abdirramani and his wife run away to Medina, but they are chased by Sufiyani and his mighty army. The poet Hemedi describes in some verses how the warriors prepare to go to fight and mentions their equipment (el Buhry 1961: 38-9):

(288) Wakaja wali tayari   They came prepared
       Kwa mikuki na khanjari   With spears, scimitars
       Na kanzu za manuwari   And all of them wore
       Jamii walizovaa   Coats of mail

In the case of the Swahili scholars who were contemporaries of
Hemedi bin Abdallah, the main difference in their compositions is
that they made more use of adaptations of personal German names
and administrative charges. The collection of poems published by
the German scholar Carl Velten, which praises German colonial
rule, in most cases dropped the nicknames of the officials and
instead 'Swahilized' their family names. Thus, this poetry, written
between 1901 and 1906, makes the following adaptations: *Wissmani*
for Hermann von Wissman, *bana Fonka* for Captain Heinrich Fonk,
bana Prinzi for Captain von Prince, *bana Sempuli* for Baron von St.
Paul, *bwana von Stranzi* for Commissioner von Strantz, *bana Saha* for
Commissioner Zache, *bwana Buruni* for the official Braun and
Veltini for Carl Velten (Velten 1907: 345, 348, 382, 384, 387, 391,
393, 395). A special case is the allusion to the German Emperor
Kaisari Wilhemu that we find in one anonymous work of the
collection of war poetry also collected by Velten. (Velten 1917: 64).

In a similar way, administrative terms were also adapted to
Swahili. Thus we read of *guverneri, jauverneri, govmani* and *govana* for
the term Governor (Velten 1907: 349, 374 and Velten 1917: 72),
maboi (from 'boy') for messenger and *sitakbazi* or *kabzeni* for the
post of District Commissioner (Velten 1907: 364). As to military
terms we can see that *manowari* is still the most used term, but new
ones appear, such as the onomatopoeic *bombom* used for shells or
machine-guns and *rakiti* for automatic rifles or machine-guns as
well (Velten 1907: 344 and 1917: 74, 79, 85, 88). One curious
aspect is the lack of unity among the poets when they refer to the
German nation and its citizens. Hemedi bin Abdallah uses the
word *Mdachi-wadachi* while Makanda bin Mwenyi Mkuu, former
fighter against the Germans and a contributor to Velten's
collection, calls them *Mdoitshi-madoitshi*, terms also used by an
anonymous poet (Velten 1917: 70, 71, 82). Alternatively, other
poets use the words *Jermani-majermani*, which denotes the clear
influence of the English language among these Swahili poets
(Velten 1907: 361, 363). It is also worth considering why the
English word for 'German' had more influence than 'Deutsch'
even in the case of poets who lived in German East Africa. Indeed,

the number of words adapted from English is greater than those taken from German. This fact suggests either that it was considered much easier to adapt English than German phonetics, or that the possibilities for having contact with or listening to the German language were fewer. Finally, it is worth noting that only one German expression, a greeting, was adapted to Swahili: *bana morne* (Guten morgen) is referred to in two anonymous poems as a way of stressing the kind attitude of two functionaries, Captain von Wissman and General von Torotha, towards their subordinates (Velten 1907: 372, 380).

The most significant and innovative adaptation of English words is found in the *Utenzi wa Mzinga wa Alhamisi* written around 1897 by Mustafa bin Kisi bin Hamadi Imutafi from Zanzibar. The poem narrates a famous episode known as the *Mzinga wa Alhamisi* (the Thursday bombardment). Soon after the beginning of the British protectorate in Zanzibar, when Sultan Ali bin Said died, the British installed Hamed bin Thuwein on the throne in spite of the opposition of Khalid bin Barghash, who claimed to be the legitimate successor of his uncle. Hamed bin Thuwein died unexpectedly on August 25th 1896. Khalid bin Barghash managed to seize the palace in an attempt to gain power. Two days later, British forces attacked the palace until Khalid surrendered. The poem of Mustafa bin Kisi is remarkable for its noticeable tendency to use similes and for its 'curious use of English expressions for effect' (Copland 1957: 66). The *utenzi* is centred on the British arrangements for the attack, the surrendering of Khalid bin Barghash and his asylum in the German consulate prior to his exile to the German colony of Tanganyika. As might be expected, words related to military activities and accessories are present in the verses, such as *mabeti* (cartridge pouch) (stanza 13) (Johnson 1939: 34), *kumpuni* (companies) (stanza 23) and the mention of military salutations: *wakapijwa folini* ('the fall-in was sounded') (stanza 15) and *Iamrishwe suluti* ('the order is given for the salute') (stanza 38). The most interesting verse is related to the orders given before the attack (Copland 1957: 72):

(39) *Thumma yakuli kuluni*	Then the colonel says,
Chifu Talian	-the Italian commander-,
Jinil sulut, ranti am,	'General salute, present arms'
Rururururururururu.	Rururururururururu.

There is also an ingenious combination of Swahili with English verbs as in the case of *wakaudiringi* (those who drank) found in a verse where the poet criticizes the disorder provoked by drunken European soldiers in the streets of Zanzibar (stanza 62). This *utenzi* also has interesting adaptations of European personal and geographic names. Thus we find *Hardingu* for Sir Arthur Hardinge, acting consul of Zanzibar (stanza 39). We also find *Jilasko*, a curious adaptation of 'Glasgow' the name of one of the British *manuwari* which participated in the bombardment of the Sultan's palace (Stanza 51). This poem is evidently richer in the use of European words than those written in German East Africa. It also reflects how the activities of the Europeans in Zanzibar are portrayed from the point of view of a Swahili eyewitness of these events.

Conclusion

A study of the vocabulary that has been adapted to Swahili from English and German certainly implies two factors: the first is the strong impression that such 'naked' military power made on the poets' minds, as has already been pointed out by one scholar (Glassman 1995: 260-1); the second is the familiarity of Swahili poets with administrative and bureaucratic matters and with German officials and scholars, as is clear in the materials collected by Velten. This is not surprising if we consider that most of the contributors to the collection worked for the Germans as scribes, translators and informants (Velten 1917: 61-3). On the other hand, the onomatopoeic words for salutations, gun machines and bombs, together with adaptation of personal names, probably arise from people's inventiveness and not from the talent of specific poets.

Although the incorporation of foreign words is a natural process in all the languages, an analysis of the type of vocabulary borrowed from a language denotes the kind of relations and contacts established between the alien and local peoples and how and why this process happens. In the case of the Portuguese presence in the area, the words of this language preserved in Swahili concern ornaments, furniture and diverse accessories, but in a colonizing context like that prevailing in East Africa at the beginning of the twentieth century, there is an obvious abundance of military, technological, commercial and bureaucratic terms, demonstrating the need to incorporate expressions for which the existing indigenous vocabulary could hardly find an equivalent.

In conclusion, this paper must be read as a proposal for a socio-linguistic approach to the vocabulary of this poetry which can give important indicators of the cultural and social life of the Swahili people at the beginning of the European colonial period. The kind of relationships which existed between Europeans and Africans can be revealed through careful research on Swahili poetry, which represents an authentic indigenous source reflecting the world, cosmogony and mentality of the Swahili.

NOTES

1. This research is derived from the main topic of my ongoing PhD dissertation on the historiography of Swahili war poetry. In this research, I have received financial support from the Consejo Nacional de Tecnologia (CONACYT) of México, the School of Oriental and African Studies, the Central Research Fund, University of London and from the British Institute in Eastern Africa.

2. Ibrahim Noor Shariff, *The Function of Dialogue Poetry in Swahili Society*, p. 88-9. Shariff gives us an example of the multiple ways in which the sentence 'I come' can be written: Mimi ninakuja (6 syllables), Mi ninakuja (5), ninakuja (4) nakuja (3) naja (2).

3. From a historiographic perspective the literary approach of Knappert is highly dubious due to his complete lack of reference for the sources of the poems or information about how they were collected. For a full critique of this approach see the reviews of his book *Four Centuries of Swahili Verse* by Shariff 1971 and 1981 and Allen 1982.

4. Abdulaziz mentions in one of his footnotes a poem of Muyaka whose content deals with the episode of the British retreat from Mombasa. Unfortunately, this poem is not included in the anthology of Muyaka's works (Abdulaziz 1979: 140).

5. Allen mentions in his glossary to el Buhry's *utenzi* that the word comes from the word 'dukhn' (el Buhry 1968: 82).

Bibliography

Abdulaziz, Mohamed H., 1979. *Muyaka: Nineteenth-Century Swahili Popular Poetry*. Nairobi: Kenya Literature Bureau.

Abedi, Kaluta Amri, 1954. *Sheria za Kutunga Mashairi na Diwani ya Amri*. Dar es Salaam, The Eagle Press.

Allen, James de Vere, 1982. 'Review of 'Four Centuries of Swahili Verse: A Literary History and Anthology', by Jan Knappert', *Research in African Literatures*, 13, 1: 142.

Allen, John W.T. (ed.), 1971. *Tendi, Six Examples of a Swahili Classical Verse Form with Translations and Notes*. London: Heineman.

Berg, Fred James, 1971. 'Mombasa under the Busaidi Sultanate: the City and its Hinterlands in the Nineteenth Century', University of Wisconsin, Ph.D. dissertation.

Biersteker, Ann, 1996. *Kujibizana. Questions of Language and Power in Nineteenth- and Twentieth- Century Poetry in Kiswahili*. East Lansing: Michigan State University Press (African Series, 4).

——, and Ibrahim Noor Shariff (eds.), 1995. *Mashairi ya Vita vya Kuduhu: War Poetry in Kiswahili Exchanged at the Time of the Battle of Kuhudu*. East Lansing: Michigan State University Press (African Historical Sources, 7).

——, and Mark Plane, 1989. 'Swahili Manuscripts and the Study of Swahili Literature', *Research in African Literatures* 20, 3: 449-472.

——, 1961. *Utenzi wa Abdirrahmani na Sufiyani*. (Translated by Roland Allen, with notes by J.W.T. Allen). Dar es Salaam: East African Literature Bureau.

el Buhry, Hemedi bin Abdallah bin Masudi, 1968. *Utenzi wa Vita vya Wadachi Kutamalaki Mrima* (translation and notes by J.W.T. Allen). Nairobi: East African Literature Bureau.

Glassman, Jonathon, 1995. *Feasts and Riot: Revelry, Rebellion and Popular Conciousness on the Swahili Coast*. James Currey: London.

Le Guennec-Coppens, Françoise, 1997. 'Changing Patterns of Hadhrami migration and social integration in East Africa', in Ulrike Freitag and William G. Clarence-Smith (eds.) *Hadrami Traders, Scholars and Statesmen in the Indian Ocean, 1750s- 1960s*, Leiden, E. J. Brill.

Harries, Lyndon, 1962. *Swahili Poetry*. Oxford: Clarendon Press.

Hichens, William, 1943 [1941] 'Swahili Prosody', *Swahili* 33, 1: 107-37.

Hinawy, Mbarak Ali, 1950. *Al-Akida And Fort Jesus, Mombasa*. London: Macmillan and Co. Limited.

Jackson, Robert D., 1970. 'Resistance to the German Invasion of the Tanganyikan Coast 1888-1891,' in Robert I. Rotberg and Ali A. Mazrui, *Protest and Power in Black Africa*. New York: Oxford University Press: 37-79.

Johnson, Frederick, 1939. *A Standard Swahili-English Dictionary*. London: Oxford University Press.

Kessel, Leo van, 1980. 'Introduction' to Mgeni bin Faqihi's *Utenzi wa Rasi 'lGhuli*. Dar es Salaam: Tanzania Publishing House.

Kieran, John A., 1970. 'Abushiri and the Germans', in Bethwell A. Ogot (ed.) *Hadith 2*. Nairobi: East African Publishing House: 157- 201.

Knappert, Jan, 1967. *Traditional Swahili Poetry*. Leiden, E. J. Brill.

——, 1971, *Swahili Islamic Poetry* (3 vols.). Leiden, E. J. Brill.

——, 1979. *Four Centuries of Swahili Verse: a Literary History and Anthology*. London: Heinemann Educational Books.

Lienhardt, Peter, 1968. 'Introduction' to Hasani bin Ismail, *Utenzi wa Swifa ya Nguvumali*. Oxford: Claredon Press: 1-80.

Massamba, David P. B., 1983. 'Utunzi wa Ushairi wa Kiswahili' in *Fasihi*, Paper for the International Seminar of Swahili Writers, Dar es Salaam, Institute of Kiswahili Research.

Mazrui, Alamin and Ibrahim Noor Shariff, 1994. *The Swahili: Idiom and Identity of an African People*. New York: Africa World Press.

Mulokozi, Mugyabuso M. and Kulikoyela K. Kahigi, 1979. *Kunga za Ushairi na Diwani Yetu*. Dar es Salaam: Tanzania Publishing House.

——, 1999. *Tenzi Tatu za Kale*. Dar es Salaam: Taasisi ya Uchunguzi wa Kiswahili, University of Dar es Salaam.

Mustafa, Kisi bin Hamadi Imutafi, 1957. 'The Bombardment of Zanzibar': a poem translated by B. D. Copland, with historical notes by John M. Gray, *Journal of the East African Swahili Committe*, 27: 66- 82.

Pouwels, Randall, L., 1987. *Horn and Crescent*. New York: Cambridge University Press.

Rosenthal, Franz, 1952. *A History of Muslim Historiography*. Leiden, E. J. Brill.

Shariff, Ibrahim Noor, 1991. 'Islam and secularity in Swahili literature: an overview', in Kenneth W. Harrow (ed.), *Faces of Islam in African Literature*. London, James Currey: 37-57.

——, 1971. 'Knappert's tales', *Kiswahili*, 41, 2: 47-55

——, 1981. 'Knappert tells more tales' *Horn of Africa* 42: 156-96

——, 1983. "The Function of Dialogue Poetry in Swahili Society", Ph.D. Thesis, New Brunswick: The State University of New Jersey.

——, 1988 *Tungo Zetu*, Trenton N. J.: The Red Sea Press.

Topan, Farouk, 2001. 'Projecting Islam: narrative in Swahili poetry', *Journal of African Cultural Studies*, 14, 1: 107- 119.

Velten, Carl, 1917, 1918. 'Suaheli-Gedichte' *Afrikanische Studien*, Mitteilugen des Seminars für Orientalische Sprachen zu Berlin, XX and XXI 61-182, 135-183.

——, 1907. *Prosa und Poesie der Suaheli*, Berlin, ne.

Whiteley, Wilfred, 1969. *Swahili: The Rise of a National Language*. London: Methuen & Co. Ltd.

Omar, Yahya Ali and Peter J. L. Frankl, 1994. 'A 12th/18th century letter from Kilwa Kisiwani', *Afrika und Übersee*, 77: 263-5.

CHAPTER 13

FROM MWANA KUPONA TO MWAVITA: REPRESENTATIONS OF FEMALE STATUS IN SWAHILI LITERATURE

Farouk Topan

Introduction

In her brief survey of the image of woman in Swahili prose fiction, Mbughuni makes three observations on the tripartite relationship between author, audience and critic which are pertinent to this paper (Mbughuni 1982: 15-24). She cautions the critic (and audience) against accepting as facts what may only be the perceptions of the authors themselves about women. She suggests that, for instance, the depiction of many female characters as prostitutes in the works of fiction that she had surveyed derives from the 'fantasies and concerns of the male sensibility which produced such an image' rather than constituting a reflection of the situation in reality (ibid: 15). Secondly, Mbughuni points out that, in the Swahili situation, only a very small proportion of the population actually reads these works of fiction, and, consequently, their influence on the larger populace needs to be viewed from that perspective. Mbughuni's third point is that the image of women projected in literature is shaped by the form of literary tradition prevalent in that particular society; the tendency, in Swahili fiction, is to be didactic, and therefore to set up stereotypical models of 'good' and 'bad' women. Thus, two images of woman, at opposite extremes, emerge from Mbughuni's survey.

At one end of the continuum is the 'saintly Mary' who is perceived as a good woman, dutifully working away in the kitchen, and obedient to the wishes of her man. Her character is considered wholesome as she helps in the maintenance of order and stability in society. However, at the other end of the continuum is the 'evil Eve', a temptress who wrecks society by leading men into crime and moral turpitude.

Much else has been published in the two decades since Mbughuni's survey. More significantly, a number of women writers have since emerged whose efforts have helped to establish a female presence in Swahili literature. Foremost among them are Penina Mlama (née Muhando), Amandina Lihamba, and Angelina Chogo, all three from Tanzania, and Ari Katini Mwachofi from Kenya. Their success has been achieved in two ways. First and foremost they have established themselves as *writers*, that is, as creative individuals in their own right whose works of fiction in Swahili focus on a variety of issues facing society, including the treatment and predicament of women[1]. They are also successful academics, dramatists, and, in Lihamba's case, an actress as well[2].

Swahili women on the coast did enjoy fame and status in the past. Literary and historical sources inform us that women occupied positions as rulers in the coastal city-states; they had the title of *mwana*, translated as 'queen' in the existing literature. Mwana Musura of Siu, Mwana Mkisi of Mombasa, and Mwana Aziza of Zanzibar (Unguja), for example, are mentioned in the poems of Muyaka (d. 1840) (Abdulaziz 1979: 147). This has led some scholars to suggest that Swahili societies might then have been matrilineal in their social organization (Shepherd 1977; Nurse and Spear 1985). Other scholars reject this, suggesting that the Swahili were and indeed still are cognatic in descent (Middleton 1992: 99; Horton and Middleton 2000: 232). Be that as it may, it is clear that, as Islam spread on the coast, its scholars established a system based on what Strobel has called a 'patriarchal ideology'(1979: 84) which gave rise to male dominance in various areas of community life. Shepherd observes that, in two of the Comoro islands, 'an underlying matrilineal organisation struggles with the strong emphasis on patrifiliation imported with Islam' (1977: 347 – see also Le Guennec-Coppens, this volume).

However, the colonial phase (1890s to 1960s) introduced notions of 'liberalism' on the coast through Western education, particularly that of girls, championed by local leaders such as Alamin Mazrui in Mombasa and Sultan Hamoud bin Ali in Zanzibar. The cosmopolitan nature of the major cities also helped to broaden the way Swahili women perceived women of other communities including Europeans, Goans, various Indian communities (both Muslim and non-Muslim), those of the immediate hinterland, and from further inland. Moreover, throughout the twentieth century, East Africa – like other areas of the Third World – has increasingly been affected by cultural influences conveyed through the media, films, songs, fashion, tourism, politics and a number of other conduits which emerge when people of different backgrounds make contact. In other words, a Swahili woman today is far from being isolated, living an existence exclusively within the confines of Swahili culture. Values from other cultures impinge and impact upon her existence.

With the above background in mind, this paper examines three Swahili texts and attempts to explore the status and empowerment of the modern woman; in doing so, it is useful to remember that modernity is a relative concept: each age is modern to itself.

Utenzi wa Mwana Kupona

I begin with the *Utenzi wa Mwana Kupona*, a classical poem popular along the coast, particularly among the northern Swahili[3]. It was composed in Pate by Mwana Kupona bint Msham (*c.* 1810-1860), a lady of noble descent (*mwungwana*) whose husband held a high-ranking position in the administration of the area. She composed the poem in 1858, two years or so before her death. It is addressed to her seventeen-year old daughter, Mwana Hashima bint Sheikh (1841-1933). The earlier translators of the poem – mainly Hichens and Werner (1934), quoted in Biersteker (1991) – have considered the subject of the poem as the advice of a mother to her daughter on 'wifely virtue'. Of its 102 verses, 24 specifically address this subject (verses 23 to 36, and 42 to 51). The relationship between husband and wife also features indirectly in other verses, e.g. 52 to 56 where Mwana Kupona speaks of her own marriage as an example to her daughter[4].

What does the poem tell us of a Swahili woman's status in the mid-nineteenth century? As noted earlier, Mwana Kupona belonged to the upper stratum of Lamu society. We know that she had servants working for her as she advises the young Hashima 'not to consort with slaves unless there is work to be done' (v. 20). Apart from this piece of advice, however, her other counsels would probably not be much different from the ones given by Swahili mothers in less exalted positions. These fall under three categories: her relationship with her husband; her interaction with other people; and taking care of her home and of her person. Of these three, the main emphasis is placed on the wife-husband relationship which, in a sense, permeates the others. An important point to note is that the advice is given within the ethical framework of Islam as perceived by Mwana Kupona. According to her,

v. 22　　*Mama pulika maneno*　　Listen to me, my dear.
　　　　kiumbe ni radhi tano　　A person needs to be blessed by five
　　　　ndipo apate usono　　(beings) before she attains peace in
　　　　wa akhera na dunia　　this world and the next.

v. 23　　*Nda Mngu na Mtumewe*　　By God and his Prophet;
　　　　baba na mama wayue　　by father and mother, you should know;
　　　　na ya tano nda mumewe　　and the fifth is by her husband,
　　　　mno imekaririwa.　　as has been stated repeatedly.

The husband's blessings are thus important not only for the wellbeing of the wife in this world but also in the Hereafter. Mwana Kupona explains:

v. 25　　*Na ufapo wewe mbee*　　If you die first,
　　　　radhi yake izengee　　seek his blessings and go with them
　　　　wende uitukuzie　　into the next world;
　　　　ndipo upatapo ndia.　　only then will you find the way.

v. 26　　*Siku ufufuliwao*　　When you rise again (in the Hereafter)
　　　　nadhari ni ya mumeo　　the choice will be your husband's;
　　　　taulizwa atakao　　he will be asked his will,
　　　　ndilo takalotendewa.　　and that will be done.

v. 27　　*Kipenda wende peponi*　　If he wishes you to go to Paradise,
　　　　utakwenda dalhini　　at once you will go;

| *kinena wende motoni* | if he says to Hell, |
| *huna budi utatiwa.* | there must you be sent. |

The husband's authority over the wife seems absolute. The only leeway granted the wife is in cases where a husband makes demands that contravene the commands of God (v.50); it would then be acceptable for the wife to defy the husband and go against his wishes.

Mwana Hashima is advised to relate to her husband in three ways. The first way concerns her behaviour towards him. She must respect him and value his opinion; she must not anger or provoke him; she must not argue with him or answer him back. Instead, she must remain silent. She should not be obstinate but should listen to her husband and consent to his wishes. When he goes out, she should see him off, and welcome him with a smile on his return. And when she decides to go out, she should first seek his permission, and she should not remain away from home beyond ten o'clock in the evening. She should praise him in the company of others.

Secondly, the daughter is advised to look after her husband's personal comforts. She should give him a massage when he is lying down. She should make arrangements for someone to fan him when he is asleep, and she herself must not disturb him by being noisy. She must serve food to him when he awakes. She should not speak to him in a loud voice when he gets up from sleep; instead, she should 'sit still and do not get up, so that when he wakes, he may find you' (v.32). She should shave him and tend to his beard. She should adorn herself for him. The third message is in relation to their home: the house must be kept clean at all times so that it reflects well on her husband; she must clean the toilets. And so the list goes on.

Critics of the poem have found such injunctions unacceptable in these modern times. Senkoro considers the counsels humiliating as they reduce a woman to being simply a 'decoration' around the house (1988: 141). Mulokozi finds that the 'image of the woman we are given by Mwana Kupona is that of a man's submissive servant and a petty, sensuous object' (1982: 43). Khatib agrees: such a woman, he says, is turned into a chattel of the husband, and their relationship becomes one of master and slave (1985: 46). These three critics are men; I have not so far come across a criticism of the poem by a Swahili woman[5]. However, a non-Swahili woman scholar has made an interesting assessment of Mwana Kupona's message to her daughter (Biersteker 1991: 59-77).

Ann Biersteker starts from the premise that the theme of the wifely duties or virtue (which covers just over a third of the poem) is not the only theme, and that another significant one emerges when one explores the sub-text of the poem. In order to access the message of the sub-text, one needs to re-read the text and examine the way Mwana Kupona has employed metaphor and irony within the structure of her poem. In other words, Mwana Kupona resorts to an 'inner language', a *fumbo*, a literary device quite prevalent in Swahili poetry whose use is well explained by Lienhardt (1968: 3):

> Both in literature and in daily speech there is a *Kiswahili cha ndani*, or 'internal Swahili', consisting of the inner meanings of words and phrases. These parts of verbal play serve the purposes of irony. Words a simpleton may take as a literal statement are recognized by others to be a metaphor implying something quite different.

When viewed in this way, what emerge in the poem are subtle traces of female superiority, humour and even empowerment through the very medium employed by the mother in her poem: the power of language. Admittedly, in a society such as the one that existed in Pate, husbands had almost unbounded authority over their wives; yet, it was possible for women to negotiate their positions without transgressing those boundaries. Be obedient, Hashima is being told, but not in matters in which you think the husband's wishes go against those of God. This leaves the door open to interpretation, to the involvement of other people in the process, even to invoking a concept feared in Swahili society: *aibu*, shame. And *aibu* is invoked through speech, and executed through gossip (Swartz 1991: 177-208). Both use a particular type of language. Hashima is advised how to behave (v.13 *uwe na adabu, mwenye ulimi wa thawabu*: be of good manners, with a sweet/discreet tongue); to present herself to people as a cheerful person who does not speak words of malice:

v. 17   *Ifanye mteshiteshi*   Make yourself amusing
        kwa maneno yaso ghashi   but using words without malice
        wala sifanye ubishi   do not be quarrelsome,
        watu wakakutukia.   making people hate you.

v. 18   *Nena nao kwa mzaha*   Talk with them [people] cheerfully
        yaweteao furaha   so as to give them pleasure;
        iwapo ya ikraha   it is better to be silent
        kheri kuinyamalia.   than to give offence.

This emphasis on the use of language, coupled with the way she is asked to behave in society, is meant to create an environment around the daughter which would in turn empower her with confidence and assurance. The husband, on the contrary, is presented as someone who is almost devoid of speech, or someone to be taken as such:

v. 35   *Mtunde kama kijana*   Tend him like a child
        asiyoyua kunena   that cannot yet speak;
        kitu changalie sana   tend with great care
        kitokacho na kungia.   that which goes in and out.

Two suggestions are presented in this verse. One is to consider the husband as a *kijana*, a child; the definition of a *kijana* includes the ability to speak, i.e. to make sense, in contrast to *mtoto mchanga*, a baby who babbles and is still making an effort to speak. It is being suggested to Mwana Hashima, rather ironically, that she should consider her husband as a *kijana* who is not yet mature. Yet he possesses 'that which goes in and out'. Allen translates this line as 'take particular care of his digestion' (1971: 63) which Biersteker does not accept; instead, she thinks that the reference here is to his sexual organ. Taken as a whole, then, the advice of the mother to the daughter is to take charge of a situation in a subtle way, without making the 'child' even aware that he is powerless, i.e. he has authority without speech.

Allen and Biersteker also differ significantly on the translation of the verse that follows the one given above. The sequence of the verses is also noteworthy. Verse 36 states:

v. 36   *Mpumbaze apumbae*   Amuse him so that he may relax
        amriye sikatae   do not oppose his command;
        maovu kieta yeye   if it is ill-advised,
        Mngu atakulipia.   God will defend you.

The above is Allen's translation. Biersteker differs from it by rendering the verb *kupumbaza* as 'to delude' thus translating the first line as advice to Hashima to delude her husband; in effect, to deceive him so that he remains deluded[6]. The husband is shown to be 'controllable and vulnerable to manipulation' (Biersteker 1991: 71). The last line is also translated differently. Biersteker translates *atakulipia* as 'he will avenge you', thus adding a stronger dimension to the divine intervention on behalf of the wife.

Kilio cha Haki

The second text, *Kilio cha Haki*, published in 1981 by Alamin Mazrui of Mombasa, is a play whose main character, Lanina of Muyaka, is placed at the centre of a complex situation. Religion does not feature in the play; the framework now is provided by politics. Mazrui does not mention Kenya or any country as such, but makes it clear that the action takes place in Africa. For the crux of the play is the exploitation of Africa by, and for the benefit of, foreigners.

Delamon is a *kaburu* (a Boer) who owns land and farms in the country. His only interest in the country is to make as much profit as possible, without a care for the rights of the workers. Lanina, a cigarette-smoking modern woman, is the elected leader of the workers' Union. She is deeply involved in the struggle to improve the conditions of her members. Her Union has called a strike, and, when the play opens, the atmosphere at Delamon's farm is tense. Delamon is prepared to negotiate with the Union leader, and is amazed to learn that she is a woman. He asks contemptuously (p.8):

Mwanamke? Yaani mzozo wote huu ni kazi ya mwanamke.	A woman? All this trouble is caused by a woman.
Mwanamke mmoja tu?	Just one woman?
Naye amewashinda?	And she has overcome you?
Hamkuweza kumnyosha?	You could not straighten her out?
Nimefanya ujinga ulioje kuwapa kazi madubu kama nyinyi!	I made a mistake to entrust this job to fools like you!

Delamon meets with Lanina but the meeting ends in failure as Lanina refuses to give way to Delamon's wishes. Some policemen come into Delamon's office and arrest Lanina and her companion after slapping her and heaping abuse upon her.

It is clear as the play progresses that Lanina is caught up in a difficult situation, mainly because she is a woman. There is conflict between her work and home. Her husband does not understand or appreciate her position as a leader. His thinking is traditional, and he expects Lanina to stay at home to cook for him and look after the children. As soon as Lanina sets foot in the room after her detention at the police station, where she had been beaten and humiliated, he pounces on her with his complaints. Lanina tries to make him understand that there is nothing wrong if he cooks now and again, or if he looks after the children. After all, it is his house as well and they are his children too. But his thinking is not swayed. He does think it proper for a man to perform such domestic chores. He is also a jealous man who cannot brook the idea of his wife dealing with men outside the home.

Lanina's father in the village thinks along the same lines as her husband. When she visits her parents, she is met with abuse from him and accusation of being *malaya*, a prostitute, for consorting with men in her work. He disowns her and even tries to beat her. Her mother is more affectionate, but even she does not understand why she should engage in activities that bring *aibu*, shame, on them. For, apparently, her parents have lost friends in the village because of reports, or rather gossip, about what she is up to in the city.

Lanina persists in her demands as a Union leader but Delamon sacks her from the farm. She takes up a job as a waitress at a 'kiosk' which serves food to workers. She tells her companions that there is no shame in doing such a job as long as it is respectable. Later, however, she is arrested and accused of murder when the police, at the instigation of Delamon through the Police Chief Henderson, are involved in a confrontation with the workers which leads to fatalities. She is held responsible for them as *mchochezi*, the instigator. The play ends with Lanina in custody awaiting a possible death sentence.

In many respects, Mazrui's characterization of Lanina is a stereotype of the woman worker who is torn between career and family. But, unlike her counterparts in the West, it is not only the pressure of time or lack of resources that is the issue, but a conflict which arises from a cultural perception that a woman should not involve herself too visibly in the public domain. Lanina goes a stage further by being a leader and involving herself in politics. Towards the end of the play her lawyer tells her (p.76):

Unajua Lanina,
ingekuwa bora kwako kama
ungejiepusha na mambo haya
ukakaa nyumbani kumtazama
mumeo na watoto wako.
Siasa ni mchezo mchafu,
na ungewaachia wanaume mchezo huo!

Do you know, Lanina,
it would have been better for you
if you had avoided all these matters
by staying at home and looking after
your husband and children.
Politics is a dirty game,
and you should have left it for men
to play!

Lanina's reply is that a woman should not be isolated from taking part in politics by being kept at home. It is her right to participate in the activities which affect her life.

Mazrui's play deals with a range of issues that face a developing African nation. There is exploitation by greedy capitalists, but there is also greed and corruption in the ranks of the workers. Lanina is betrayed by Tereki, her companion, when he is offered material gains that would normally be out of his reach. The police, too, are in the control of the capitalists; their commander, Henderson, is a willing partner of Delamon in suppressing the workers. Lanina, a woman, thus stands out as a beacon of hope for the future.

Mama ee

Mama ee, a play written by Ari Katini Mwachofi (from Teita) and published in 1987, represents by far the most insightful work of Swahili fiction written by a woman into the plight and suffering of a wife. Unlike Mazrui's play, where the action of the plot emanates from the public domain of a workers' Union, Mwachofi's play addresses the domestic problems of husband and wife.

Mwavita is married to Kinaya; they have one child, Juma. She works in an office in the city where she is very much appreciated. Kinaya also has a good position but spends his time and money getting drunk and going out with other women. (Mwavita thinks that he has two other 'wives' or kept women in town). Despite this, he expects Mwavita to serve him food when he returns home, even in the early hours of the morning. He tells his wife (p. 3):

Mimi ni mume wako na ndiye mwenye amri katika nyumba hii yangu.
Lazima ufanye nisemalo. Usifikiri hiyo elimu yako na kazi ya mshahara

imekufanya mume sawa na mimi. Tangu zamani, mabibi zetu waliwatii mababu zetu. Vivyo hivyo lazima nawe unitii mimi.

I am your husband and I am the one who has authority in this house of mine. You must do as I say. Don't think that your education and your salaried job turns you into a husband equal to me. From long ago, our grandmothers have been obedient to our grandfathers. In the same way, you must obey me.

Mwavita replies with contempt and asks him to forget the old days of their grandparents. 'This is a totally different century', she tells him. She also corrects his thinking that, having paid *mahari* (bridewealth), he has 'purchased' a wife. They quarrel, and he beats her so harshly that she loses two teeth and has a miscarriage. The case is taken to the village elders who decide in favour of Mwavita. The husband is asked to pay compensation over a period of time; Mwavita may only return to her husband after that has been paid. Mwavita, however, misses her child, Juma, and agrees to return to Kinaya (and in reality to Juma) before he has paid the amount fully.

The next scene takes place a year later. She is pregnant once again, and is at a stage when she is frequently sick. She curses herself for allowing herself to get into that condition, especially as her husband has returned to his old ways of drinking and partying. She feels trapped. She thinks of herself as being worse than a slave (p.46):

Mtumwa huwa anajuwa kuwa yeye ni mtumwa lakini
mke hajui kuwa yeye ni mtumwa!

A slave knows that she is a slave, but a wife does not
know that she is one.

Her husband then comes home smelling of drink, and is furious to learn that his suit has not been pressed. He blames her and his sister-in-law whom he calls a whore because she had a baby without getting married. There is a quarrel, and Mwavita and her sister leave the house.

We learn in the next scene, which takes place a few months later, that Mwavita had given birth prematurely, and that the baby had died a fortnight later. She now lives in a smaller but smarter place, and seems to be in a much happier state of mind. Kinaya still wants her to return to him. A Minister from the church pays her a visit to persuade her to return to her husband. He tells her that marriage is a sacrament and should be for life. This angers her, and it is interesting to compare her attitude to religion with that of Mwana Kupona; she tells him:

> ...*kama kukubali kuwa mmoja wa wafuasi wa kanisa lako ni kukubali utumwa, kunyanyaswa, kuonewa, kupuuzwa, sina haja kuwa katika kundi lako takatifu.*

> ... if to be a follower of the Church means to [agree to] be a slave, to be humiliated, to be victimized, to be slighted and ignored, then I have no need of being a member of your holy group.

Mwavita takes Kinaya to court for the custody of Juma. She loses her case as the judge (a drinking friend of her husband's) decides that it is in the interests of the child that he remains with the father. The play ends with a scene in which the two women — Mwavita and her sister — physically beat up Kinaya who comes to Mwavita's house to ask her to return to him.

The play raises issues of gender relations within marriage, of the impotence of the village elders to enforce their decisions, and the necessity of taking recourse to the laws of the land for justice. In this respect, the play moves further than Mazrui's as it considers issues which women face in real life. Although the character of Mwavita seems bitter at times, her bitterness is justified in the face of the treatment she gets from her husband, a person meant to love and protect her. Mwachofi is not against men as such; she would rather see women united to fight for their rights, and hence the closing line of the play:

> *Umoja wa wanawake. Hoyee!*   The unity of women. Hurrah!

Conclusion

Two interesting considerations emerge from a discussion of these texts. Women writers have now broken through the barrier imposed by the etiquette of culture. Mwachofi does not need to resort to an inner Swahili as did Mwana Kupona; her language is open and forthright. The second point, perhaps even more significant, is the attitude of men towards issues of gender. Mazrui is not the only writer to have taken a stand against the exploitation of women. In his own way, so has Kezilahabi in *Rosa Mistika*; indeed, Bertoncini's *Vamps and Victims* is a testimony to this change of perception on the part of male writers. For those wishing to sample the contents, an excellent start is Muhammed Said Abdulla's 'Mke wangu' [My wife] (Bertoncini 1996: 74-81).

NOTES

1. Their publications, mostly plays, are cited in the bibliography. See Bertoncini (1989) for brief biographical notes on the Tanzanian writers.

2. Lihamba won the award for Best Actress at the Zanzibar International Film Festival, 1998, for her role in the film *Maangamizi – the Ancient One.*

3. One wonders whether the poem has retained its popularity into the twenty-first century, especially among the younger generation. I have not come across references to it in conversations with ordinary people in recent times (i.e. from the 1980s onwards), compared, say, to the 1960s. However, its popularity among scholars continues: the latest version has been published in an anthology of three poems (*tenzi*) by Mulokozi (1999).

4. I follow the version edited by Allen (1971: 55-75), retaining and adapting his translation where appropriate.

5. It may be worthwhile to reproduce here a quotation of Flora Nwapo given in Bertoncini (1996: 10). The quotation is from Nwapo's interview in 1993 in which she explains the different emphases in the writings of Western and non-Western women:

> For us, the first generation writers, we do not think much of feminism as the West thinks of it. Each time we go to conferences and we are confronted by these feminists, we tell them that we are not feminists. (...) There is not that need for aggressiveness that feminism in the West projects. (...) I tell [the Western women] that their problems are not my problems because their world is different.

6. We may note that, in the play to be discussed later, Mwachofi opens the first scene with a quotation from this verse.

Bibliography

Abdulaziz, Mohammed H., 1977. *Muyaka: Nineteenth century Swahili Popular poetry.* Nairobi: East Afrcan Publishing House.

Allen, John W.T., 1971. *Tendi.* New York: Africana Publishing Corporation.

Bertoncini-Zúbková, Elena, 1989. *Outline of Swahili literature.* Leiden: E.J.Brill.

———, 1996. *Vamps and Victims.* Cologne: Rudiger Koppe Verlag.

Biersteker, Ann, 1991. 'Language, poetry and power: A reconsideration of "Utendi wa Mwana Kupona"'. In Kenneth W. Harrow (ed.) *Faces of Islam in African Literature.* Portsmouth: Heinemann.

Hichens, William, and Alice Werner, 1934. *Advice of Mwana Kupona upon the Wifely Virtue.* Medstead, Hampshire: Azania Press.

Horton, Mark, and John Middleton, 2000. *The Swahili. The Social Landscape of a Mercantile Society.* Oxford: Blackwell.

Khatib, Mohamed Seif, 1985. 'Utenzi wa Mwana Kupona', *Mulika*, 17: 46-52.

Lienhardt, Peter, 1968. *The Medicine Man. Swifa ya Nguvumali.* Oxford: The Clarendon Press.

Mazrui, Alamin, 1981. *Kilio cha Haki.* Nairobi: Longman.

Mbughuni, Patricia, 1982. 'The image of woman in Swahili prose fiction'. *Kiswahili.* 49, 1: 15-24.

Middleton, John, 1992. *The World of the Swahili: An African Mercantile Civilization* New Haven: Yale University Press.

Mulokozi, Mugyabuso M., 1982 'Protest and resistance in Swahili poetry'. *Kiswahili.* 49, 1: 25-54.

———. 1999. *Tenzi tatu za kale.* Dar es Salaam: Taasisi ya Uchunguzi wa Kiswahili, Chuo Kikuu cha Dar es Salaam.

Mwachofi, Ari Katini, 1987. *Mama ee.* Nairobi: Heinemann Kenya.

Nurse, Derek, and Thomas Spear,1985. *The Swahili: Reconstructing the history and language of an African society, 800-1500.* Philadelphia: University of Pennsylvania Press.

Senkoro, F.E.M.K., 1988. 'Mwana Kupona Nana: Utenzi wa Mwana Kupona'. In *Ushairi: Nadharia na Tahakiki.* Dar es Salaam: Dar es Salaam University Press.

Shepherd, Gillian, 1977. 'Two marriage forms in the Comoro Islands: An investigation' *Africa* 47, 4: 344-358.

Swartz, Marc J., 1991. *The way the world is. Cultural processes and social relations among the Mombasa Swahili.* Berkeley: University of California Press.

INDEX